110650091

Reid's Read-Alouds 2

Other *Booklist* Publications

The Back Page, by Bill Ott

Reid's Read-Alouds: Selections for Children and Teens, by Rob Reid

Writing Reviews for Readers' Advisory, by Brad Hooper

Reid's Read-Alouds 2

Modern-Day Classics from
C. S. Lewis to Lemony Snicket

Rob Reid

American Library Association
Chicago   2011

Rob Reid is the very popular author of numerous books on children's programming for ALA Editions. He has also written resources for Upstart Books and is the author of two picture books. In addition, he writes regular columns on programming and children's literature for *LibrarySparks* magazine and has a column in *Book Links* magazine titled "Reid-Aloud Alert." Reid is a Senior Lecturer at the University of Wisconsin–Eau Claire, and he conducts workshops across North America on ways to make literature come alive for children. He can be contacted through www.rapnrob.com.

Copyright © 2011 by the American Library Association. Any claim of copyright is subject to applicable limitations and exceptions, such as rights of fair use and library copying pursuant to Sections 107 and 108 of the U.S. Copyright Act. No copyright is claimed in content that is in the public domain, such as works of the U.S. government.

Printed in the United States of America
15 14 13 12 11   5 4 3 2 1

While extensive effort has gone into ensuring the reliability of the information in this book, the publisher makes no warranty, express or implied, with respect to the material contained herein.

ISBN: 978-0-8389-1072-6

Library of Congress Cataloging-in-Publication Data
Reid, Rob.
  Reid's read-alouds 2 : modern day classics from C.S. Lewis to Lemony Snicket / Rob Reid.
    p. cm.
  Includes bibliographical references.
  ISBN 978-0-8389-1072-6 (alk. paper)
1. Children--Books and reading--United States. 2. Children's literature--Bibliography. 3. Young adult literature--Bibliography. 4. Oral reading. 5. Children's libraries--Activity programs--United States.
6. School libraries--Activity programs--United States. I. Title.
  Z1037.R542 2011
  011.62--dc22   2010028985

Cover design by Kristin Krutsch
Book design in Garamond and Interstate by Roslyn Broder

♾ This paper meets the requirements of ANSI/NISO Z39.48-1992 (Permanence of Paper).

ALA Editions also publishes its books in a variety of electronic formats.
For more information, visit the ALA Store at www.alastore.ala.org and select eEditions.

To my past, present, and future students
at the University of Wisconsin–Eau Claire

ALA Editions purchases fund advocacy, awareness,
and accreditation programs for library professionals worldwide.

Contents

Acknowledgments

I'd like to thank the following:

My colleague and friend Tamara Lindsey, who constantly told me to include "this book and that book" in this collection

Laura Tillotson, for giving me the "Reid-Aloud Alert" column in *Book Links* magazine

Eloise L. Kinney, who should be a goalie—nothing gets past her

Stephanie and Michael and the whole ALA Editions gang

The McIntyre Library staff for the resources to help locate the titles in this book, particularly the wonderful Children's Literature Comprehensive Database

Every library staff person in the member libraries of the MORE system in western Wisconsin who put their hands on the books that traveled from a shelf somewhere and wound up in my hands

The Cooperative Children's Book Center (CCBC), for being just about the best invention ever

My wife of thirty years, Jayne

My children, Laura, Julia, Alice, and Sam—we've shared a lot of books together

My grandson, Parker—we're just getting started

Introduction

The first edition of *Reid's Read-Alouds* (ALA Editions, 2009) profiled children's and young adult books published between the years 2000 and 2008. This companion volume showcases two hundred strong read-aloud books that were published from 1950 to 1999.

This project turned into both a scavenger hunt and a trip down memory lane. I revisited books that I had read to groups of young people during my years as a junior high school English teacher and also as a youth services public librarian. I looked at books I had never read before but were recommended to me by other professionals as successful read-alouds. I examined books that were read to me as a child to see if they were still relevant to today's youth. I read and reread approximately four hundred fiction chapter books, folklore collections, informational books, and biographies before selecting the two hundred titles found in this collection.

During my "hunt," I looked for a variety of genres and age levels and a good balance between male and female protagonists. I looked for literary aspects that would connect with the modern child, particularly avoiding concepts and language that might seem dated. I looked for a wide representation of authors, limiting myself to selecting one or two of their works, although many authors have several more titles that are superb read-alouds. I looked for representative books from each of the five decades, but I quickly realized that it would be impossible to try to have equal numbers from each decade. In fact, you'll find more titles from the 1990s than from the other decades added together. The simple reason is that there are more books from the 1990s still in print, another requirement for a title to be included in this book. So many wonderful read-alouds from the 1950s, 1960s, and 1970s in particular are no longer in print, although one may find them in libraries or find used copies through the Internet. Even some favorites from the 1980s and 1990s are no longer available. I realized this while poring over back issues of the annual *Choices*, published by the Cooperative Children's Book Center (CCBC) at the University of Wisconsin–Madison.

I discarded many older titles, too, because of racial stereotypes. Many times, ethnic characters were given pidgin English dialect or were misrepresented in other ways. I relied heavily on both the CCBC and the Oyate website for their insights on books by and about people of color. In all but a few examples regarding books featuring minority protagonists, I went with insider author perspectives. Unfortunately, this decision highlights the scarcity of books written by authors of color before the year 2000.

I also chose not to include works that had excessive swearing, sexual incidents, or characters dealing with personal private matters, such as puberty. These books are better suited to be read by individuals. There are indeed some titles in this collection that contain some strong language. I highly recommend that one preview an entire book before reading it aloud to children or teens.

The focus of the two *Reid's Read-Alouds* books as well as the "Reid-Aloud Alert" column in *Book Links* magazine is on finding wonderful titles to read to *groups* of young people. The titles have been considered for flowing text, engaging storytelling, and appeal to a wide range of young listeners. The suggested grade levels listed with each annotation are listening levels, not reading levels. Through the years, I have read these books to children at public library programs and tours, in classrooms, in detention centers, in camps, in parks-and-recreation programs, and to neighborhood kids and homeschooled children.

Finally, the unique feature that sets my books and column apart from other read-aloud resources are the "10 Minute Selections." These are captivating episodes taken from the books that can be read in one brief sitting. In reality, these selections can range from five minutes to fifteen minutes. The "10 Minute Selection" feature originated during my time as a children's librarian, when I had limited times with visiting groups. Looking back, I also realized I employed them during my teaching years, when we took a break from other studies and shared quality oral-literature moments. Even though I no longer work in a public library or in a classroom for younger kids, I continue to read to the young. I have spent the last few years sharing these modern-day classics, both old favorites and those "new" to me, with many groups of kids in a variety of settings.

All of the books in this collection are kid-tested. Some of the books made us laugh; some made us cry. They all touched us in one way or another. Their worth cannot be overestimated, and for that, I thank the wonderful authors featured here for sharing their talents.

Authors and Titles at a Glance

Alexander, Lloyd. *Time Cat: The Remarkable Journeys of Jason and Gareth*. Holt, 1963.

Almond, David. *Skellig*. Delacorte, 1999.

Armstrong, Jennifer. *Shipwreck at the Bottom of the World: The Extraordinary True Story of Shackleton and the* Endurance. Crown, 1998.

Avi. *Poppy*. Orchard, 1995.

———. *Romeo and Juliet—Together (and Alive!) at Last*. Orchard, 1987.

Ayer, Eleanor. *Parallel Journeys*. Atheneum, 1995.

Babbitt, Natalie. *Kneeknock Rise*. Farrar Straus Giroux, 1970.

———. *Tuck Everlasting*. Farrar Straus Giroux, 1975.

Ball, Zachary. *Bristle Face*. Holiday House, 1962.

Bauer, Joan. *Rules of the Road*. Putnam, 1998.

Bauer, Marion Dane. *On My Honor*. Clarion, 1986.

Bellairs, John. *The House with a Clock in Its Walls*. Dial, 1973.

Berry, James. *Ajeemah and His Son*. HarperCollins, 1991.

Bloor, Edward. *Tangerine*. Harcourt, 1997.

Blume, Judy. *Fudge-a-Mania*. Dutton, 1990.

Bond, Michael. *A Bear Called Paddington*. Houghton Mifflin, 1958.

Boston, L. M. *The Children of Green Knowe*. Harcourt, 1955.

Brittain, Bill. *Dr. Dredd's Wagon of Wonders*. Harper and Row, 1987.

Bruchac, Joseph. *Eagle Song*. Dial, 1997.

Bruchac, Joseph, and James Bruchac. *When the Chenoo Howls: Native American Tales of Terror*. Walker, 1998.

Bunting, Eve. *Someone Is Hiding on Alcatraz Island*. Clarion, 1984.

Burch, Robert. *Ida Early Comes over the Mountain*. Viking, 1980.

———. *Queenie Peavy*. Viking, 1966.

Burnford, Sheila. *The Incredible Journey*. Little, Brown, 1960.

Butterworth, Oliver. *The Enormous Egg*. Little, Brown, 1956.

Byars, Betsy. *The Pinballs*. Harper and Row, 1977.

Cameron, Ann. *The Stories Julian Tells*. Knopf, 1981.

Cameron, Eleanor. *The Wonderful Flight to the Mushroom Planet*. Little, Brown, 1954.

Cassedy, Sylvia. *Behind the Attic Wall*. Crowell, 1983.

Catling, Patricia Skene. *The Chocolate Touch*. Morrow, 1979.

Chew, Ruth. *The Wednesday Witch*. Scholastic, 1969.

Christopher, John. *The White Mountains*. Macmillan, 1967.

Cleary, Beverly. *The Mouse and the Motorcycle*. Morrow, 1965.

———. *Ramona the Pest*. Morrow, 1968.

Cleaver, Vera, and Bill Cleaver. *Where the Lilies Bloom*. Harper and Row, 1969.

Clements, Andrew. *Frindle*. Simon and Schuster, 1996.

Clifford, Eth. *Help! I'm a Prisoner in the Library*. Houghton Mifflin, 1979.

Cooney, Caroline B. *The Fog*. Scholastic, 1989.

Cooper, Susan. *The Boggart*. Margaret K. McElderry, 1993.

———. *The Dark Is Rising*. Simon and Schuster, 1973.

Creech, Sharon. *Chasing Redbird*. HarperCollins, 1997.

Curtis, Christopher Paul. *The Watsons Go to Birmingham—1963*. Delacorte, 1995.

Cushman, Karen. *Catherine, Called Birdy*. Clarion, 1994.

Dahl, Roald. *The BFG*. Farrar Straus Giroux, 1982.

———. *Fantastic Mr. Fox*. Knopf, 1970.

Danziger, Paula. *Amber Brown Is Not a Crayon*. Putnam, 1994.

DeFelice, Cynthia. *Weasel*. Macmillan, 1990.

DeJong, Meindert. *The Wheel on the School*. Harper and Row, 1954.

Deuker, Carl. *On the Devil's Court*. Little, Brown, 1988.

Dickinson, Peter. *Chuck and Danielle*. Delacorte, 1996.

Dorris, Michael. *Morning Girl*. Hyperion, 1992.

———. *Sees Behind Trees*. Hyperion, 1996.

Duncan, Lois. *Don't Look Behind You*. Delacorte, 1989.

English, Karen. *Francie*. Farrar Straus Giroux, 1999.

Enright, Elizabeth. *Gone-Away Lake*. Harcourt, 1957.

Erdrich, Louise. *The Birchbark House*. Hyperion, 1999.

Estes, Eleanor. *The Witch Family*. Harcourt, 1960.

Farmer, Nancy. *The Ear, the Eye and the Arm*. Orchard, 1994.

Fitzhugh, Louise. *Harriet the Spy*. Harper and Row, 1964.

Fleischman, Paul. *The Half-a-Moon Inn*. Harper and Row, 1980.

Fleischman, Sid. *By the Great Horn Spoon*. Little, Brown, 1963.

————. *The Whipping Boy.* Greenwillow, 1986.

Fleming, Ian. *Chitty-Chitty-Bang-Bang.* Random House, 1964.

Fox, Paula. *One-Eyed Cat.* Bradbury, 1984.

Gallo, Don, ed. *Ultimate Sports: Short Stories by Outstanding Writers for Young Adults.* Delacorte, 1995.

Gannett, Ruth Stiles. *The Dragons of Blueland.* Random House, 1951.

George, Jean Craighead. *My Side of the Mountain.* Dutton, 1959.

Giff, Patricia Reilly. *Lily's Crossing.* Delacorte, 1997.

Greenfield, Eloise. *Koya Delaney and the Good Girl Blues.* Scholastic, 1992.

Grimes, Nikki. *Jazmin's Notebook.* Dial, 1998.

Haddix, Margaret Peterson. *Just Ella.* Simon and Schuster, 1999.

Hahn, Mary Downing. *Wait Till Helen Comes.* Clarion, 1986.

Hamilton, Virginia. *The House of Dies Drear.* Macmillan, 1968.

————. *The People Could Fly: American Black Folktales.* Knopf, 1985.

Hautzig, Esther. *The Endless Steppe: Growing Up in Siberia.* Crowell, 1968.

Henkes, Kevin. *The Zebra Wall.* Greenwillow, 1988.

Henry, Marguerite. *Brighty of the Grand Canyon.* Rand McNally, 1953.

Herrera, Juan Felipe. *Crashboomlove: A Novel in Verse.* University of New Mexico Press, 1999.

Hesse, Karen. *Out of the Dust.* Scholastic, 1997.

————. *Sable.* Holt, 1994.

Hinton, S. E. *The Outsiders.* Viking, 1967.

Ho, Minfong. *The Clay Marble.* Farrar Straus Giroux, 1991.

Hoban, Russell. *The Mouse and His Child.* Harper and Row, 1967.

Hobbs, Will. *Far North.* Morrow, 1996.

Holman, Felice. *Slake's Limbo.* Macmillan, 1974.

Horvath, Polly. *The Trolls.* Farrar Straus Giroux, 1999.

Howe, Deborah, and James Howe. *Bunnicula: A Rabbit-Tale of Mystery.* Atheneum, 1979.

Hunt, Irene. *Across Five Aprils.* Follett, 1964.

Hurwitz, Johanna. *Russell and Elisa.* Morrow, 1989.

Huynh, Quang Nhuong. *The Land I Lost: Adventures of a Boy in Vietnam.* Harper and Row, 1982.

Ibbotson, Eva. *The Secret of Platform 13.* Dutton, 1994.

Jacques, Brian. *Redwall.* Philomel, 1986.

Jiménez, Francisco. *The Circuit: Stories from the Life of a Migrant Child.* Houghton Mifflin, 1997.

Johnson, Angela. *Heaven.* Simon and Schuster, 1998.

Jordan, Sherryl. *The Raging Quiet.* Simon and Schuster, 1999.

Juster, Norton. *The Phantom Tollbooth*. Random House, 1961.

Kennedy, Richard. *Inside My Feet: The Story of a Giant*. Harper and Row, 1979.

Kerr, M. E. *Gentlehands*. Harper and Row, 1978.

King-Smith, Dick. *Babe the Gallant Pig*. Crown, 1985.

Kjelgaard, Jim. *Outlaw Red*. Holiday House, 1953.

Klause, Annette Curtis. *The Silver Kiss*. Delacorte, 1990.

Kline, Suzy. *Herbie Jones*. Putnam, 1985.

Konigsburg, E. L. *About the B'Nai Bagels*. Atheneum, 1969.

————. *From the Mixed-Up Files of Mrs. Basil E. Frankweiler*. Atheneum, 1967.

Korman, Gordon. *Why Did the Underwear Cross the Road?* Scholastic, 1994.

Krull, Kathleen. *Lives of the Musicians: Good Times, Bad Times (and What the Neighbors Thought)*. Harcourt, 1993.

Le Guin, Ursula K. *A Wizard of Earthsea*. Parnassus, 1968.

L'Engle, Madeleine. *Meet the Austins*. Farrar Straus Giroux, 1960.

————. *A Wrinkle in Time*. Farrar Straus Giroux, 1962.

Lester, Julius. *More Tales of Uncle Remus*. Dial, 1988.

Levine, Gail Carson. *The Fairy's Mistake*. HarperCollins, 1999.

Lewis, C. S. *The Lion, the Witch and the Wardrobe*. Macmillan, 1950.

Lindgren, Astrid. *Ronia, the Robber's Daughter*. Viking, 1983.

Lisle, Janet. *Afternoon of the Elves*. Orchard, 1989.

Lowry, Lois. *All about Sam*. Houghton Mifflin, 1988.

————. *Number the Stars*. Houghton Mifflin, 1989.

MacLachlan, Patricia. *Sarah, Plain and Tall*. Harper and Row, 1985.

Magorian, Michelle. *Good Night, Mr. Tom*. Harper and Row, 1981.

Maguire, Gregory. *Seven Spiders Spinning*. Clarion, 1994.

Mahy, Margaret. *The Great Piratical Rumbustification and The Librarian and the Robbers*. Dent, 1978.

Manes, Stephen. *Be a Perfect Person in Just Three Days*. Clarion, 1982.

Marsden, John. *Tomorrow, When the War Began*. Pan Macmillan, 1993.

Marshall, James. *Rats on the Roof and Other Stories*. Dial, 1991.

Mazer, Harry. *Snow Bound*. Delacorte, 1973.

Mazer, Norma Fox. *Good Night, Maman*. Harcourt, 1999.

McKay, Hilary. *The Exiles*. Margaret K. McElderry, 1992.

McKinley, Robin. *Beauty: A Retelling of the Story of Beauty and the Beast*. Harper and Row, 1978.

Merrill, Jean. *The Pushcart War*. Scott, 1964.

Morey, Walt. *Kavik the Wolf Dog*. Dutton, 1968.

Mowat, Farley. *Owls in the Family*. Little, Brown, 1962.

Murphy, Jim. *The Great Fire*. Scholastic, 1995.

Myers, Walter Dean. *Scorpions.* Harper and Row, 1988.

Naidoo, Beverly. *Journey to Jo'burg: A South African Story.* Lippincott, 1986.

Namioka, Lensey. *Yang the Youngest and His Terrible Ear.* Little, Brown, 1992.

Napoli, Donna Jo. *Zel.* Dutton, 1996.

Naylor, Phyllis Reynolds. *Shiloh.* Atheneum, 1991.

————. *Witch's Sister.* Simon and Schuster, 1975.

Nix, Garth. *Sabriel.* HarperCollins, 1995.

Nixon, Joan Lowery. *The Kidnapping of Christina Lattimore.* Harcourt, 1979.

Norton, Mary. *The Borrowers.* Harcourt, 1952.

Nye, Naomi Shihab. *Habibi.* Simon and Schuster, 1997.

O'Brien, Robert C. *Mrs. Frisby and the Rats of NIMH.* Atheneum, 1971.

Ortiz Cofer, Judith. *An Island like You: Stories of the Barrio.* Orchard, 1995.

Park, Barbara. *Junie B. Jones Has a Monster under Her Bed.* Random House, 1997.

Paterson, Katherine. *Bridge to Terabithia.* Crowell, 1977.

————. *Lyddie.* Lodestar, 1991.

Paton Walsh, Jill. *A Parcel of Patterns.* Farrar Straus Giroux, 1983.

Paulsen, Gary. *Hatchet.* Simon and Schuster, 1987.

————. *The Voyage of the* Frog. Orchard, 1989.

Pearce, Philippa. *Tom's Midnight Garden.* Lippincott, 1958.

Peck, Richard. *The Ghost Belonged to Me.* Viking, 1975.

————. *A Long Way from Chicago.* Dial, 1998.

Peck, Robert Newton. *Soup.* Knopf, 1974.

Pellowski, Anne. *Betsy's Up-and-Down Year.* Philomel, 1983.

Peterson, John. *The Littles.* Scholastic, 1967.

Phelps, Ethel Johnston, ed. *Tatterhood and Other Tales.* Feminist Press, 1978.

Philbrick, Rodman. *Freak the Mighty.* Scholastic, 1993.

Pinkwater, Daniel. *The Hoboken Chicken Emergency.* Atheneum, 1977.

Pullman, Philip. *The Ruby in the Smoke.* Random House, 1985.

Qualey, Marsha. *Thin Ice.* Delacorte, 1997.

Rawls, Wilson. *Where the Red Fern Grows.* Delacorte, 1961.

Rockwell, Thomas. *How to Eat Fried Worms.* Watts, 1973.

Rowling, J. K. *Harry Potter and the Sorcerer's Stone.* Scholastic, 1998.

Rylant, Cynthia. *Every Living Thing.* Bradbury, 1985.

Sachar, Louis. *Holes.* Farrar Straus Giroux, 1998.

————. *Sideways Stories from Wayside School.* Morrow, 1978.

San Souci, Robert D. *Cut from the Same Cloth: American Women of Myth, Legend, and Tall Tale.* Philomel, 1993.

Scieszka, Jon. *Knights of the Kitchen Table.* Viking, 1991.

Silvey, Anita, ed. *Help Wanted: Short Stories about Young People Working*. Little, Brown, 1997.

Singer, Isaac Bashevis. *Zlateh the Goat and Other Stories*. Harper and Row, 1966.

Smith, Dodie. *The Hundred and One Dalmatians*. Viking, 1956.

Smith, Janice Lee. *The Monster in the Third Dresser Drawer and Other Stories about Adam Joshua*. Harper and Row, 1981.

Sneve, Virginia Driving Hawk. *High Elk's Treasure*. Holiday House, 1972.

Snicket, Lemony. *The Bad Beginning*. Scholastic, 1999.

Soto, Gary. *Baseball in April and Other Stories*. Harcourt, 1990.

———. *Crazy Weekend*. Scholastic, 1994.

Speare, Elizabeth George. *The Witch of Blackbird Pond*. Houghton Mifflin, 1958.

Spinelli, Jerry. *Maniac Magee*. Little, Brown, 1990.

———. *Who Put That Hair in My Toothbrush?* Little, Brown, 1984.

Steig, William. *Abel's Island*. Farrar Straus Giroux, 1976.

Streatfield, Noel. *Skating Shoes*. Random House, 1951.

Taylor, Theodore. *The Trouble with Tuck*. Doubleday, 1981.

Temple, Frances. *Grab Hands and Run*. Orchard, 1993.

Thomas, Jane Resh. *The Comeback Dog*. Clarion, 1981.

Uchida, Yoshiko. *Journey to Topaz*. Scribner, 1971.

Van Draanen, Wendelin. *Sammy Keyes and the Hotel Thief*. Knopf, 1998.

Voigt, Cynthia. *Bad Girls*. Scholastic, 1996.

———. *Homecoming*. Atheneum, 1981.

Vuong, Lynette Dyer. *The Brocaded Slipper and Other Vietnamese Tales*. Addison-Wesley, 1982.

Walter, Mildred Pitts. *Justin and the Best Biscuits in the World*. Lothrop, Lee and Shepard, 1986.

Werlin, Nancy. *The Killer's Cousin*. Delacorte, 1998.

White, E. B. *Charlotte's Web*. Harper and Row, 1952.

White, Ruth. *Belle Prater's Boy*. Farrar Straus Giroux, 1996.

Williams, Vera. *Scooter*. Greenwillow, 1993.

Wrede, Patricia C. *Dealing with Dragons*. Harcourt, 1990.

Wright, Betty Ren. *Christina's Ghost*. Holiday House, 1985.

Yee, Paul. *Tales from Gold Mountain: Stories of the Chinese in the New World*. Macmillan, 1989.

Yep, Laurence. *The Ghost Fox*. Scholastic, 1994.

Yolen, Jane. *Briar Rose*. Tor, 1992.

———. *The Devil's Arithmetic*. Viking, 1988.

The Read-Alouds

Alexander, Lloyd. *Time Cat: The Remarkable Journeys of Jason and Gareth.* **Holt, 1963. 206 p. Gr. 3–5.**
Jason discovers that his cat, Gareth, not only has the ability to talk but also is able to transport both of them through time. They visit several places—from ancient Egypt, where cats were held in high esteem, to seventeenth-century Germany, where cats were hunted, accused of being witches' demons. The two also visit Rome, Great Britain, Ireland, Japan, Italy, Peru, and the Isle of Man. Before returning home, they help the rebels' cause during the American Revolution in 1775.

10 Minute Selection: Read chapter 1, "The Visitors." After a particularly rough day, Jason learns that Gareth can talk. He also discovers that Gareth "can visit nine different lives. Anywhere, any time, any country, any century." Continue reading chapter 2, "The Sacred City of Cats." Egyptians grab Jason and urge him to bring his cat to meet the Lord of the Two Lands of Egypt. If not, Jason will be thrown to the crocodiles. Jason protests when he learns that the ruler plans to take possession of the cat. Jason is thrown into a tiny room. The end of this passage makes for a good cliff-hanger. However, if time allows, include chapter 3, "Neter-Khet." The pharaoh demands that Gareth entertain him. Of course, cats do only what they want to do. In the end, the ruler Neter-Khet learns that "not even Pharaoh can give orders to a cat."

Almond, David. *Skellig.* **Delacorte, 1999. 182 p. Gr. 5–8.**
Michael moves into a new house. He and his parents are worried about his baby sister, who is seriously ill. Michael meets a homeschooled girl named Mina, who becomes his friend. There is a dilapidated garage on the property. Michael finds a mysterious man or a humanlike beast in the garage. The creature, known as Skellig, hardly moves because of arthritis. Skellig likes to eat Chinese food as well as bluebottle flies and spiders. And it appears that Skellig has wings. Is he a man, an

owl, an angel? The way that Skellig interacts with Michael, Mina, and eventually the baby makes this magical realistic book a powerful read-aloud.

10 Minute Selection: Read the very short chapter 3. Michael is exploring the garage. "I leaned across a heap of tea chests and shined the flashlight into the space behind and that's when I saw him." The man keeps asking, "What do you want?" Move on to chapter 7, another short excerpt. Michael ventures into the garage again and talks to the stranger. Michael also meets Mina. Finally, read chapter 20. Michael takes Mina to meet Skellig for the first time. Skellig refuses to answer the children's questions, but he accepts their food and medicine. When Mina tells him that he must let them help him, he replies, "Do what you want."

Armstrong, Jennifer. *Shipwreck at the Bottom of the World: The Extraordinary True Story of Shackleton and the* **Endurance. Crown, 1998. 126 p. Gr. 5–12.**

Sir Ernest Shackleton and his crew left England in 1914 and set off to Antarctica. In 1915, their ship, the *Endurance,* was trapped in the ice and crushed. "What he and his crew did succeed in doing in 1915–1916 was one of the most incredible feats of survival ever recorded. Every stage of their journey seemed more remarkable than the last." Every single member of the twenty-four-man crew survived some of the world's harshest conditions. Author Armstrong does a remarkable job of conveying the excitement and emotions of this true event as fine as any fictional survival story.

10 Minute Selection: Inform your audience that this story really happened to a crew that was stranded in Antarctica around the time of World War I. Read the last half of the chapter titled "Winter on the Pack," beginning with the sentence, "The Boss found ways of maintaining a routine in order to keep the crew from going crazy with cabin fever." These activities included mandatory haircuts, lectures, theatrical productions, and dog races. The running joke was that the men would make a toast "to our sweethearts and wives—may they never meet!" The chapter ends with the ominous line, "Outside in the darkness, the endless mass of pack ice was grinding against itself like a restless giant breaking mountains in its sleep."

Second 10 Minute Selection: Read the second half of the chapter titled "Pressure," beginning with the sentence, "The afternoon of September 30 brought an enormous ice floe bearing down on the ship from the port side." This passage shows the *Endurance* tilting from the pressure of the ice. "Everything that wasn't nailed down slid, slithered, and crashed against the bulwark. Dogs and men all went head over heels in a mass of howling confusion." Later on, Shackleton gives the order to abandon ship. "Then they went over the side, leaving *Endurance* to die in the grip of the ice."

Avi. *Poppy.* **Orchard, 1995. 147 p. Gr. 3–5.**
Mr. Ocax is an owl who rules the mice under his "protection." The mouse family has grown so large that some members need to move and locate a new food supply. Mr. Ocax forbids the move, but a young mouse named Poppy travels to the New House "on the northern side of Dimwood Forest." It's a dangerous journey. She narrowly escapes a fox and runs into a log belonging to Ereth, a porcupine. Poppy has always heard that porcupines eat mice. Poppy soon learns that Mr. Ocax is the one eating the mice, and she faces him in a showdown. The other titles in the Tales from the Dimwood Forest series include *Poppy and Rye* (1998), *Ragweed* (1999), *Ereth's Birthday* (2000), *Poppy's Return* (2005), and *Poppy and Ereth* (2009).

10 Minute Selection: Read the last few pages of chapter 10, "Dimwood Forest," beginning with the sentence, "Poppy made her way northward through the forest in short runs." A fox chases her into a log. The chapter ends with, "She was trapped." Read the entire following chapter, titled "Erethizon Dorsatum." Poppy meets Ereth. His dialogue is a delight to read aloud. "What the bee's butt are you doing here, fur ball?" Ereth chases the fox away. Poppy believes the porcupine will eat her and hides further in the smelly log. The chapter ends with Ereth asking, "Poppy . . . you wretched excuse for a runt, why the devil are you hiding in my toilet?"

Avi. *Romeo and Juliet—Together (and Alive!) at Last.* **Orchard, 1987. 122 p. Gr. 5–8.**
Eighth-grader Pete Saltz has a crush on Anabell Stackpoole, but he's too shy to tell her. His buddy, narrator Ed Sitrow, creates a plan to cast Saltz as Romeo and Anabell as Juliet in a quickly thrown-together, student-driven production of Shakespeare's play. Sitrow soon finds himself in over his head. Saltz's rival, Hamilton, tries to sabotage the play; the spotlight girl has a crush on Sitrow (and doesn't know how to operate the spotlight); and the set and costumes aren't ready until the actual production. This leads to the play hilariously featuring everything from log-cabin sets to costumes with jingling bells on pointy-toed shoes and paper crowns from Burger King. The characters also appear in the book *S.O.R. Losers* (1984).

10 Minute Selection: Read the very short chapter 3. Sitrow looks up the definition of *love* in the dictionary. He informs other students that Saltz is in love. He quotes the dictionary definition when he tells them that Saltz "has an attraction, desire, or affection for her, too. And while I know it's hard to believe, she seems to be arousing delight, admiration, tenderness (of an elicit kind), sympathetic interest, as well as benevolence and devoted affection." Move on to chapter 5. Sitrow calls for a secret meeting and sets up the grand plan. Finally, read chapter 18. Saltz is worried about the kissing scene. He's never kissed a girl before. Neither has Sitrow, who nonetheless instructs Saltz to scrunch and suck and practice on either a Cabbage Patch Kid or a dog.

Ayer, Eleanor. *Parallel Journeys*. Atheneum, 1995. 228 p. Gr. 6–12.
Author Ayer delivers a clear-cut look at World War II in Europe, supplemented with the first-person accounts of Jewish survivor Helen Waterford and Alfons Heck, who became a high-ranking officer of the Hitler Youth. "One followed Hitlerism, the other the Holocaust, along a parallel journey through history." The two met several years after the war and collaborated to tell their stories, giving unique perspectives of the events that happened. There are several German names and phrases throughout the book.

   10 Minute Selection: Inform your audience that the following excerpt is a real account, not a work of fiction. Read most of chapter 14, "Our Journey to Heaven," beginning with the sentence, "The women in Helen's group, having lived through their first selection, now rejoined the men." Helen learns that she is in "Birkenau, one of the forty camps at Auschwitz." She recognizes Anne Frank's mother talking to another prisoner. Helen gives an account of the conditions the prisoners faced. At the end of the chapter, Helen tells how Mrs. Frank died and how Anne was shipped to another camp. End the passage with the line, "Helen and her group of 300 waited, wondering what fate the Germans had in store for them next."

   Second 10 Minute Selection: If time allows, read a passage that shows the rare perspective of a former Nazi. Read the long chapter 13, "A Meeting with *Mein Führer*." Alfons, a sixteen-year-old member of the Hitler Youth, is stunned to learn that the Allies are very close to Germany. He is also surprised when he is named the new *Gefolgschaftsführer*, "a rank nearly equal to an army captain, in charge of 150 to 190 boys." At one point, he orders his boys to shoot an elderly teacher if he comes back and interferes. Alfons is taken to a train where he meets Albert Speer, "one of the two or three most powerful men in Germany." Despite their losing efforts, Speer asks the Hitler Youth to fight on. At the end of his speech, Speer introduces "somebody very special. The door opened and in walked Adolf Hitler."

Babbitt, Natalie. *Kneeknock Rise*. Farrar Straus Giroux, 1970. 118 p. Gr. 3–6.
The village of Instep is situated below a cliff in the Mammoth Mountains known as Kneeknock Rise. Legend has it that the terrible Megrimum lives on Kneeknock Rise. The villagers hear it moan when the weather gets bad. A young boy named Eagan is sent to visit his Instep relatives—Aunt Gertrude, Uncle Anson, and cousin Ada. Another relative, Uncle Ott, is missing and has left his dog, Annabelle, behind. One day, Ada teases Eagan, saying that he is too afraid to climb up

Kneeknock Rise. Eagan heads "toward the cliff, fearless and wild, and the old dog ran after him." When Eagan's aunt hears that he is climbing up to the Megrimum, she drops "in a faint to the floor."

10 Minute Selection: There are no numbered chapters in the book. Start reading the beginning. Through Babbitt's wonderfully descriptive writing, we learn about Kneeknock Rise, the Megrimum, and the cast of characters. One night, Eagan wakes up to "a violent crash of thunder." Ada joins him, and they listen for the Megrimum. "Just then, from somewhere high up in the night, a thin, wailing sound came riding down the wind." They spot a figure climbing down the mountain during a flash of lightning. Aunt Gertrude comes in and screams. She sees something outside of the window and faints. End the passage with the line, "And Annabelle, emerging from under the cot, stood with her front paws on the windowsill, barking on and on against the glass, which now showed nothing but the empty, drizzling dark."

Babbitt, Natalie. *Tuck Everlasting.* **Farrar Straus Giroux, 1975. 139 p. Gr. 4–8.**
The book starts with one of my favorite opening sentences: "The first week of August hangs at the very top of summer, the top of the live-long year, like the highest seat of a Ferris wheel when it pauses in its turning." One August, Winnie Foster is walking through her family's woods when she comes upon a teenage boy drinking from a spring. The boy—Jesse Tuck—and his family kidnap Winnie; they want to explain why she should not drink from the spring nor tell anyone about it. The Tucks had found a spring that gives eternal life. A strange man in a yellow suit shows up with evil intentions to own the woods and sell the water to "certain people, people who deserve it. And it will be very, very expensive." Winnie has to decide if she will take a drink of the special water.

10 Minute Selection: Read chapters 7 and 8. Winnie learns the story of the Tuck family and how they came to understand they would live forever. Jesse states, "As far as I know, I'll stay seventeen until the end of the world." The passage ends with "not one of them noticed that the man they had passed on the road, the man in the yellow suit, had crept up to the bushes by the stream and heard it all, the whole fantastic story."

Ball, Zachary. *Bristle Face.* **Holiday House, 1962. 206 p. Gr. 4–8.**
Jase is a fourteen-year-old runaway who adopts a funny-looking dog he names Bristle Face. "He looked like he had started out to be a hound, then decided he'd look better as a porcupine." The two befriend Lute, a fairly lazy store owner who has decided to run for sheriff. Bristle Face is good at digging up box turtles, but Jase has dreams of Bristle Face becoming a fox hound. Rad Toler, the current sheriff, shows up at Lute's store one day. "He pointed to Bristle Face and said, 'That one. I'm takin' him with me.'"

10 Minute Selection: This is actually just a four-minute passage. Start well into chapter 3, "Old Red Snow," beginning with the sentence, "Right then a terrible squawking set up amongst the chickens." Bristle Face is chasing Widow Jarkey's rooster and then spots a rabbit. He runs into a clothesline and finds himself "head and front feet into a pair of the Widow's bloomer kind of underpants." The story turns into a slapstick chain of events. The passage ends with, "The Widow was still laughing too, and she told me she'd had so much fun out of Bristle Face that she wasn't even mad about her clean clothes getting dirty."

Second 10 Minute Selection: Read the middle portion of chapter 6, "Cat Fight," starting with the sentence, "We followed the creek to the big pool." Jase is deep in the woods trying out a fishing hole for the first time. As he's about to bait his hook, he gets a strange feeling. "Eight or ten feet in front of me, crouched down on a flat rock that was about two feet above me, yellowish eyes looking like two fire coals there in the daylight, was a panther." The panther attacks, but Bristle Face charges. Jase gets slashed by the panther's claws and falls into the water. He's aware that Bristle Face and the panther have also fallen in. End the passage with this cliff-hanger line: "I watched them and waited for Bristle Face and the panther to come to the top. But they didn't."

Bauer, Joan. *Rules of the Road.* **Putnam, 1998. 201 p. Gr. 6–12.**
Jenna has had her driver's license for only six months when Mrs. Gladstone, the head of the Gladstone Shoe Stores, hires Jenna to be her driver. Mrs. Gladstone had noticed Jenna's head for business and employs the teen's help to thwart a company takeover by her son, Elden. They take a cross-country trip in Mrs. Gladstone's Cadillac from Chicago, Illinois, to Dallas, Texas. Jenna is hesitant about taking the job, but she needs to get away from her alcoholic father. The two unlikely travelers become strong allies against Elden and the stockholders. Jenna and Mrs. Gladstone reappear in the book *Best Foot Forward* (2005).

10 Minute Selection: Read the opening chapter. We see Jenna in action as a top-notch shoe saleswoman. "My grandmother always said that everyone needs something in life that they do pretty well. For me, it's selling shoes." Jenna is nervous because Mrs. Gladstone, the company president, is in the store watching everything. Jenna is horrified when her father shows up at the store drunk, hollering her name. Move on and read a brief passage from chapter 2, beginning with the sentence, "The phone rang." Mrs. Gladstone hires Jenna as a driver. Jenna is not sure. "'Mrs. Gladstone, I've only driven a twelve-year-old Honda Civic, never a Cadillac.' 'That will change tomorrow, won't it? Good night.' 'But—' Click." End with the sentence, "'You've never been in a Cadillac,' Faith countered, grabbing half my sandwich."

Bauer, Marion Dane. *On My Honor.* **Clarion, 1986. 90 p. Gr. 4–5.**
Joel isn't crazy about Tony's suggestion to bike to Starved Rock State Park, but he gives in. Joel's father makes him promise to stick to the plan. "'On your honor?' Joel's father said. 'You won't go anywhere except the park?' 'On my honor,' Joel repeated." Before they arrive at the park, Tony stops his bike by a river and convinces Joel to go swimming. Tragically, while trying to show off his swimming abilities, Tony disappears in the water. Joel panics. A teen couple stops and unsuccessfully helps Joel search for Tony. Joel convinces them that he'll contact the police. Instead, he bikes home and tells everyone that Tony went to the park ahead of him. Now he has to get through the next few days with this terrible secret.

10 Minute Selection: Read chapter 3. Tony climbs into the Vermillion River. Joel hesitates. "It's really dirty. And the worst of the stuff, chemicals and sewage, you can't even see." Tony, as usual, gets his way and Joel enters the water. The two get into an argument. Joel loses his temper and challenges Tony to swim out to a sandbar. Continue reading chapter 4. Joel swims to the sandbar. He makes it and looks back to brag. "Behind him stretched the river, smooth and glistening, reddish brown, but there was no sign of Tony."

Bellairs, John. *The House with a Clock in Its Walls.* **Dial, 1973. 179 p. Gr. 4–7.**
Lewis goes to live with his uncle Jonathan in Michigan after his parents are killed in a car crash. Jonathan has purchased an old mansion that belonged at one time to the wizard Isaac Izard. Lewis meets Mrs. Zimmerman, Jonathan's next-door neighbor, who just happens to be a witch. Jonathan himself has dabbled in magic. Lewis learns that Izard had placed a mysterious clock somewhere in the house; they can hear the ticking. They hurry to locate it after Lewis discovers the following passage, written by Izard: "Doomsday not come yet! I'll draw it nearer by a perspective, or make a CLOCK that shall set all the world on fire upon an instant." There are nineteen books in the series. The second title is *Figure in the Shadows* (1975). Some of the latter books were written by Brad Strickland from Bellairs's notes.

10 Minute Selection: As setup, inform your audience that Lewis has told a boy named Tarby that he is able to raise the spirits of dead people. Read chapter 5. Lewis has arranged to meet Tarby in a cemetery at midnight. They are sitting in front of a tomb. Lewis draws the proper symbols, but he becomes stumped at one point. "Lewis had read in Jonathan's book that you were supposed to fill in the space with the name of the dead person." Lewis doesn't know the name, but his hand is guided to write the name Selanna. There is a loud booming noise from the tomb. "The iron doors jolted, as if they had been struck a blow from inside. The chain rattled, and there was a clunk on the pavement. The padlock had fallen." The boys run.

Berry, James. *Ajeemah and His Son.* **HarperCollins, 1991. 83 p. Gr. 6–12.**
It is 1807 in Africa. Ajeemah is accompanying his son Atu as they go to present a dowry to Atu's future stepfather—a dowry of two gold coins hidden in Ajeemah's shoe. Along the way, the two are captured by slave traders and shipped to Jamaica. They are sold and separated. They never see each other again. Ajeemah wants to set his owner's plantation on fire. Atu wants to run away. He goes so far as to steal a gun. Atu eventually dies. Years later, Ajeemah remarries and slavery is outlawed. He recounts his story at his daughter's wedding. "Then the people stood, looking at Ajeemah. They didn't seem to know what to do, how to love him and honor him. . . . Obviously overcome by the moment, Ajeemah merely stood there. Somebody began to clap. And everybody clapped." Despite its slim size, there is a lot of emotion packed into this book.

    10 Minute Selection: There are no chapters. Start at the beginning and read through to the line, "And as the coast of Africa disappeared, a long-drawn-out groan of grief rose up together steadily from the people one after another, till all died away into silence." These first few pages tell of the kidnapping of Ajeemah and Atu.

Bloor, Edward. *Tangerine.* **Harcourt, 1997. 294 p. Gr. 7–10.**
Paul and his family move to Florida, where part of Paul's middle school has been destroyed by sinkholes. He transfers to Tangerine Middle School and joins the soccer team. His achievements are overshadowed by his older brother Erik's accomplishments on the high school football team. Paul is bothered by Erik's cruel tendencies. Even though he is an athlete, Paul has been legally blind since he was five years old. He functions well enough with his thick glasses. Throughout the story, Paul is bothered by hidden memories that eventually reveal the real cause of his disability.

    10 Minute Selection: Read the chapter titled "Friday, September 22." It is Paul's first soccer game for his new team, the War Eagles. They are on the road, facing the Whippoorwills, a team known for its dirty tactics. "I don't know why—maybe they were mad about having such a wimpy nickname—but these guys turned out to be really nasty. So did their fans." Paul's team gets tripped, elbowed, spit upon, and cursed. Paul goes in the game during the second half when his teammate Tino retaliates by throwing punches at an opponent. A fullback for the other team knocks Paul down, "stretched out my goggles from my face, scooped up a handful of mud, and smeared it in my eyes. *In my eyes!* I went berserk!" Paul gets taken out for throwing punches. Paul is finally told by a teammate that he's a true War Eagle and that he has brothers to back him up.

Blume, Judy. *Fudge-a-Mania.* **Dutton, 1990. 147 p. Gr. 1–4.**
The Tubman and Hatcher families decide to take a vacation together in Maine. This upsets Peter Hatcher since Sheila Tubman is his sworn enemy. The summer house is very full with two grandparents, several pets, and Peter's guest Jimmy Fargo. Even Jimmy's father decides to join them at the last minute and sleeps on the couch. Peter's little brother Fudge loses his pet mynah bird Uncle Feather, gets sick from eating too many blueberries, gets stuck in a folding bed, and plans on marrying Sheila so she can keep away monsters at night. The other books featuring Peter, Fudge, and Sheila are *Tales of a Fourth Grade Nothing* (1972), *Otherwise Known as Sheila the Great* (1972), *Superfudge* (1980), and *Double Fudge* (2002).

10 Minute Selection: Read the first three chapters, which are very short. Chapter 1, "Who's the Lucky Bride?" finds Fudge declaring his plans to marry Sheila Tubman. Peter pretends to faint every time Sheila's name is mentioned. Chapter 2, "Pete and Farley," finds the Hatcher family trying to have a quiet meal at Tico-Taco. Fudge asks the waiter if he has cooties. Chapter 3, "The Most Disgusting of Them All," has the Hatcher family showing up in Southwest Harbor, Maine. While the Tubmans come out to greet them, Peter's dog, Turtle, runs into a skunk. Have fun reading the dialogue of the characters, who speak as they hold their noses. "'Thith ith too nautheating for wordth,' Libby said, grabbing Jake and running back into the house. 'Do thomething, Peter!' Sheila yelled. 'What am I thuppoth to do?'"

Bond, Michael. *A Bear Called Paddington.* **Houghton Mifflin, 1958. 128 p. Gr. K–4.**
Mr. and Mrs. Brown encounter a small, polite bear in London's Paddington Station. He tells them that he has arrived from Darkest Peru. Mr. and Mrs. Brown find a note on the bear's suitcase that reads "Please look after this bear. Thank you." They do just that and name the bear after the train station. Paddington becomes a part of the family, which includes the children, Judy and Jonathan, and the housekeeper, Mrs. Bird. Paddington has several small adventures, including taking a difficult bath, going shopping and winding up in the store's front window, helping Mr. Brown win a painting competition, attending a play and impressing the cranky lead actor, getting lost at the beach, and performing magic tricks that don't always work. Paddington is featured in several more chapter books and picture books. The second chapter book in the series is *More about Paddington* (1959).

10 Minute Selection: Read chapter 3, "Paddington Goes Underground." Paddington is served breakfast in bed, which proves to be harder to eat than it looked. Judy and Mrs. Brown are impatient to take Paddington shopping, so the young bear puts his bacon in his travel case. They are followed by dogs. Paddington has trouble navigating the crowds and escalators in the Underground. He gets separated from his companions and runs into trouble with an inspector. Mrs.

Brown and Judy come to the rescue. The inspector has other things on his mind. "Judging by the noise coming from the top of the escalator there was some sort of dog fight going on. It needed investigating."

Boston, L. M. *The Children of Green Knowe*. Harcourt, 1955. 183 p. Gr. 3–5.
A little boy named Tolly moves to Green Noah, once known as Green Knowe. His great-grandmother Oldknow welcomes him, as do the spirits of three children—Toby, Linnet, and Alexander—who all lived there in the seventeenth century. They had all died in the Great Plague. Great-grandmother Oldknow spins stories about the three children; their horse, Feste; and the events surrounding the old manor. Tolly learns of a curse put on the house by a gypsy woman many years before. The big tree called Green Noah is dangerous. It even has a song about it. "Green Noah / Demon Tree / Evil Fingers / Can't catch me!" The other books in the series include *Treasure of Green Knowe* (1958), *The River at Green Knowe* (1959), *A Stranger at Green Knowe* (1961), *An Enemy at Green Knowe* (1964), and *The Stone of Green Knowe* (1976).

   10 Minute Selection: Read the chapter titled "Toby's Story." Once upon a time, Linnet was ill, and Toby had to ride on the horse, Feste, to find the doctor. When they reached the bridge over the river, Feste refused to go on it, even after Toby hit the horse. Instead, Feste jumped in the river. When they made it safely to land, Toby yelled at the horse. "Suddenly there came a hair-raising scream, the scream of rending wood, sounding like an animal in panic. The wooden bridge twisted and cockled under his eyes and, with cracks like cannon fire, collapsed and was swept in a tangled mess downstream." The horse had saved Toby, and they made it to the doctor's home in time. End with the sentence, "The next thing that Toby knew was that Feste was blowing down his neck as if to say: 'That supper was splendid, but how about breakfast?'"

Brittain, Bill. *Dr. Dredd's Wagon of Wonders*. Harper and Row, 1987. 179 p. Gr. 3–8.
The townspeople of Coven Tree are suffering from a great drought. A mysterious man named Dr. Dredd shows up promising rain. A boy named Calvin, who belongs to Dredd, has the ability to make it rain. Calvin runs away from his cruel master. The citizens of Coven Tree protect him once they learn Dredd is in league with the devil. Dredd, in turn, unleashes a series of horrors on the town, including a strongman, a black knight, and a fire-breathing dragon. This is the second book in the Coven Tree series. The other titles are *The Wish Giver* (1986) and *Professor Popkins' Prodigious Polish* (1990).

   10 Minute Selection: Read a short portion of chapter 1, "Strangers," beginning with the line, "Ladies and gentlemen, I am Dr. Hugo Dredd." Dredd shows the folks of Coven Tree the wonders inside his wagon. They learn about the suit of armor that once belonged to the Black Knight of Etherium. The suit of armor is split up. End the passage with the sentence, "Legend has it that if the two sections of armor were to be joined, the Black Knight would rise again to scourge the countryside." Move on to chapter 5, "No Holds Barred." Begin halfway through the chapter with the line, "By the middle of the afternoon, Calvin had mended a squeaky stair tread, fashioned a new handle for the grain shovel and fixed a broken harness in the barn." Dr. Dredd has brought his strongman, Antaeus, to battle Sven the blacksmith over Calvin. Ellen, Calvin's friend, helps discover the secret to defeating Antaeus. Dr. Dredd retreats back to his wagon. The chapter ends with Dredd talking to the suit of armor that once belonged to the Black Knight. "From somewhere deep within the armor came a low, hideous moaning."

Bruchac, Joseph. *Eagle Song.* **Dial, 1997. 79 p. Gr. 1–4.**
Fourth-grader Danny and his family left their home on the Mohawk reservation to live in Brooklyn. The other students tease Danny. "Hey, Chief, going home to your teepee?" His father visits Danny's classroom and shares a story and some information about the Iroquois. The other students are very receptive to the presentation, and Danny wonders if he'll be treated better. He learns the answer to that question when he's injured by a basketball that is thrown at him. Things get worse when Danny's mother gets a call that his father was injured in a construction accident. A glossary and a pronunciation guide are provided.

10 Minute Selection: Read chapter 4, "The Visit." Danny's father is the guest speaker in Danny's classroom. He holds up a wampum belt. "To us it is like a book because it tells a story." At this point, go back to chapter 3, "The Great Peace," and read the story that Danny's father shares with the class, the story of the peacemaker Aionwatha (Hiawatha). End with the sentence, "So the Great League of Peace was formed by our Iroquois people long ago," and jump back to read the rest of chapter 4. Danny's father goes on to tell how the founders of the United States used Iroquois symbols. At the end of the day, "the class exploded into applause. . . . It was great his father had come to school. But would the kids treat him better now?"

Bruchac, Joseph, and James Bruchac. *When the Chenoo Howls: Native American Tales of Terror.* **Walker, 1998. 131 p. Gr. 4–8.**
These twelve traditional and original Native American stories feature such creatures as the Stone Giant, the Flying Head, Ugly Face, Man Bear, the Spreaders, the title character, and more. The stories come from several Northeast Woodland Native American cultures, including the Abenaki, Seneca, Mohawk, Lenape, Oneida, Onondaga, Penobscot, and Passamaquoddy. In the story "Amankamek," a snake disguises itself as a human and takes a girl named Red Flower from her

family. In "Toad Woman," three contemporary friends are exploring a cedar bog when one of the boys goes under the water. Another boy believes he "saw something move just under the surface. It looked almost like a brown, long-fingered hand." A pronunciation guide is provided.

10 Minute Selection: Read the story "Keewahkwee." Little Weasel is a boy who lives with Older Sister. She keeps her face covered with her long hair. A rabbit informs Little Weasel that Older Sister is really Keewahkwee, a cannibal ogre who is fattening him up to eat. The boy runs away but is pursued. He is helped along the way by Porcupine and Heron before he finds his grandfather and a tiny dog. Older Sister catches up and is ready to eat them all when Little Dog shakes himself four times, grows larger with each shake, and destroys Keewahkwee.

Bunting, Eve. *Someone Is Hiding on Alcatraz Island*. Clarion, 1984. 136 p. Gr. 5–8.
Danny is being pursued by the Outlaws gang because he saved a mugging victim from the brother of a gang member. They spot him on Fisherman's Wharf in San Francisco. He manages to jump aboard a departing tourist boat to Alcatraz Island. The four gang members follow on the next boat, forcing Danny to hide on the island overnight. The Outlaws catch Danny and a young park ranger named Biddy. They lock the two in cells while they look for one of their missing companions. Danny manages to escape and looks for a way to overthrow the gang and rescue Biddy.

10 Minute Selection: Read chapter 5. Danny is looking for a place to hide, knowing that the Outlaws are prowling the island. He is excited when he spots a group of rangers, but before he shouts, he realizes that the Outlaws have broken into the ranger station and are the ones wearing the ranger jackets. Danny climbs a water tower to better monitor the Outlaws. He soon hears a voice below him. It is Jelly Bean, one of the gang members. The chapter ends with Jelly Bean, who talks like his nose is stuffed, taunting Danny. "There you are Daddy-Boy. I'b cubbing to get you."

Burch, Robert. *Ida Early Comes over the Mountain*. Viking, 1980. 145 p. Gr. 3–5.
During the Great Depression in Georgia, a tall countrywoman named Ida Early shows up one day at the Sutton household looking for work. The children, tired of their bossy aunt Earnestine, who took over the household after their mother passed away, are immediately attracted by Ida's tall tales and playful character. One day, some classmates make fun of Ida's odd appearance. The Sutton children feel bad that they didn't come to her defense. Ida is no longer playful and prefers to go to bed early. Ida saves the day during a school program when a child's pet bear suddenly attacks one of the students. The sequel is *Christmas with Ida Early* (1983).

10 Minute Selection: Read the short chapter titled "The Stew-Making Fool." Aunt Earnestine has instructed Ida to make lunch while she and Mr. Sutton are in town. Read the next chapter, titled "The Tiddlywinks Champion of the Whole Wide World." Ida plays tiddlywinks with the children instead of preparing lunch. She tricks young Ellen into browning the meat while waiting for her turn. "Unless you think you might not be quite old enough to shoulder such a responsibility." When Ellen returns, Ida convinces Randall to peel the potatoes. The two children go back and forth between the game and kitchen. When Earnestine and Mr. Sutton arrive home, the children are noisy and lunch is ready. Earnestine complains that she hoped the children hadn't been carrying on all morning. Ida replies, "I don't think they have. But to tell you the truth, I've been so busy cooking I've hardly had time to notice."

Burch, Robert. *Queenie Peavy*. Viking, 1966. 151 p. Gr. 4–6.
Thirteen-year-old Queenie Peavy has been sent to the principal's office more than one dozen times in her first month of eighth grade. She's very sensitive about her father being in prison, and her temper gets out of hand. Queenie chews tobacco, and she can "also spit it—with deadly aim." She is also very accurate when throwing rocks. She arranges for an accident to happen to one of her chief tormentors. She gets in trouble not only for that incident but also for breaking a church window, something she denies doing. She prepares herself for a visit to the reformatory.

10 Minute Selection: Read the chapter titled "The Trick on Cravey Mason." Cravey constantly teases Queenie. When the class is on a field trip, Queenie sets up a log rail near a stream bank and dares Cravey to walk on it. When he does, Queenie gives the base of the log a kick, knocking Cravey into the water. Unfortunately, the log falls on his leg, breaking it. Continue reading into the next chapter, "Them Promises I Never Kept." Queenie is in trouble for breaking Cravey's leg. Cravey's father threatens to send the medical bill to Queenie's mother. Queenie is ordered to apologize to Cravey, but when Cravey states that they'll send her mother to prison with her father, Queenie states, "All I've got to say is that if you don't leave me alone I may decide to break your other leg, too!"

Burnford, Sheila. *The Incredible Journey*. Little, Brown, 1960. 145 p. Gr. 3–6.
Three pets—an old bull terrier, a young Labrador retriever, and a Siamese cat—leave the home of their caretaker and set off to find their owners. Their travels take them over two hundred miles of Canadian wilderness. In addition to coming into contact with several humans, the animals also encounter a porcupine, a wolf, a bobcat, and bears. They are occasionally separated, but eventually they meet up and take care of each other.

10 Minute Selection: Read chapter 3. The terrier is feeling the effects of its old age in the wilderness. Food is scarce. The old dog collapses. A bear cub finds him and injures the dog with its claws. "The smell of the drawn blood excited the cub further; he straddled the dog's body and started to play with the long white tail, nibbling at the end of it like a child with a new toy." The cat attacks the cub, which attracts the attention of the mother bear. The retriever and the cat prevent the mother bear from attacking the helpless terrier. The cat finds food for the old dog. The chapter ends with the line, "But the cat purring against his chest and the young dog curled at his back were wakeful and alert most of the remaining night; neither moved from his side."

Butterworth, Oliver. *The Enormous Egg.* **Little, Brown, 1956. 188 p. Gr. 3–5.**
Nate Twitchell and his family are surprised when one of their hens lays "the biggest egg I'd ever seen." Nate and the hen take good care of the egg but are shocked when a strange-looking creature emerges. A vacationing paleontologist, Dr. Ziemer, confirms that the creature is indeed a triceratops dinosaur. Nate names the dinosaur Uncle Beazley after a distant relative. "If I recollect his picture, there is a certain resemblance between the two." Uncle Beazley grows too big to stay at the farm. He is 3,176 pounds and more than seventeen feet long when they ship him first to the National Museum in Washington, D.C., and then to the zoo. Uncle Beazley's life is in danger when a senator tries to pass a bill that ensures that all dinosaurs remain extinct.

10 Minute Selection: Read most of chapter 13, beginning with the sentence, "Well, we decided that the best time to exercise Uncle Beazley was early in the morning, before people were out on the streets." Nate and the triceratops get into trouble when the driver of a pickup truck honks his horn and Uncle Beazley knocks the truck over. Continue reading into chapter 14. Dr. Ziemer gets a phone call from a police captain about the incident. End the passage with the lines, "Then there was an even longer pause. Finally the police captain said, 'I'd better come over and see you about this,' and then he hung up."

Byars, Betsy. *The Pinballs.* **Harper and Row, 1977. 136 p. Gr. 4–6.**
Three children arrive at a foster home. Harvey's mother left him and never made contact again. Harvey's father just broke his son's legs by running over him with the car while drunk. Thomas J was abandoned as a baby and raised by two elderly ladies who found him in front of their farmhouse. Thomas J arrived at the foster home after both sisters broke their hips. Carlie is an outspoken girl who is staying at the foster home "until the home situation stabilizes." Her stepfather is physically abusive. The three kids slowly bond, not without difficulties, with each other and the foster parents. The last line of the book, where Thomas J says, "Let's go

home," will touch many hearts. Some of the media references are dated—Sonny and Cher, Tony Orlando and Dawn—but these won't distract from the story.

10 Minute Selection: Read the first chapter, which introduces each child and explains how each one came to the foster home. Move to chapter 13. Inform your audience that Harvey hasn't been truthful to Carlie about his legs. He has told her that he broke both legs playing football. In this chapter, Carlie is pushing Harvey up a hill to the public library. Carlie jokes that they should scare Mrs. Mason. "We could get a dummy, dress him up in your clothes and push him down the street." The two begin to talk about their fathers. Carlie never knew her real father. Harvey tells Carlie the truth about his legs.

Cameron, Ann. *The Stories Julian Tells*. Knopf, 1981. 71 p. Gr. K–3.
Julian shares stories about himself, his younger brother Huey, his parents, and his new friend Gloria. One story concerns the boys eating pudding that was made for their mother and being punished for it. In another story, Huey believes that the word *catalog* means something concerning cats. He's upset when the catalog arrives and there's nary a picture of a cat. In other stories, Julian loses a tooth, he meets the new girl who moves to his block, and the boys plant a garden. The other books featuring Julian, Huey, and Gloria are *More Stories Julian Tells* (1986), *Julian's Glorious Summer* (1987), *Julian, Secret Agent* (1988), *Julian, Dream Doctor* (1990), *The Stories Huey Tells* (1995), *More Stories Huey Tells* (1997), *Gloria's Way* (2000), and *Gloria Rising* (2002).

10 Minute Selection: Read the very first story, titled "The Pudding like a Night on the Sea." Father declares that he's going to make a wonderful pudding that "will taste like a whole raft of lemons. It will taste like a night on the sea." The boys watch him make the pudding. Before Father takes a nap, he warns the boys to leave the pudding alone. The boys find it hard to resist. They each take a taste . . . and wind up eating most of the pudding. Father threatens to beat and whip them. The boys are afraid. "'Now it's time for your beating!' my father said." Huey has to beat eggs with an eggbeater. "I hope you're ready for your whipping!" Julian whips the egg whites. The boys are tired from the work and turn down their father's offer to taste the new pudding. Their mother, however, is pleased. "'Why, this tastes like a whole raft of lemons,' she said. 'This tastes like a night on the sea.'"

Cameron, Eleanor. *The Wonderful Flight to the Mushroom Planet*. Little, Brown, 1954. 195 p. Gr. 3–5.
David finds an unusual notice in the newspaper asking for a small spaceship to be delivered to Mr. Tyco M. Bass. He and his friend Chuck build a spaceship out of material they find around their homes. Mr. Bass is delighted and adds some final touches to it. He sends the boys into outer space to explore an unknown planet that Mr. Bass calls Basidium-X. The boys meet the inhabitants and work to

save the planet. Although the book is certainly a product of its time—one of the characters actually says "Gee whillikers"—its environmental message is very relevant today. This is the first book in the Mushroom Planet series, which includes *Stowaway to the Mushroom Planet* (1956), *Mr. Bass's Planetoid* (1958), *A Mystery for Mr. Bass* (1960), and *Time and Mr. Bass* (1967).

10 Minute Selection: Tell your audience that two boys just landed their spaceship on a strange planet. Begin reading the last few pages of chapter 11, "The Pale Planet," beginning with the sentence, "Come on Chuck—leave the bag here." The chapter ends with the boys seeing two strange men who are moaning and groaning. Continue reading chapter 12, "The Wise Men Who Weren't Very Wise." The strange men tell the boys that they haven't been able to solve the problems their planet is facing. Their leader, the Great Ta, has threatened to behead them. They go on to tell them what that problem is. The boys meet a man "only slightly taller than themselves." End with the lines, "'I am Ta,' said the man in deep tones. 'I greet you.'"

Cassedy, Sylvia. *Behind the Attic Wall*. Crowell, 1983. 315 p. Gr. 4–6.
Twelve-year-old Maggie has been kicked out of several boarding schools. She is a loner and doesn't get along with anyone. She is sent to Adelphi Hills but is surprised that the former school is now her new home. She lives there with her two strict aunts, who constantly criticize her. Maggie eventually hears strange voices. She finds a secret room that contains two dolls. "'She's here at last.' The voice came—could that be?—from the woman doll—from inside her head or something, because her lips didn't move, but she was speaking, saying real words—a doll." And then, the dolls began to move.

10 Minute Selection: Read chapter 12, which begins with the beautifully written sentence, "The thing was that it all happened little by little, the way lights go down in an auditorium, so slowly you aren't sure that they're going down at all, but by the time everything is finally dark you feel no surprise." Maggie begins to hear voices and wonders who else is in the house. Her aunts simply tell her that she is high-strung. Maggie continues to hear the voices and searches the entire house. "What *were* they? Voices without people?" The chapter ends with Maggie remembering that she had seen a face in a high window on the day she arrived.

Catling, Patricia Skene. *The Chocolate Touch*. Morrow, 1979. 126 p. Gr. K–4.
Young John Midas loves chocolate—so much so that he eats too much of it. He sneaks extra chocolate when his parents aren't looking. One day, he finds a mysterious coin and spends it at a candy store that he's never seen before. He buys a box of chocolates, but finds only one piece inside. However, "it was the most chocolaty chocolate he had ever encountered." Things start going wrong. Everything he eats and drinks turns into chocolate. Soon, everything he touches turns

into chocolate. When his mother turns into "a lifeless statue of chocolate," John heads back to the strange candy store for help.

10 Minute Selection: Read chapter 5. John sits down in class and gets ready to take a test. John is nervous so he asks permission to get a drink of water. Unfortunately, the water "turned into ice-cold chocolate water, thin and sweet." He returns to class, but his pencil turns into chocolate. Move on to chapter 7. John is in the school cafeteria, and he's sick of the taste of chocolate. He's looking forward to eating food he normally dislikes. "John took a plate of cold chicken and ham, potato chips, and a crisp, moist lettuce-and-tomato salad. . . . He also took a pint of milk, a thick-crusted whole-wheat roll and a cool pat of butter, a tumbler of water with ice cubes clinking against the glass, and a dish of fresh fruit—slices of orange and grapefruit and banana and grapes." Everything turns to chocolate. John cries out, "Oh, dear, oh, dear! What is going to happen to me?"

Chew, Ruth. *The Wednesday Witch*. Scholastic, 1969. 128 p. Gr. 2–4.
Hilda is a Wednesday Witch who rides around on a vacuum cleaner. "Her magic is at its best on Wednesday. The rest of the week she works on her spells. On Wednesday she comes out of her cave and looks for mischief." Hilda shows up at Mary Jane's door after the young girl opens her mother's bottle of Mischief perfume. Mary Jane doesn't let herself be tricked by the witch. In fact, the witch's cat, Cinders, prefers to stay with Mary Jane. "All she feeds me is toads—when she remembers to feed me at all." Eventually, Mary Jane takes possession of the vacuum cleaner and the witch herself, whom Mary Jane shrunk small enough to fit inside a doll house.

10 Minute Selection: Read the chapter titled "The Magic Scissors." Hilda notices her cat is missing. "There was no little cat to send for firewood, so Hilda had to go herself. . . . In the end Witch Hilda had a cold snack of grasshopper legs." She finds her magic scissors and commands her vacuum cleaner to find mischief. They return to Mary Jane's house. The witch demands the return of her cat. She takes the scissors, which have the power to shrink things with each snip. Soon "the cat was only one inch high." The witch leaves her vacuum cleaner behind but steals Mary Jane's roller skates. The chapter ends with Cinders the cat curling up on a miniature sofa in Mary Jane's dollhouse.

Christopher, John. *The White Mountains*. Macmillan, 1967. 164 p. Gr. 4–8.
The world is controlled by large metallic machines known as the Tripods. Young Will runs away from home before he is Capped, a ritual young people go through to become passive servants of the Tripods. He learns of a resistance group that resides far away in the White Mountains. He is joined on this dangerous journey by his nemesis, Henry, and another boy Will calls Beanpole. As they get nearer to the White Mountains, they are pursued by a Tripod. The other books in the series

are *The City of Gold and Lead* (1967), *The Pool of Fire* (1968), and the prequel, *When the Tripods Came* (1988).

10 Minute Selection: I rarely pick a selection so close to the book's climax, but this passage will certainly hook young listeners without ruining the ending for them. Read the last section of chapter 9, "We Fight a Battle." Begin with the sentence, "We were continuing to climb over rough, but mostly open country." The boys hear something. "It came from behind, faint but seeming to grow louder every instant: the hideous warbling ululation which we had heard in the cabin of the *Orion*—the hunting call of the Tripods." The boys have "metal eggs," which today's young readers will recognize as hand grenades. The eggs have no effect on the Tripod. A tentacle grabs Will and brings him up into the air. Will manages to throw his egg into an opening, where it explodes and shuts down the machine. The chapter ends with the line, "Our tormentor would not torment us again."

Cleary, Beverly. *The Mouse and the Motorcycle*. Morrow, 1965. 158p. Gr. K–3.
Ralph is a mouse who lives in the Mountain View Inn. He meets a boy named Keith, who is traveling with his mother and father. The two strike up a friendship when Keith encourages Ralph to ride a toy motorcycle. "'You have to make a noise,' the boy explained matter-of-factly. 'These cars don't go unless you make a noise.'" Feel free to make any noise to accompany the book's "Pb-pb-b-b" motorcycle noise. Ralph feels bad when he loses Keith's motorcycle. He then puts his family in danger when he chews some hotel sheets. "It means war on mice. . . . It means traps, poisons . . ." Ralph eventually comes to the rescue when Keith develops a fever. Ralph also appears in *Runaway Ralph* (1970) and *Ralph S. Mouse* (1982).

10 Minute Selection: Read the entire chapter 5, "Adventure in the Night." Ralph takes the motorcycle out for a nocturnal spin through the hotel. He is terrified when a man appears with his pet dog. He next finds Keith's door shut, but he is helped by the kindly bellboy Matt. Ralph is spotted by Keith's mother in the chapter's funny conclusion. "'But I'm positive—' insisted the boy's mother. 'That you saw a mouse on a little red motorcycle,' finished the boy's father and laughed even harder."

Cleary, Beverly. *Ramona the Pest*. Morrow, 1968. 192 p. Gr. K–4.
Ramona Quimby is one of the most popular characters in the world of children's literature. Her year in kindergarten makes this one of the funniest books on the market. The climax comes when Ramona fails to stop pulling another girl's curls and becomes, in the words of her older sister Beatrice, "a kindergarten dropout." Ramona appears in the Henry Huggins books as well as *Beezus and Ramona* (1955). She also stars in her own series, which includes *Ramona the Brave* (1975), *Ramona and Her Father* (1977), *Ramona and Her Mother* (1979), *Ramona Quimby Age 8* (1981), *Ramona Forever* (1984), and *Ramona's World* (1999).

10 Minute Selection: Read the last section of the first chapter, titled "Ramona's Great Day." Start with the lines, "'All right, class,' said Miss Binney briskly. 'Let's go outside and play Gray Duck.'" Ramona gets into trouble because she pulls Susan's hair. She is forced to sit on the bench while the other children play their game. Two preschoolers look at Ramona, and one says, "She's sitting there because she's bad." During naptime, Ramona tries to show how she's "the best rester" by snoring. The other children giggle and snore themselves. "They led to more and more, less and less delicate snores until everyone was snoring except the few who didn't know how to snore." The chapter ends with Ramona thinking kindergarten didn't turn out like she thought it would but hoping tomorrow would be better.

Cleaver, Vera, and Bill Cleaver. *Where the Lilies Bloom.* Harper and Row, 1969. 174 p. Gr. 5–8.
Fourteen-year-old Mary Call is trying to keep her family together after their father has passed away. They live in the Great Smoky Mountains in a shack their land-lord, Kiser, owns. Mary Call saves Kiser's life and gets him to agree to sign the house and land over to her. Kiser wants to marry Devola, Mary Call's eighteen-year-old sister, who folks feel is "womanly in form but with a child's heart and a child's mind." Mary Call does her best to keep her father's death a secret so the family isn't turned over to the county. She almost gives up when she learns Kiser doesn't truly own the house and land, and the paper he signed is worthless. The sequel is *Trial Valley* (1977).

10 Minute Selection: Read chapter 10. Winter is coming, and the children are arguing as they scramble to get ready for lean times. "He was afraid and I was afraid, for winter in all its savage efficiency was upon us though the calendar didn't say so and our preparation for it had fallen some short of planning." They move the cow indoors along with the rooster and pig. That night, the roof collapses under the weight of the snow. A fox jumps in and attacks the pig and rooster. Mary Call defeats the fox and feels good, despite the fact there is a "sliver in the soft, fleshy part of my hand, embedded deep, about a half-inch wide and thick."

Clements, Andrew. *Frindle.* Simon and Schuster, 1996. 105 p. Gr. 3–6.
Nick Allen, who "had plenty of ideas, and he knew what to do with them," is beginning fifth grade. He meets his match with his language-arts teacher, Mrs. Granger. "She was small, as teachers go . . . but Mrs. Granger seemed like a giant." Nick gets an idea to call pens "frindles," an action that bothers Mrs. Granger. "It was a chess game, Nick against Mrs. Granger." Nick gets everyone else to do the same thing, and the story becomes known across the nation. It even makes Nick rich. As he gets older, Nick learns that Mrs. Granger was secretly rooting for him. The book is a great ode to education.

10 Minute Selection: Read the first chapter, titled "Nick," which describes Nick's playfulness in school. He creates an entire South Seas activity complete with white sand in his third-grade class. He even knows how to turn up the thermostat with a screwdriver. A year later, Nick learns how to drive his teacher, Mrs. Avery, crazy by imitating a blackbird's "peep." Move on to chapter 3, "The Question." Nick meets Mrs. Granger and tries to use his patented "delaying question—also known as the teacher-stopper, or the guaranteed-time-waster." The whole class knows what Nick is up to. "Unfortunately, so did Mrs. Granger." She successfully turns his antics into an extra homework assignment for him. The chapter ends with, "Everything he had heard about this teacher was true—don't mess around with The Lone Granger."

Clifford, Eth. *Help! I'm a Prisoner in the Library.* **Houghton Mifflin, 1979. 103 p. Gr. 2–5.**
Two sisters, Mary Rose and Jo-Beth, find themselves locked overnight in a library while a blizzard rages outside. The two girls had found refuge in the library just as it was closing. Miss Finton, the librarian, had earlier shut the door on their frantic father, who was searching for them, insisting no one was still in the building. The power and the phone lines are dead. Out of desperation, the girls make a sign that reads "Help! I'm a Prisoner in the *Liberry*" and place it in a window. In the darkness, the girls are spooked by display dummies, a strange voice that turns out to be a mynah bird, a mysterious thump overhead, and a banshee cry from the basement.

10 Minute Selection: Read chapter 3, "Off With Their Heads." The girls find a telephone and call the police, shouting, "We're prisoners in the library!" A police officer warns them to stop playing around. Jo-Beth makes the sign for the window, while Mary Rose tries the phone again. "Without warning, the phone went dead." The power goes out, too. The chapter ends with the lines, "She didn't know what Mary Rose was going to say because at that exact moment, there was a heavy thud over their heads, as if someone had fallen down. The moaning started almost at once."

Cooney, Caroline B. *The Fog.* **Scholastic, 1989. 218 p. Gr. 6–8.**
Christina has spent her childhood on an island off the coast of Maine. Now, she is starting junior high on the mainland. She and the three other island kids live with the innkeepers, the Shevvingtons, who are also the school's principal and English teacher. Christina learns quickly that the Shevvingtons are evil, and she tries to prove to others that they move from town to town, "destroying the souls of innocent victims." The adults, including her parents, don't believe her. Christina's friend Anya is slowly becoming obsessed with the sea and one stormy night starts walking into it. Christina pleads with the Shevvingtons to help, but instead, they

lock Christina out of the house. This is the first of the Point Horror Trilogy, and even though we don't learn the true nature of the Shevvingtons, it makes a satisfying stand-alone read. The other titles are *The Snow* (1990) and *The Fire* (1990).

10 Minute Selection: Read the last section of chapter 11. We see cruel Mrs. Shevvington in action. Begin with the sentence, "In English, Mrs. Shevvington discussed a poem by Carl Sandburg." The students write poems and read them aloud in class. Mrs. Shevvington makes cruel remarks to the students throughout. The strange school counselor, Miss Frisch, comes for Christina. As Christina leaves, she gets a warning from a classmate. Continue reading a few pages into chapter 12. Christina is in the clutches of Miss Frisch and Mr. Shevvington. End with the lines, "She lost control. 'I am not violent!' shrieked Christina, hitting him with her book bag."

Cooper, Susan. *The Boggart.* Margaret K. McElderry, 1993. 196 p. Gr. 3–7.
A Boggart is a fun-loving but mischievous ancient spirit. The Boggart finds itself in Canada with a new family. He's excited about new things, like pizza and electricity. However, his Old Magic combined with modern technology causes problems. The Boggart eventually becomes homesick for Scotland and finds a technological answer to its problems. The sequel to this book is *The Boggart and the Monster* (1997).

10 Minute Selection: Explain to your audience that a Boggart, an invisible and mischievous spirit, is living with two Canadian children, Jessup and Emily. Read the last half of chapter 6, beginning with the line, "He sat there all through a history lesson about the Roman Empire, which—having lived in the Roman Empire, for the four hundred years during which it included the British Isles—he found inaccurate and boring," and read to the end of the chapter. The Boggart watches a game of hockey, which he compares to a medieval joust. He is hit with a puck, turns into one himself, and flies about the stadium to the surprise of witnesses. Read the first few pages of chapter 7. Jessup is in trouble because of the hockey incident. The Boggart feels sorry and tries to rectify things by making a peanut-butter and jelly sandwich for Jessup. Jessup winds up sitting on the sandwich. End with the sentence, "The Boggart had carefully left his gift in the place where he felt Jessup was most likely to see it—his computer chair."

Cooper, Susan. *The Dark Is Rising.* Simon and Schuster, 1973. 244 p. Gr. 4–9.
Will Stanton, the seventh son of a seventh son, is the last of the Old Ones. Will is charged with finding the great Signs of the Light in the ancient battle the Old Ones have waged against the Dark. Will is assisted by the Old One known as Merriman. The Dark threatens Will's world by inflicting a cruel, cold winter. Later, Will's sister is kidnapped. It is not necessary to read the first book in the series, *Over Sea, Under Stone* (1965), in order to understand *The Dark Is Rising,*

the second in the series. The other titles are *Greenwitch* (1974), *The Grey King* (1975), and *Silver Tree* (1977).

10 Minute Selection: Read the first chapter in the book, "Midwinter's Eve." Something strange is happening in Will's world as his eleventh birthday approaches. Animals seem to fear him, the radio blares when he walks past it, and a strange man is hovering nearby in the fields. A neighbor gives Will a cryptic warning that "the Walker is abroad. . . . And this night will be bad, and tomorrow will be beyond imagining." The neighbor also gives Will a strange ornament, "made of black metal, a flat circle quartered by two crossed lines." As Will walks home with his brother, they witness a flock of rooks diving after the strange man in the fields. End the passage with the lines, "His fingers closed round the iron circle in his pocket and held it tightly. This time, the iron felt warm."

Creech, Sharon. *Chasing Redbird.* **HarperCollins, 1997. 261 p. Gr. 5–8.**
Thirteen-year-old Zinnia becomes obsessed with clearing an overgrown, forgotten twenty-mile trail that begins behind her family's farm. As she works on the trail, she tries to make sense of her life. "I only knew I had to undertake this mission. I had to. . . . It didn't occur to me that I might be escaping something or even chasing something."

10 Minute Selection: Read chapter 13, "Bingo." A local boy named Jake brings Zinnia a puppy as a gift. She learns that another family lost their puppy, whose name is Gobbler. "When I got home, the puppy was sleeping on the blanket in the kitchen. 'Gobbler,' I called. 'Gobbler—' His ears perked up, his eyes opened, and he ran to me." Inform your audience that Zinny is furious to learn Jake stole the puppy. Move to the end of chapter 15, "Lost and Found," beginning with the sentence, "At the Hiddle Farm, I was once again greeted by the broom-waving Old Mrs. Butler." Zinny writes a letter to Jake that reads "IF YOU BRING THAT DOG BACK AGAIN, I'LL PUNCH YOUR BRAINS OUT." Finally, read the second half of the very short chapter 21, "Wanted." Zinny thinks she needs a horse to help her clear the trail. She puts up a sign asking for a horse. "I hoped Jake would see it. I hoped he would bring me a horse, and I didn't care if he had to *steal* it."

Curtis, Christopher Paul. *The Watsons Go to Birmingham—1963.*
Delacorte, 1995. 210 p. Gr. 4–8.
Ten-year-old Kenny Watson narrates the story of his family and their trip from Flint, Michigan, to visit Grandma Sands in Alabama. Kenny's older brother Byron has gotten on his parents' nerves because of his misbehavior. The parents decide a summer with Grandma Sands will help straighten out Byron. "There're so many

things that can go wrong to a young person and Byron seems bound and determined to find every one of them. . . . So hopefully, the slower pace in Alabama will help him by removing some of those temptations." The comic tone of the first part of the novel shifts to seriousness when Kenny almost drowns and then is traumatized by the fatal 1963 Birmingham bombing of the church that resulted in the deaths of four young girls.

10 Minute Selection: This selection is a no-brainer. Read the extremely popular scene where Byron gets his lips stuck to the frozen outside mirror of the Watsons' car. Begin by informing your audience that Kenny and his mean older brother Byron have been told to scrape the ice off their car. Read the last half of chapter 1, "And You Wonder Why We Get Called the Weird Watsons." Start with the sentences, "The next time I took a little rest Byron was still calling my name but sounding like he had something in his mouth. He was saying, 'Keh-ee! Keh-ee! Hel'. . . hel'. . . !'" Their father runs out and immediately begins to laugh. "This little knucklehead was kissing his reflection in the mirror and got his lips stuck!" Unfortunately, the only way they can free his lips is with "a good hard snatch."

Cushman, Karen. *Catherine, Called Birdy.* **Clarion, 1994. 205 p. Gr. 6–10.**
Catherine is thirteen years old when she begins her journal in 1290 England and fourteen when she finishes it. She longs for more in life than what is available to her. "'You are so much already, Little Bird. Why not cease your fearful pounding against the bars of your cage and be content?' I do not know exactly what this means but it troubles me." Her father plans to give her hand in marriage to someone wealthy, but Catherine finds ways to drive away her suitors. She fears that she will be forced to marry a man from the north "because his manor lies next to my mother's and my father lusts after it." Catherine calls him Shaggy Beard. "The man was a pig, which dishonors pigs."

10 Minute Selection: Read several entries that show some of Catherine's successful efforts to chase away potential suitors, beginning with the entry dated "23rd Day of September" and ending with the "26th Day of September" entry. Catherine blacks out her front teeth with soot and places mouse bones in her hair. "I smiled my gap-tooth smile at him and wiggled my ears. My father's crack still rings my head but Master Lack-Wit left without a betrothal." Move on and read the entries for the "5th Day of October" through the "9th Day of October." Catherine is "mucking about to mix the puddle of mud, straw, cow hair, and dung into daub for covering the walls." A potential suitor spots her but doesn't know her true identity. She convinces him that "Catherine" is lacking her wits and has a stooped back. The last entry to read is from the "3rd Day of February," when Catherine sets fire to the privy another suitor is using at the time.

Dahl, Roald. *The BFG.* **Farrar Straus Giroux, 1982. 219 p. Gr. 2–5.**
The BFG is a Big Friendly Giant, the only giant that doesn't eat "human beans."
He is also the smallest of the giants. "I is the titchy one. I is the runt." He kidnaps
an orphan girl named Sophie because she witnessed him putting good dreams
into children's heads while they slept. However, they become best friends. She's
in danger, however, from the other giants. They'll eat her if they find her. She
and the BFG come up with an ingenious plan—a plan that involves the queen of
England—to stop the other giants from eating any more people. The BFG's dialogue is a treat to read aloud.
  10 Minute Selection: Read the chapters titled "Snozzcumbers" and "The Bloodbottler." Snozzcumbers are a disgusting vegetable the BFG eats because he won't
eat humans. "'It's disgusterous!' the BFG gurgled. 'It's sickable! It's rotsome! It's
maggotwise!'" The Bloodbottler is a bully of a giant. Sophie hides in a snozzcum-
ber. However, the Bloodbottler takes a bite of the disgusting food with Sophie in
it. The Bloodbottler spits it out, sending Sophie flying across the room.
  Second 10 Minute Selection: Read the scary chapter titled "Who?" Sophie first
sees the BFG outside of her window in the middle of the night. She's horrified
when the giant turns his head, "and the eyes were staring straight at Sophie." She
hides under her blankets. Skip ahead and read the hilarious chapter titled "Frobscottle and Whizzpoppers." Sophie tells the BFG about soda and how it causes one
to burp. The giant thinks burping is "filthsome." The BFG drinks "frobscottle,"
a fizzy drink that causes one to make "whizzpoppers." A "whizzpopper" happens
when soda bubbles go down instead of up, and "they'll be coming out somewhere
else with an even louder and ruder noise."

Dahl, Roald. *Fantastic Mr. Fox.* **Knopf, 1970. 81 p. Gr. 1–5.**
Mr. Fox lives in a hole with "Mrs. Fox and their four Small Foxes." He constantly
steals chickens, turkeys, geese, and ducks from three nasty farmers—Farmer Bog-
gis, Farmer Bunce, and Farmer Bean. The farmers have had enough, and they
pursue Mr. Fox into his den. The foxes are forced to dig deeper. The farmers
dig the entire hill away with heavy machinery. Other burrowing animals are also
trapped. They are all in danger of starving to death. Mr. Fox tunnels to the farms
and brings back not only poultry but vegetables (for the rabbits) and cider. The
book ends with the animals feasting underground and the farmers sitting outside
the hole in the rain "waiting for the fox to come out. And so far as I know, they
are still waiting."
  10 Minute Selection: Read the short chapter 2, "Mr. Fox." Mr. Fox demonstrates
his skills at stealing poultry. The farmers decide to shoot him. Continue with
chapter 3, "The Shooting." The farmers shoot off Mr. Fox's tail. They plan on digging the fox out of his hole. Move on to chapter 5, "The Terrible Tractors." The
farmers are tired of digging with shovels. They leave and come back with Cater-

pillar tractors. Mr. Fox is horrified. "Dig for your lives! Dig, dig, dig!" Finish the passage by reading the short chapter 6, titled "The Race." The farmers remove the entire hillside in pursuit of the foxes. People from the surrounding villages come and make fun of the farmers for going to all of this trouble to catch one fox. The farmers are more determined to succeed.

Danziger, Paula. *Amber Brown Is Not a Crayon.* **Putnam, 1994. 80 p. Gr. K–3.** Third-grader Amber Brown is having a rough year. "This is definitely the worst year of my life . . . the very, very, very, very worst." First, her parents get divorced. Then her father moves to France. And now, her best friend, Justin, is moving to Alabama. Amber is upset when she tries to help Justin pack and he wants to throw away "the chewing gum ball we have been adding to for a year and a half." The two friends don't know how to handle their emotions and stop talking to each other. They eventually "link pinkies" and say they are going to miss each other. Justin gives her a present—the chewing gum ball. This is the first of fifteen Amber Brown books. The second in the series is *You Can't Eat Your Chicken Pox, Amber Brown* (1995).

10 Minute Selection: Read chapters 3 and 4. The passage opens with Justin and Amber sharing an Oreo cookie. Amber eats the cream center and Justin eats the "cookie parts." Amber is hoping that the lady looking at Justin's house doesn't buy it. "I hope you don't mind alligators in the toilet," she tells the woman. Later, the two kids are walking home from school. Actually, Justin is hopping like a kangaroo. "Ka-thwonk. Ka-thwonk." They take a bow when Hannah Burton calls them immature. The two children stop in their tracks when they see the "SOLD" sign in front of Justin's house.

DeFelice, Cynthia. *Weasel.* **Macmillan, 1990. 119 p. Gr. 4–7.** A strange mute man named Ezra shows up in the middle of the night and beckons eleven-year-old Nathan and his sister Molly to follow him. He leads them to their father, who has been missing for days. The father had been caught in a trap by a man known as Weasel. Weasel stole the father's gun and left him to die. Later, Weasel traps Nathan and holds him prisoner. When Nathan escapes, all he can think about is killing Weasel. The sequel is *Bringing Ezra Back* (2006).

10 Minute Selection: Read the first two short chapters. We learn the setting is 1839 Ohio. Nathan and his sister hear a knock on the door. A strange man standing outside holds something in his hand. The first chapter ends with Nathan crying, "Mama's locket!" The second chapter lets us know that the children's father had gone hunting, but he never returned. The children follow the strange man, hoping to find their father. Move on to chapter 9. Nathan is alone in the woods in the middle of the night. He realizes that something or someone is stalking him. "A voice broke the stillness and sent a chill racing down my spine. 'You gonna hide there all night, boy?'" It's Weasel, pointing a rifle at him. The chapter ends with, "The last thing I remember was hearing a rifle shot and a long, loud scream, and wondering if it was my voice or Weasel's."

DeJong, Meindert. *The Wheel on the School.* Harper and Row, 1954. 298 p. Gr. 3–5.
Lina, the lone girl in a school of six children in the Dutch fishing village of Shora, writes a composition about storks. The great birds don't nest in Shora. The teacher challenges the children to learn all about storks. This leads to a search for wheels to place on the buildings' steep roofs so the storks will make their nests. While the children look throughout the town and the countryside, they get to know some of the adults better, including a tin man, Grandmother Sibble, Old Douwa, and Janus, the meanest man in the village. At one point in the story, Lina and Old Douwa are stranded by the incoming tide. "It was a crazy procession that stormed into Shora and along the road to the dike." The tin man's horse and wagon come to the rescue with Janus in his wheelchair hanging on behind.

10 Minute Selection: Read the second half of chapter 5, "Pier and Dirk and the Cherry Tree," beginning with the sentence, "Back in the fenced-in yard the tin began rattling and clattering once more." The boys confront Janus, who fiercely guards his cherry tree from birds and little boys. Janus has them trapped but is impressed when he hears their story about searching for a wheel for the storks. The boys had heard that Janus lost both legs to a shark when, in reality, Janus lost them to blood poisoning. "Janus had become real; he had become a part of the village. He wasn't a fearsome ogre to be hated and outwitted. . . . He had become a friend!"

Deuker, Carl. *On the Devil's Court.* Little, Brown, 1988. 252 p. Gr. 7–12.
Seventeen-year-old Joe Faust is the new kid in his school. He studies Marlowe's *The Tragical History of the Life and Death of Doctor Faustus* in English and is interested in the likeness of his family name with that of the book's protagonist. While shooting baskets in an abandoned building, he makes a pact with the devil in his mind. "Give me a full season, give me twenty-four games of this power, and my soul is yours." Joe goes on to move up from junior varsity to breaking scoring records and leading his team to the state championship. His father, meanwhile, has a heart attack, and Joe worries that this may be part of his bargain with the devil.

10 Minute Selection: Read the end of part 2, beginning with the sentence, "I wish the day had ended right there, but I still had gym class." Joe worries about being a senior stuck on junior varsity. The two-page passage ends with the line, "But that's when it really began." Continue reading part 3, chapters 1 through 3. Joe notices a weird shadow while he's shooting baskets in the abandoned gym. He thinks back to Dr. Faustus and then proceeds to hit perfect shots. That's when he makes his vow to the devil. He also gains confidence in other aspects of life. He easily handles a gang of thugs who threaten him. His coach moves him up to varsity. Stop short of the end of chapter 3 at the sentence, "The whole thing was impossible, but I was so incredibly happy I decided if I had sold my soul, my only regret was that I hadn't done it sooner."

Dickinson, Peter. *Chuck and Danielle.* **Delacorte, 1996. 115 p. Gr. 3–6.**
Chuck is a whippet who is afraid of everything, including paper bags, pigeons, supermarket carts, cats, teddy bears, and motorcycles. Her owner Danielle's friend's sister calls her a "whimpet." Despite her timid dog, Danielle has a running bet with her mother that Chuck will someday save the universe, at which point Danielle's mother will owe her a Big Mac. Throughout these seven short stories, Chuck knocks over a purse snatcher, starts a cow stampede, and wins an obstacle-course race.

10 Minute Selection: Read the first chapter, "Chuck Saves the Universe." We meet Chuck, whose full name is Golden Hazelwood Mungo Paternoser, and Danielle, who "lives with her mum in an apartment at the bottom of an old house in a large town in England." Chuck worries a lot. When she worries, she "bolts to the end of her lead. If anyone's in the way, she bolts between their legs and trips them up." Danielle has joined her friend Jenny in a tree house. They spot Jenny's grandmother heading their way when the poor woman is knocked down. A man on a motorbike heads over to help her up when a second man grabs her bag and runs off. Chuck, who is frightened by the motorbike—"it gave a dreadful whippet-eating roar"—knocks down the robber, who is then given the boot by the man on the motorbike.

Dorris, Michael. *Morning Girl.* **Hyperion, 1992. 74 p. Gr. 4–8.**
Morning Girl is a twelve-year-old Taino girl living with her family in the Bahamas in 1492. She received her name because "I open my eyes as soon as the light calls through the smoke hole in the roof, sift the ideas that have come to me in the night and decide which one to follow first." Alternate chapters are told by her younger brother Star Boy, who prefers the night. In the evening, "there are special things to see if you watch closely." The two talk about their daily life on the island. The book ends with strangers approaching in a canoe. The final two pages contain a chilling excerpt from the log of Christopher Columbus.

10 Minute Selection: Read chapter 5, told by Morning Girl. She tries hard to understand what she looks like. The water isn't still enough for her to see her reflection. Her mother tells her "to close your eyes and think with your fingers." Her brother and father tease her, yet it is her father who suggests that Morning Girl look into his eyes. "Suddenly I saw two tiny girls looking back. . . . They were pretty." Continue reading chapter 6. Star Boy describes a terrific storm that hit the island. He runs away from the rest of the family and finds shelter in "the one tree that would surely remain tomorrow in the same spot it had been today." The spirit of his grandfather comforts him.

Dorris, Michael. *Sees Behind Trees*. Hyperion, 1996. 104 p. Gr. 4–7.
Walnut is an American Indian who has trouble with his sight. His parents and "the weroance, our most important person, the expert on hunting," recognize his talents. They name him Sees Behind Trees. He goes on a journey to help Gray Fire, an elderly man. Gray Fire has not been able to find the place where he cut off his toes to escape a trap. Along the way, the two meet some strangers who have a baby. Tragedy comes to both Gray Fire and the baby's parents. Sees Behind Trees must safely find his way back home with the baby.

10 Minute Selection: Read the first chapter, where we meet Walnut. He is having trouble hitting a target with his bow and arrow. The weroance declares a special test at the coming-of-age trials. Walnut wins because he is able to identify Gray Wolf entering the village from the south. "'Sees Behind Trees,' the weroance pronounced, 'is now a young man.'"

Second 10 Minute Selection: Read most of chapter 4, beginning with the sentence, "I walked through the village, not even speaking to people I passed because I knew if I did I would say another stupid thing." Sees Behind Trees hears the story of how Gray Wolf, once the fastest runner, found a special place, "a land of water." Gray Wolf's foot slipped between two rocks and got caught. In desperation, Gray Wolf cut his off toes to free himself. Continue reading to the end of the chapter. Sees Behind Trees promises to help Gray Wolf find the land of water once again.

Duncan, Lois. *Don't Look Behind You*. Delacorte, 1989. 172 p. Gr. 7–12.
High school senior April's life is turned upside down when her family is forced to go into the government's Witness Protection Program. There was an attempt on her father's life because he was a witness against drug lords. April gives up her boyfriend, prom, graduation, her tennis championship, and her college plans. Her name is changed to Valerie, and her family is relocated from Virginia to Florida. A hit man named Vamp has already made one attempt on her family's lives. April makes some crucial mistakes that put Vamp back on their trail.

10 Minute Selection: Introduce this passage by telling your audience that April and her family are hiding in a hotel under the Witness Protection Program and that they are being guarded by a man named Jim. Read a section of chapter 5, beginning with the sentence, "'Jim's gone out,' he said." April and her brother hear a knock at their hotel door. April looks through the peephole, sees a maid, and starts to open the door. However, something's not quite right. With the chain still in place, the maid—a man disguised as a maid—tries to ram through the door. The family bodyguard, Jim, comes down the hall, and the door slams shut. April hears "a thump and a curse, followed by a pop, like the sound of a cork coming out of a champagne bottle." More help arrives, but Jim and the intruder are nowhere to be found. The family is hustled out of the hotel. The chapter ends with another agent stating, "His name's Mike Vamp. I should have guessed that he'd be the one they'd send for you."

English, Karen. *Francie.* **Farrar Straus Giroux, 1999. 199 p. Gr. 5–10.**
Francie lives with her mother and brother in segregated Noble, Alabama. She is a good student and helps her mother do a variety of chores for several white families. Francie teaches an older student, Jesse, to read, but Jesse is pulled from school by his father. Later, Jesse is accused of hitting a white man and is pursued by the law. Francie sets food out for him in the woods and this action puts her own family in jeopardy.

10 Minute Selection: Read a short piece from the chapter titled "School," beginning with the sentence, "Augustine Baker was hissing at me." Augustine is a bully who has it in for Francie, especially after Francie refuses to give her an answer for the test. Finish with the sentence, "I think you done all there is to do, Francie," and move on a few pages to, "Then I noticed someone coming up the road." It is our introduction to Jesse, an illiterate sixteen-year-old who wants to attend school. Francie is instructed to help him learn how to read. After school, Augustine and her sister Mae Helen confront Francie. They knock her to the ground when "Jesse, appearing out of nowhere it seemed, grabbed her [Augustine] from behind, nearly lifting her off her feet before setting her aside. She went down on her butt hard, her eyes wide with surprise." End with the line, "Me and Prez started for home."

Enright, Elizabeth. *Gone-Away Lake.* **Harcourt, 1957. 256 p. Gr. 3–5.**
Portia is exploring a swampy area with her cousin Julian when they come across several dilapidated homes in the middle of nowhere. They are surprised to find a reclusive elderly brother and sister—Minnehaha and Pindar—living there, in separate houses. The older siblings are delighted to have young folks around, while the children have an exciting summer exploring this location, which was once a vibrant lake community. Portia and Justin try to keep their daily excursions a secret from the rest of the family, but when an emergency arises, Minnehaha and Pindar leave their hidden world and become good friends with everyone, including Portia's little brother Foster. The sequel is titled *Return to Gone-Away* (1961).

10 Minute Selection: Read the second half of chapter 9, "The Gulper." Begin with the sentence, "Foster knew he was going to find something on that island, but he didn't know what," and read to the end of the chapter. Foster discovers an abandoned house and enters it to escape a thunderstorm. He's frightened not only of the storm but also of the dark, creepy aspect of the house. When the storm subsides, Foster becomes braver and explores the rest of the house. He eventually feels ownership. "'Good-bye house, I'll be back soon,' he said to it, feeling as though the nice sheltering little place were really his own." Foster heads back but steps onto a patch of mud and starts sinking. The chapter ends with Foster crying for help.

Erdrich, Louise. *The Birchbark House.* **Hyperion, 1999. 239 p. Gr. 4–6.**
Omakayas and her family are members of the Ojibwa people. The story follows the joys and hardships of the year 1847 on their island home on Lake Superior. Omakayas has a way with animals and healing. She makes a pet of an injured crow and also has a tense encounter with two bear cubs and their mother. Her whole family comes down with smallpox during the winter, and their food supply is perilously low. With the help of the huntress Old Tallow and her grandmother Nokomis, Omakayas learns more about her past and the skills she'll need in the future. The other titles in the series are *The Game of Silence* (2004) and *The Porcupine Year* (2008).

10 Minute Selection: Read part of chapter 2, "Old Tallow," beginning with the sentence, "Before she went back on the trail, Omakayas rinsed off the old candy lump in the lake," and read until the end of the chapter. Omakayas finds two bear cubs in the woods. She plays with them until she is pinned underneath the mother bear. Continue reading into the next chapter, "The Return," until the sentence, "Her mother promised her a very special pair of winter makazins and Angeline even braided her hair with one of her own red ribbons." Omakayas reflects on her encounter with the bears and concludes that it was a good thing.

Estes, Eleanor. *The Witch Family.* **Harcourt, 1960. 223 p. Gr. 2–5.**
Amy and Clarissa are two young girls who love to draw and tell stories about Old Witch. Amy decides to "banquish" (a combination of *banish* and *vanquish*) Old Witch to a glass hill so she will learn to be good. The girls later add Little Witch Girl to live with Old Witch. A bee named Malachi is created to keep Old Witch in line. Malachi learns how to spell, thus becoming a spelling bee. The book is full of wordplay and imagination. Amy's real world seems to collide with her imaginative world, and she finds herself in trouble on the glass hill.

10 Minute Selection: Inform your listeners that a little witch is going to school for the first time, and she knows a friendly bee named Malachi. Read a selection from chapter 4, "The Witch School." Begin with the sentence, "In her picture Amy quickly drew the little witch girl flying in the schoolroom window, the new little witch girl flying into a new school, alone, and late." The other witch students are mean to Little Witch Girl. "Because Little Witch Girl was new, they were all resolved not to like her." We learn that witches subtract when they add, they exercise by stomping around the room, and they spell words backward. They also learn "witchiplication" (magical spells). Malachi stings the other students whenever they try to cast spells on Little Witch Girl. End the passage with the line, "So, in honor both of the brilliant new pupil and the epidemic of invisible bee bites, she dismissed the class."

Farmer, Nancy. *The Ear, the Eye and the Arm*. Orchard, 1994. 301 p. Gr. 5–8.
Tendai, Rita, and Kuda, the sheltered children of General Amadeus Matsika, who is the chief of security for the Land of Zimbabwe, are kidnapped. They are forced into labor by an evil woman known as the She Elephant. They escape, only to find themselves through a gate into a world that reflects Africa's past. Once they find their way out, they are taken in by Mrs. Horsepool-Worthingham, who tells them lies and keeps them from their parents. Three mutant detectives—the title characters—are one step behind the children, who unfortunately fall once more into the clutches of the She Elephant. The children prove to be very resourceful, even when they face death at the hands of the general's enemies, known as the Masks.
    10 Minute Selection: Inform your audience that three children have been initially kidnapped by a strong woman known as the She Elephant and are now being held against their will by another woman. Read most of chapter 31, beginning with the sentence, "'I don't want children underfoot,' said Mrs. Horsepool-Worthingham." The woman has invited several guests over for tea. The chapter ends with the line, "In the gateway, nearly filling the gateway, stood the big black shape of the She Elephant." Continue reading chapter 32. The two women battle over the children. The chapter ends with the She Elephant making off with the children in a taxi.

Fitzhugh, Louise. *Harriet the Spy*. Harper and Row, 1964. 298 p. Gr. 3–5.
Eleven-year-old Harriet M. Welsch loves spying on people in her New York neighborhood and writing down her observations in her notebooks. She even comments on her classmates. One day, Harriet loses her notebook, and her fellow students read the not-too-flattering things she has written about them. They plot revenge, which causes Harriet to misbehave in destructive ways. It's not until she receives a letter from her former nanny Ole Golly that Harriet apologizes to her classmates and channels her writing talent as the class paper editor.
    10 Minute Selection: Read a section of chapter 2, beginning with the sentence, "At the entrance of her school a group of children crowded through the door." Harriet writes some scathing comments about her classmates and her teachers. "MISS WHITEHEAD'S FEET LOOK LARGER THIS YEAR. MISS WHITEHEAD HAS BUCK TEETH, THIN HAIR, FEET LIKE SKIS, AND A VERY LONG HANGING STOMACH." End this section with the line, "Assembly was over," and move on to the beginning of chapter 10. Harriet loses her notebook

in the schoolyard. She finds Janie Gibbs reading from the notebook to the other students. "They just looked and looked, and their eyes were the meanest eyes she had ever seen." Finish the passage where Janie tells Harriet to "go over there on that bench until we decide what we're going to do to you."

Fleischman, Paul. *The Half-a-Moon Inn*. Harper and Row, 1980. 88 p. Gr. 3–6.
Aaron lives with his mother by the ocean. He writes on a slate "for Aaron had been born unable to speak." He is left alone when his mother goes on a journey to sell her cloth. She warns him to stay out of the woods, for they are "full of wolf packs and bears, and a-crawling with brigands like a corpse full of maggots." Aaron sets off in a snowstorm when his mother fails to return. He accompanies an illiterate ragman to an inn deep in the woods. He becomes a prisoner of the evil Miss Grackle, who has the ability to read people's dreams and steal their money. His life is also in danger when he spills soup on the notorious robber Lord Tom. Aaron learns that the villain plans on "entering a room where the boy slept in a bed and with a vengeful smile, driving a knife in his back."
    10 Minute Selection: Read chapter 4. Aaron arrives at the Half-a-Moon Inn with the ragman. The door opens, and Aaron sees "a bear-sized woman wrapped in shawls like a mummy." It's Miss Grackle, the proprietor of the inn. She seems happy to learn that Aaron knows how to build a fire and that he is mute. She finds a bed for him and Aaron falls asleep. Continue reading chapter 5. Aaron finds that his winter coat, sack, stockings, and boots are missing. We learn that there is a family curse that prevents Miss Grackle from lighting a fire to warm the inn. Aaron is forced to work for Miss Grackle and help her steal from the guests.

Fleischman, Sid. *By the Great Horn Spoon*. Little, Brown, 1963. 193 p. Gr. 3–5.
Young Jack and his butler, Praiseworthy, travel to the California gold rush to save Aunt Arabella's dwindling fortune. They hide in barrels of potatoes as stowaways on the ship *Lady Wilma*. They soon make themselves known to the captain and demonstrate their worth by solving problems. After a 15,000-mile, five-month voyage, the ship finally reaches California. Praiseworthy earns the nickname Bullwhip when he hits a robber with his glove filled with gold dust and knocks the man up a tree. After striking gold, the two are heading back to Boston to save Aunt Arabella when disaster strikes. Their boat sinks, and the two must loosen their money belts to reach the surface. Jack and Praiseworthy maintain their optimism and, once again, turn disaster into opportunity.
    10 Minute Selection: Read most of chapter 2, "How to Catch a Thief." Begin with the sentence, "The following day, toward dusk, Jack was washing up in a

bucket of sea water when Praiseworthy was struck as if by lightning," and read to the end of the chapter. Praiseworthy devises a clever plan to catch the man who stole their money, causing them to become stowaways. The plan involves a pig covered with coal dust.

Second 10 Minute Selection: Read the first section of chapter 4, "The Pig Hunt." Jack has grown fond of the pig named Good Luck. However, the cook plans on turning the pig into Sunday dinner. Jack hides Good Luck and tries to push it through a window. "But Good Luck got stuck half in and half out." Luckily for Jack, both Praiseworthy and a prospector named Mountain Jim help hide the porker. End the passage with the line, "Sunday passed without roast pork for dinner and the following night the Lady Wilma anchored off the green coast of Brazil."

Fleischman, Sid. *The Whipping Boy*. Greenwillow, 1986. 89 p. Gr. 3–6.
Jemmy, a former rat catcher, is a whipping boy. Whenever the prince misbehaves, which is quite often, Jemmy is the one who is physically punished. "It was forbidden to spank, thrash, cuff, smack, or whip a prince." Prince Brat, as he is known to everyone but himself, decides to run away from the castle, and he takes Jemmy with him. They are kidnapped and held for ransom by the highway robbers Cutwater and Hold-Your-Nose Billy. The boys are rescued by a girl and her trained bear, but they are still in danger.

10 Minute Selection: Read the first five chapters of the book. We are introduced to the two main characters. The prince is spoiled rotten and is angry that Jemmy doesn't make a sound when he is whipped. "It's pure spite that you won't howl." While the prince ignores his tutor, "the whipping boy learned to read, write, and do sums." The prince runs away because of boredom and makes Jemmy carry "a wicker basket the size of a sea chest." Jemmy plans to sneak away from the prince and go back to his former life. Before he can make his move, the two are confronted by the highwaymen. The passage ends with the two ruffians trying to decide how much gold they could get for the prince.

Fleming, Ian. *Chitty-Chitty-Bang-Bang*. Random House, 1964. 114 p. Gr. 3–5.
Inventor Caractacus Pott, his wife, Mimsie, and the twins Jeremy and Jemima find a car. "It shouldn't be just ANY car, but something a bit different from everyone else's." The car happens to be "a twelve-cylinder, eight-liter, supercharged *Paragon Panther*. This is the only one in the world." When the car starts up, it goes "CHITTY-CHITTY-BANG-BANG," thus its name. The Pott family also discovers the car has many special features, such as the ability to fly and turn into a hovercraft. CHITTY-CHITTY-BANG-BANG comes to the rescue when the children are kidnapped by the notorious Joe the Monster and his gang.

10 Minute Selection: Read the first part of chapter 3. Joe the Monster kidnaps Jeremy and Jemima. "Fortunately, CHITTY-CHITTY-BANG-BANG had smelled trouble." The car raises a tracking device and is able to follow the movements of the evil gang. The car eventually alerts the children's parents. "Commander Pott and Mimsie were instantly awake, and with, I am sorry to say, a very powerful swear word (it was 'Dash My Wig and Whiskers,' if you want to know)." The passage ends with the line, "As each fork or turning in the road came up, he followed the direction indicated by the radar scanner, and with CHITTY-CHITTY-BANG-BANG going lickety-split, lickety-split, lickety-split, they hurtled on towards the gangster hideout where Jeremy and Jemima had been locked into a bare, cell-like room at the back of the deserted warehouse."

Fox, Paula. *One-Eyed Cat.* **Bradbury, 1984. 216 p. Gr. 4–7.**
Ned lives with his minister father, his bedridden mother, and the sharp-tongued housekeeper, Mrs. Scallop. Ned's uncle Hilary gives him a Daisy air rifle for his eleventh birthday to his father's disapproval. Ned spots a cat missing one eye and feels responsible. He takes to lying, something he rarely did before. "Each lie he told them made the secret bigger, and that meant even more lies. He didn't know how to stop." Ned befriends an elderly man named Mr. Scully. The two of them leave food and a blanket outside for the cat. Mr. Scully has a stroke, and Ned visits him in the nursing home, letting the old man know that the cat is still hanging on to life. Ned still worries about the secret building inside of him and continues to tell lies. "He wondered if there was anything he couldn't lie about now. It seemed to him he didn't even care anymore." Ned finally confesses first to Mr. Scully, who can't respond, and then to his mother.

10 Minute Selection: Read the second half of chapter 2, "The Gun." Start when Uncle Hilary says, "Neddy, I must give you your birthday present," and read to the end of the chapter. Reverend Wallis puts the rifle in the attic and tells Ned he can have it when he's older. Ned sneaks up to the attic that evening, takes the rifle outside, and shoots at a shadow. As he's walking back home, he thinks he sees a face looking through a window at him.

Gallo, Don, ed. *Ultimate Sports: Short Stories by Outstanding Writers for Young Adults.* **Delacorte, 1995. 333 p. Gr. 6–12.**
Sixteen stories feature a wide variety of sports from football and basketball to scuba diving, Hawaiian canoe racing, and even science-fiction virtual games. Both male and female protagonists are featured. Editor Gallo asked contributors to write about "believable teenagers involved in challenging activities that reveal their motivations and show their emotional as well as their physical conflicts." Most stories are wonderful read-alouds. Authors featured in this compilation include

Robert Lipsyte, Chris Lynch, Norma Fox Mazer, Graham Salisbury, Todd Strasser, and Virginia Euwer Wolff.

10 Minute Selection: Share "Stealing for Girls," by Will Weaver, which takes approximately twenty-five minutes to read. Sun and her brother Luke are both basketball players. Sun is upset that her parents spend more time at Luke's games. She is angry when she learns their father taught Luke two ways to steal the ball from an opponent. To make it up to Sun, her father leaves her a note that reads "Dear Sun: There is a third type of steal . . ." The two set up a practice session. "Outside, for want of five offensive players, my father presses into service a saw-horse, three garbage cans, and my mother." There is a dilemma when the family learns that both kids' final games of the season will be held at the same time in two different locations.

Gannett, Ruth Stiles. *The Dragons of Blueland.* **Random House, 1951. 88 p. Gr. K–3.**
A blue-and-yellow baby dragon named Boris tries to make his way back to his mountain home. Boris learns that his family is trapped in a cave. Several men plan to capture the dragons and sell them to zoos. Boris flies off to find his human friend Elmer for advice. Boris first met Elmer in *My Father's Dragon* (1948), and the two also have adventures in *Elmer and the Dragon* (1950). *The Dragons of Blueland,* the last book in the trilogy, works well as a stand-alone read.

10 Minute Selection: Read the first chapter. We meet the baby dragon and learn that he is excited about seeing his "six sisters and seven brothers, and my gigantic mother and father." Boris is careful not to be seen by humans, but he needs to find a place to rest. At last, he finds a large culvert, curls up, and falls asleep. Read all of chapter 2. It turns out that someone did indeed see him—a farmer named Mr. Wagonwheel (don't you love this name?). After the farmer milks the cows and eats his hard-boiled eggs, he grabs his rifle in pursuit of "the large blue monster." Meanwhile, the farmer's cows have made friends with the dragon and huddle "around the opening to the culvert" to block the farmer's view. The chapter ends with the farmer shooting wildly into bushes and "Mrs. Wagonwheel . . . in bed with a case of the nerves."

George, Jean Craighead. *My Side of the Mountain.* **Dutton, 1959. 166 p. Gr. 4–8.**
Sam runs away from his home in New York City and lives off the land deep in the Catskill Mountains. His family owns land there, and Sam knows deep inside that this is where he belongs. He slowly develops strong wilderness survival skills—making fire, building a good shelter, hunting, and knowing which plants to eat. He catches and trains a falcon chick he names Frightful. He meets different people who are wandering in the woods. Sam is concerned when newspapers start report-

ing about a strange boy living in the wilderness. He's afraid he'll be found and made to return to New York City. The companion books are *On the Far Side of the Mountain* (1990), *Frightful's Mountain* (1999), and *Frightful's Daughter* (2002).

10 Minute Selection: Read the longish chapter titled "In Which I Find a Real Live Man." Sam hears police sirens in the distance. He meets a stranger and wonders if this man is running from the law. It turns out that the man, whom Sam dubs Bando, is really a college English teacher who got lost in the woods. He becomes fascinated by Sam's lifestyle and calls him "Thoreau." Bando stays with Sam for a few days and promises to return at Christmas. The passage ends with Sam settling in with Frightful as well as a neighboring raccoon and weasel.

Giff, Patricia Reilly. *Lily's Crossing.* **Delacorte, 1997. 180 p. Gr. 4–6.**
Lily is upset when her father goes overseas during World War II. She feels guilty that she didn't even say good-bye to him. She and her grandmother are spending the summer in their vacation home in Rockaway. Their neighbors take in a Hungarian refugee boy named Albert. His sister is still in France, and he wants desperately to be with her. Lily tells him a lie. "At night. I'm going to row right out, and swim the last bit. I'll have a rubber bag with dry clothes. . . . I'm going to take a ship to my father, no one will stop to take me back." Later, she regrets telling "the worst lie she had ever told," especially when Albert tries that very thing and is caught in a rowboat during a storm. The sequel is *Willow Run* (2005).

10 Minute Selection: Tell your audience that Lily has just gotten a letter from the mailman. Read the last part of chapter 9, starting with the line, "She headed for the fishing dock, looking back once to wave at him." She sees two people. Albert is running after someone on a bicycle. The bike rider throws something into the water. Continue reading chapter 10. Lily learns the bike rider threw a kitten in a paper bag into the ocean. "She was in the water in an instant." She and Albert decide to take care of the kitten together.

Greenfield, Eloise. *Koya Delaney and the Good Girl Blues.* **Scholastic, 1992. 124 p. Gr. 4–6.**
Sixth-grader Koya loves to laugh and puts a positive spin on everything. She is excited about her celebrity cousin, Del, coming to visit but is worried that too many people will find out. Of course, she helps exacerbate the problem by telling too many classmates to keep her secret. She eventually becomes angry, which is against her nature, when her time alone with Del is taken from her. She is also caught between a fight that her sister Loritha is having with their mutual friend Dawn.

10 Minute Selection: Read chapter 9. The girls are in a large gym for a double Dutch jump rope contest. Loritha has just been informed by her coach that she won't be in the freestyle competition. Loritha blames Dawn for not contacting her about the special practice session the team had. Loritha and Koya realize that Dawn intentionally didn't contact Loritha. The competition is among the "six schools that would be competing to be the best in the city." Loritha successfully participates in the first round of competition but has to sit out during the freestyle round. Dawn and another girl don't pull off the trick because their ropes become entangled. Loritha does well in the final round, which involves speed jumping. The team finishes in second place, which makes them all proud. Koya puts her arm around Dawn. The chapter ends with the sentence, "And that's when she saw Loritha's eyes, looking at her from a few feet away."

Grimes, Nikki. *Jazmin's Notebook.* **Dial, 1998. 102 p. Gr. 6–10.**
Jazmin's inner strength and determination shine in this book set in the 1960s. She lives with her sister CeCe after their father dies and their mother is sent to Bellevue Hospital. Jazmin loves to write and shares her talent in this book. She faces down the school bully, gets out of two potentially dangerous situations with older men, and even challenges one of her school counselors to change her schedule to include college-track classes. The book ends with her admiration of a blank notebook page. "I love how smooth, and crisp, and clean it is. I love how this plain and perfect piece of paper seems to be just waiting for me to baptize it with ink, to put my own special mark on it, to make it mine. And now that I think of it, that's exactly what I love about tomorrows."

10 Minute Selection: Read the "June 10" entry, beginning with Jazmin's poem "Central Park Lesson." Jazmin has an idea for a poem but no writing materials. She grabs a candy bar wrapper and gets transported writing her ideas down. She loses the poem, but "I'm going to enjoy every good thing that comes my way, as much as I can, for as long as I can. I plan to treat each thing as if it's gossamer, or mist. Just in case." Continue reading the next entry, "July 17," beginning with the poem "Night Noise." CeCe and Jazmin are having a poker party at their place when a guest named T. C. pulls a gun on another player.

Haddix, Margaret Peterson. *Just Ella.* **Simon and Schuster, 1999. 218 p. Gr. 5–10.**
Ella Brown is now known as Princess Cynthiana Eleanora in this remake of the traditional fairy tale "Cinderella." The book picks up where the fairy tale ends. Unfortunately, Ella is not sure life as a princess is for her. She is bored by the routine and aches for a chance to do things herself. She isn't even allowed to light a fire on cold mornings. She must wait for the servants to do it. Life "isn't what I'd imagined at the ball." She is amused by the rumors going around the palace that she had the help of a fairy godmother to win the heart of the prince. "'Someone . . . someone . . . actually . . . believes that?' I finally sputtered between giggles." She

eventually decides that she doesn't love the prince—she calls him Charm, but not to his face—and tries to get out of the marriage.

10 Minute Selection: Read chapter 17. Ella confronts the prince. "I—I know you won't like hearing this, but I must tell you. I can't marry you." The prince is puzzled. "You *will* marry me." He throws a fit. He's not sure what to do. He pushes her down, rips her petticoat, and uses the cloth strip to tie her wrists. "When I started to protest, he tore off another ruffle and tied it around my mouth." The chapter ends with the prince binding her ankles and leaving the room. Skip ahead to chapter 19. Ella finds herself in the dungeon. Madame Bisset, the woman in charge of molding Ella into the perfect princess, informs Ella, "You're going to stay here until you realize you have only one choice. . . . And then you'll marry the prince."

Hahn, Mary Downing. *Wait Till Helen Comes.* **Clarion, 1986. 184 p. Gr. 4–7.** Molly and her family have trouble getting along with her new stepsister Heather. The blended family moves into an old converted country church. Heather is drawn to the nearby cemetery. She meets a malevolent ghost named Helen. Molly learns that Helen died in a fire one hundred years ago and that she may be responsible for the drowning deaths of several children over the last few years. Molly is afraid that Helen will make Heather her next victim. This was probably the most popular scary book to read aloud and recommend to kids during my years as a children's librarian.

10 Minute Selection: Read the last few pages of chapter 9, beginning with the line, "Before closing my eyes, I looked at Heather." Heather sneaks out of the house. Molly follows and sees the ghost Helen for the first time. "Too frightened to breathe, I saw the glimmer of blue light shape itself into the figure of a girl no bigger than Heather." Heather asks Helen to do something bad to Molly and Michael. Later, when both girls are back in bed, Heather whispers in Molly's ear, "Just wait till Helen comes. You'll be sorry then for all the things you've done to me." Read the first section of chapter 11. Molly and Michael are returning from the woods when they hear noises from inside the house. Molly sees "a pale figure emerge from the back door." They find their possessions destroyed along with their mother's paintings. End with the lines, "You're there, aren't you? I thought. Watching all of this, enjoying it even more than Heather."

Hamilton, Virginia. *The House of Dies Drear.* **Macmillan, 1968. 246 p. Gr. 5–8.** Thirteen-year-old Thomas Small and his family move to a new home in Ohio. The house, once used in the Underground Railroad, has hidden rooms and passages. Supposedly, it is haunted by the ghost of the abolitionist Dies Drear and two slaves; all were murdered. Thomas gets caught up in the history of the house as well as the unique people in his new community, such as Mr. Pluto, who lives in a cave. One day, the Smalls return to find that their kitchen has been vandalized. Someone wants them to leave their new home. The sequel is *The Mystery of Drear House* (1987).

10 Minute Selection: Tell your audience that young Thomas is exploring his new home, which has tunnels and hidden passages and was once used for the Underground Railroad. Read the second half of chapter 4, beginning with the sentence, "Thomas didn't say anything." Thomas has just fallen five feet down into a hole beneath some steps. He finds a stairway cut out of rock under the house's foundation. While exploring, he loses his flashlight and hears an "ahhh, ahhh" sound. He runs up a path and finds a wall. He cries for help and hears a scream. The wall slides up. The passage ends with the lines, "'Thomas Small!' his mother said. 'What in heaven's name do you think you are doing inside that wall!'"

Hamilton, Virginia. *The People Could Fly: American Black Folktales.* **Knopf, 1985. 173 p. Gr. K–12.**
There's something here for all ages. Hamilton retells two-dozen African American stories grouped under four categories: "Animal Tales"; "Tales of the Real, Extravagant, and Fanciful"; "Tales of the Supernatural"; and "Slave Tales of Freedom." Highlights include a variation of the popular "Brer Rabbit and the Tar Baby" story titled "Doc Rabbit, Bruh Fox, and the Tar Baby"; a variation of "Taily-po" titled "The Peculiar Thing"; "Wily, His Mama, and the Hairy Man"; "How Nehemiah Got Free"; and "The Most Useful Slave."

10 Minute Selection: Read the title story, which opens with the lines, "They say the people could fly. Say that long ago in Africa, some of the people knew magic." Sarah is a slave with an infant. The overseer tells her to "keep that thing quiet" and begins to whip them both. An old man named Toby walks over to Sarah and tells her that "the time is come. . . . Go, as you know how." Sarah flies over the trees. The next day is hot. Some slaves fall from the heat. Toby helps others fly away. The master tries to kill Toby, but the old man laughs and rises with other slaves. "Say they flew away to *Free-dom.*" Be sure to read Hamilton's notes about this tale to your audience. She says the story "is a powerful testament to the millions of slaves who never had the opportunity to 'fly' away. 'The People Could Fly' was first told and retold by those who only had their imaginations to set them free."

Hautzig, Esther. *The Endless Steppe: Growing Up in Siberia.* **Crowell, 1968. 243 p. Gr. 5–12.**
In 1941, the Russians sent many Polish citizens to labor camps in Siberia. Ten-year-old Esther recounts her years there in this autobiography. Her family was accused of "being capitalists and therefore enemies of the people." Her grandfather is separated from them at the train station. After a long time packed in train cars,

they arrive in Siberia and are forced to work inside a gypsum mine. They are still in exile even when they are freed from that task. They try to survive the harsh conditions of Siberia with little money, food, heat, or shelter. They move from shack to shack, living with other families. Throughout the ordeal, Esther is brave and resourceful. She values her education and friends so much that, when they are permitted to return to Poland, she pleads with her parents to stay in Siberia.

10 Minute Selection: Read the second half of chapter 1, beginning with the sentences, "Mama, the doorbell is ringing. Didn't you hear it? Shall I open the door?" Esther and her mother find Father with two Russian soldiers. The family is forced to pack and allowed to bring only a few belongings. They ride in trucks to the railroad station. The chapter ends with, "Ahead of us the cattle cars were waiting for their human cargo."

Henkes, Kevin. *The Zebra Wall.* **Greenwillow, 1988. 147 p. Gr. 3–5.**
The Vorlob family is expecting another baby girl. There are already five girls in the family: Adine, Bernice, Carla, Dot, and Effie. The entire family is suggesting names that begin with the letter *F.* Adine is angry that her aunt Irene has not only moved in with the family to help with the new baby but is sharing Adine's bedroom. She and her sisters make plans to drive Aunt Irene out of the house. Everyone is surprised when a baby boy arrives on the scene. His parents call him Baby. Adine is further upset that Aunt Irene receives the honor of naming the boy—a name that begins with the letter *Z.* "Then there'd be Vorlobs from A to Z."

10 Minute Selection: Read chapter 8, "The Flowers." "Aunt Irene was taking over. Everything. Boxes of her belongings were stacked up under the windows in Adine's bedroom, and her outlandish clothes now took up half the space in Adine's shallow closet." Aunt Irene shuts down a moneymaking operation run by Bernice and Carla. The two girls join Adine and think of ways to make Aunt Irene go away. "'She's so *bossy,*' said Adine." The girls make horrible pictures of Aunt Irene. "'How's this?' Bernice asked, leaning back so Adine could read the sign she had just finished. It said WE ONLY HAVE ONE MOTHER AND HER NAME IS NOT IRENE." Adine feels tremendously guilty after the girls place the sign under Irene's pillow.

Henry, Marguerite. *Brighty of the Grand Canyon.* **Rand McNally, 1953. 222 p. Gr. 3–5.**
Brighty, short for Bright Angel, is a wild burro living in the Grand Canyon. Although he is not domesticated, he has several human friends, including a prospector named Old Timer. A bad man named Jake Irons kills Old Timer and eludes the law in the canyon. Meanwhile, Brighty has several adventures, including becoming a burro pack leader, losing his status as leader, and meeting Teddy

Roosevelt. Brighty meets up again with Jake Irons, and the two become stranded in a blizzard with Brighty's friends Homer Hobbs and Uncle Jim.

10 Minute Selection: Read the short chapter titled "A Free Spirit." Brighty is enjoying his freedom when he comes upon two photographers. They use Brighty to help carry their equipment. Brighty has other plans. He rolls over in Bright Angel Creek and cracks a camera. The men are furious as Brighty "daintily stepped out of the ropes and kicked the pack, sending it rolling and tumbling downward until it caught in a juniper bush." Next, read the chapter titled "The Fight in the Cave." Brighty has found refuge in a cave when he is attacked by a mountain lion. The cat leaps on Brighty's back and has a tight grip when Brighty rolls over, pinning the mountain lion beneath him in a pool of water. "For long minutes he held her there. Then gradually the claws eased, and at last they fell away."

Herrera, Juan Felipe. *Crashboomlove: A Novel in Verse.* **University of New Mexico Press, 1999. 155 p. Gr. 9–12.**
César, a tenth-grade Mexican American, lives with his mother, Lucy, in California. His father is living with and supporting a second family in Denver. César gets involved with drugs, fighting, and theft, but he struggles to do the right thing. "I don't want this. I tell myself. / Every day, I get further and further / from home, from school. / How do I get back?" César falls into a coma after a joyriding crash, but he slowly heals. There is hope at the end when César is in the choir with other tough kids, all singing "Swing Low, Sweet Chariot." "I am standing tall with my voice growing / out of me, a flame, a spark, a corn plant in green gold . . . I am singing out." There are many Spanish words and phrases in the text.

10 Minute Selection: Read the following six poems from this novel-in-verse: "White Boy Shoes," "Behind the Target," "Erase Everything after School," "Broken Fingernails," "Fly into a Sock," and "Goldfish." After the vice principal breaks up a fight between César and a Hmong boy, a new tenth-grade student challenges César. The new kid beats up César behind Lucky's Mini-Mart in front of a crowd. Later, in school, César is sniffing airplane glue. While high, César sees the new kid playing basketball and slams him into a locker. "Why don't you rebound this? Kick him. / Why don't you rebound this? Slam his head. / Why don't you . . . / Mr. Stanton, the school cop, / grabs me from behind."

Hesse, Karen. *Out of the Dust.* **Scholastic, 1997. 227 p. Gr. 5–8.**
Billie Jo describes herself as a "redheaded, freckle-faced, narrow-hipped girl / with a fondness for apples, / and a hunger for playing fierce piano." She lives with her farming family in the Oklahoma Panhandle during the Dust Bowl years. On top of the drought, Billie Jo and her family suffer a horrific, sudden, tragic accident. I'm intentionally trying to be vague here because I was breathless when I first read this book and came upon this scene. One unfortunate result of the accident was

that Billie Jo's hands became badly scarred from burns. It hurts too much to play the piano. She yearns to get "out of the dust," but when she does leave, she quickly turns around to go back home. "What I am, I am because of the dust."

10 Minute Selection: Read several of the short poems that comprise this novel, starting with "Rules of Dining." The family jokes in the face of the dust. "Daddy says, / 'The potatoes are peppered plenty tonight, Polly,' / and / 'Chocolate milk for dinner, aren't we in clover!'" Move on to the poem titled "Fields of Flashing Light," where Daddy could have cried tears of mud from a dust storm. Next, read "Wild Boy of the Road." A passing boy works on the farm for a day. Billie Jo's mother says, "His mother is worrying about him." Finally, read a string of poems, starting with "Guests" and also including "Family School," "Birth," and "Time to Go." Billie Jo and her classmates and teacher are surprised to find a family has moved into their classroom during the night.

Hesse, Karen. *Sable.* Holt, 1994. 81 p. Gr. 2–4.

Tate convinces her parents to let her keep a stray dog she names Sable. Sable has a tendency to run around while Tate is in school. Tate's mother dislikes the dog and wants her gone. The dog brings home souvenirs from her travels, including someone's "brand-new mat that people use to wipe their feet on." After receiving complaints from neighbors, Tate's father gives the dog to a doctor in Concord. Tate is angry and builds a fence for Sable out of wood all by herself. She goes to visit the doctor, hoping to return with Sable, but learns that the dog has run away. Sable eventually makes her way back to Tate. The book ends with Tate catching her mother slipping Sable a bite of meat.

10 Minute Selection: Read chapter 1, "The Arrival." Tate finds a sad-looking dog outside. While petting the newcomer, Tate notices the dog's ears are very soft. "They reminded me of the trim on the sweater Pap got for Mam one year. Pap said the trim was a kind of fur called sable." The chapter ends with Tate naming the dog Sable. Move on to chapter 3, "The Bed." Tate wants to build a doghouse but has to settle for putting sawdust into a cardboard box. She sneaks a quilt into the box for Sable. Tate hopes the dog won't be any trouble. "Mam and Pap hadn't said I could keep her. But they hadn't said I couldn't, either."

Hinton, S. E. *The Outsiders.* Viking, 1967. 180 p. Gr. 6–10.

Ponyboy is a greaser, as are his friends and brothers. The greasers battle the Socs, "the Socials, the jet set, the West-side rich kids. It's like the term 'greaser,' which is used to class all us boys on the East Side. We're poorer than the Socs and the middle class. I reckon we're wilder, too." Ponyboy and his friend Johnny kill a Soc in self-defense and flee to the country. They return as heroes, but at a great cost. It's hard to imagine that author Hinton wrote this touchstone novel while in her teens. This is the book that ushered in the modern-day young adult novel.

10 Minute Selection: Read most of chapter 6, beginning with the sentence, "Man, this place is out of it." A greaser named Dallas has helped Ponyboy and Johnny find their hiding place in the country. He is checking up on them when Johnny declares that he wants to turn himself in. They head back to the abandoned church, which has been their refuge, only to find it on fire. Some children from a school picnic are caught inside the church. Johnny and Ponyboy race inside. They save the children but a burning beam falls on Johnny. Dallas pulls him out. An adult asks Ponyboy if they are professional heroes. "'No, we're greasers,' I said." End the passage with the line, "I guess that guy knew how close to hysterics I really was, for he talked to me in a low soothing voice all the way to the hospital."

Ho, Minfong. *The Clay Marble*. Farrar Straus Giroux, 1991. 163 p. Gr. 5–8.
Dara and her family are forced to leave their Cambodian village in the early 1980s. They are out of food and trying to reach the border. They find temporary relief, and Dara befriends Nea and Jantu and their family. The fighting intensifies, and Dara is separated from her family. She eventually finds them with what she believes is the magic of a clay marble Jantu made. Dara is upset to learn that her brother Sarun has forgotten their plans to return home and plant rice. He wants to join the army instead. Jantu fights for her life when she is shot by sentries who "had mistaken us for enemies in the dark." One of the sentries is Sarun. Dara learns that the magic was not in the clay marble but in Jantu herself.
    10 Minute Selection: Read most of chapter 7, beginning with the sentence, "Late one morning, shortly after Sarun had returned from the second mass distribution with hoe heads and fishnets, we heard the sounds of gunfire and bombing in the distance." The refugees flee the battle on foot. "So that was what it meant to be a refugee. We were farmers who had been displaced from our old land and yet prevented from settling on any new land." A shell explodes and injures Jantu's baby brother. The chapter ends with Dara running for help.

Hoban, Russell. *The Mouse and His Child*. Harper and Row, 1967. 181 p. Gr. 2–5.
A tramp alters two windup toy mice so that they may travel. "'Be tramps,' he said, and turned and walked away with the dog at his heels." The two windups are held captive in a dump by the evil rat Manny. They escape and find themselves first in the middle of a shrew war, then part of a theatrical performance, and next at the bottom of a pond. They are pursued by Manny throughout the story simply because he wants to smash them. The windups meet several new friends, try to reunite with other toys, become self-winding, and finally seek out their own territory. This leads to a fight with Manny and other rats at a dump.

10 Minute Selection: Read the last section of chapter 2. Inform your audience that a toy mouse and his child are forced to help rob a bank by some rats. Begin reading with the sentence, "The sky was beginning to pale, and the air was sharp with morning as Ralphie and the mouse and his child came through the woods along a path to the Meadow Mutual Hoard and Trust Company, an earthen bank beside a stream." Ralphie the rat threatens a chipmunk employee. The chipmunk steps on an alarm twig. A badger guard gobbles up Ralphie. A bullfrog helps the windup mouse and his child get ready for their long trip. A blue jay announces to the world, "RAT SLAIN IN BANK HOLDUP ATTEMPT. WINDUPS FLEE WITH GETAWAY FROG." The chapter ends with Manny the Rat hearing the blue jay. He vows to smash the windups or he knows that he'll become the laughingstock of the dump.

Hobbs, Will. *Far North*. Morrow, 1996. 224 p. Gr. 6–12.
Fifteen-year-old Texan Gabe finds himself fighting for survival in the Canadian Northwest Territories. The plane carrying Gabe, his school roommate Raymond, and Raymond's uncle Johnny Raven crashes and is swept downstream by the Nahanni River. Johnny sets up a winter camp. Gabe and Raymond convince Johnny to go with them down the frozen river, but their troubles are only beginning.

10 Minute Selection: Read the last part of chapter 6, beginning with the sentence, "Now we could see where the whitewater was heading as it sluiced down the gorge at a steeper and steeper angle." Clint, the pilot, is showing his passengers the breathtaking Virginia Falls. He has landed the plane on the river when, suddenly, the engine quits. "The only sound to be heard was the dull roar of the falls." Continue reading into the next chapter. As the plane drifts down the river toward the gorge, everyone grabs as much gear as possible. Gabe, Raymond, and Johnny make it to shore, but Clint is still on the plane. The selection ends with the lines, "I saw only the briefest glimpse of Clint being pitched into the whitewater, and then he was gone. 'Clint!' I yelled. 'Clint!'"

Holman, Felice. *Slake's Limbo*. Macmillan, 1974. 117 p. Gr. 6–12.
Because of his small stature, thirteen-year-old Aremis Slake is often bullied by others. "Anyone could beat him for any reason or non-reason, and did, when they could catch him. . . . When not shunned entirely, he was hunted and hounded for sport." He finds refuge in the city's subway system. "He stayed one hundred and twenty-one days." Slake finds a small enclosure down a track tunnel. It becomes his shelter. He starts selling used newspapers to regular customers—enough to buy some food in a subway luncheonette. The shop's manager gives him a job sweeping and enough food to survive. After an accident closes off the subway tunnel, Slake is worried that workers will find his shelter.

10 Minute Selection: Inform your audience that a teen named Slake has found a hidden room down in a subway tunnel. Read most of chapter 4. Although Slake is worried that police will find his new home, he experiences a kind of freedom that is new to him. Slake finds a clean bathroom and readies himself for the day. He's staring at a man who ordered a cup of coffee and left it on the counter after taking a few sips. Slake quickly takes the man's place and claims the coffee. Afterward, Slake picks up discarded newspapers and "three buttons, a pencil, and the head of a plastic doll." When a man grabs him, Slake freezes until the man indicates he wants to buy one of the teen's papers. End the passage with the sentence, "Slake knew he was in business."

Horvath, Polly. *The Trolls.* Farrar Straus Giroux, 1999. 135 p. Gr. 3–5.
Mr. and Mrs. Anderson are in a quandary. They are going on a trip to Paris, and their regular babysitter has come "down with a mild case of the bubonic plague and called tearfully to say she didn't want to spread the buboes around." They reluctantly ask Aunt Sally—Mr. Anderson's sister—to babysit Melissa, Amanda, and Frank, also known as Pee Wee. Aunt Sally regales the three children with wild stories—some funny and some fairly rough—about eccentric family members, finger-biting clams, cougar hunters, dog murders, and, of course, trolls.

10 Minute Selection: The chapter titled "Greens" is without a doubt one of my favorite passages of all time to read aloud to audiences. Aunt Sally and the children sit down to dinner. The children dislike beans, so Aunt Sally puts them all on her plate. She then begins a long, convoluted story about "Great-uncle Louis, who came for two weeks and stayed for six years" and Louis's efforts to make his nephew Edward eat fiddlesticks. "Think of the fiber. Are you mad to avoid such fibrous vegetation, you little anti-herbivore?" Aunt Sally plays with her green beans while telling the story. The children are fascinated as she knits with the beans, makes walrus tusks out of them, and drops them in her mouth "like clothespins into a bottle." Of course, the children want green beans and are dismayed to learn that Aunt Sally has eaten them all. "You are the strangest children I ever saw. . . . If you wanted beans, why did you give me yours?"

**Howe, Deborah, and James Howe. *Bunnicula: A Rabbit-Tale of Mystery.*
Atheneum, 1979. 98 p. Gr. K–5.**
Harold the dog narrates this story of the Monroe family and their newest pet—a bunny that the Monroes found in a movie theater. The family's cat, Chester, is suspicious of the new arrival. Chester is convinced that the bunny is really a vampire. He is further convinced when vegetables turn up white and drained of their juice. The cat tells Harold that they all should wear garlic to ward off the rabbit, but this only earns Chester a bath from Mrs. Monroe. Harold notices Bunnicula is becoming sick. Chester is preventing the rabbit from eating. In the end, the

bunny is content drinking vegetable juice, Harold becomes friends with the rabbit, and Chester sees "a cat psychiatrist to work out what the doctor called a case of sibling rivalry with Bunnicula." There are many Bunnicula chapter books and picture books. The second chapter book in the series is *Howliday Inn* (1982).

10 Minute Selection: Read the second half of chapter 4, "A Cat Prepares," beginning with the sentence, "'Well, you certainly took your time,' Chester snapped as I sauntered casually into the room." Chester is trying to convince Harold that Bunnicula is a vampire. He sleeps all day, he has "funny little sharp teeth," and he was found at the movie theater that was showing the movie *Dracula*. Furthermore, the rabbit had a note tied around its neck. Chester deduces that the note is written in an "obscure dialect of the Carpathian mountain region," in other words, Transylvania. Chester also points out that Bunnicula's food has been turning white. The chapter ends with the two animals hearing something in the kitchen and finding a white zucchini.

Hunt, Irene. *Across Five Aprils*. Follett, 1964. 188 p. Gr. 5–7.

Jethro and his family are living in southern Illinois when the Civil War begins, in 1861. His older brothers sign up for the army. One brother joins the Rebs, and the entire family faces scorn from some of their neighbors. Another brother deserts his post, and the Federal Registrars stop by. "You fail to report him, and you and your family will be up to your necks in trouble. Do you understand?" Jethro and his family follow the various battles through a series of letters and newspaper accounts.

10 Minute Selection: This is a long passage. Read the middle section of chapter 5, beginning with the sentence, "A half dozen men sat around the fireplace at one end of the stove or leaned against the counters and cracker barrels." Jethro is confronted by a man named Wortman, who insults Jethro's father for not denouncing Bill, the brother who joined the Southern army. End this passage with the line, "'I've learned that—by talkin' with ye jest a little. Well,' he pulled on a jacket as he spoke, 'where's the team?'" Move ahead to the sentence, "The two-mile stretch of woods road was just ahead—the hardest two miles of the trip if one considered the terrain." Jethro is joined on his ride home by Dave Burdow, a man who has been known to be an enemy of Jethro's family. Burdow assures Jethro that he means him no harm. Burdow foils an ambush by Wortman, and Jethro makes it safely home. End with the line, "He mounted his horse and, without looking around, started back over the road they had just traveled."

Hurwitz, Johanna. *Russell and Elisa*. Morrow, 1989. 88 p. Gr. K–2.

Three-year-old Elisa gets a package from her grandmother that contains a rag doll. Elisa names the doll Airmail "because she came to me in the mail in an airplane." Elisa has a series of adventures with Airmail, her friends, and her family. Elisa's older brother is Russell. He is not always impressed with his little sister. At one point, Elisa loses Airmail at the library. Russell feels guilty because he knew when and where Elisa lost Airmail but kept quiet because "he liked walking along with his mother and his sister without the doll." In the end, Russell comes up with a plan to help Elisa get through the long night without her doll. This is one of fourteen books in the Riverside Kids series. The first in the series is *Busybody Nora* (1976).

10 Minute Selection: Read chapter 2, "The Haircut." Elisa's friend Annie comes over to play. They give Airmail a pretend haircut. Russell gets his sharper scissors and gives Airmail "a real haircut." The kids decide Russell can give Annie a haircut, too. "'I won't cut it all off,' Russell promised. He was enjoying this game that Elisa began." Of course, Russell and Elisa's mother is upset when she learns that the kids have been playing "barbershop." Luckily, Annie's mother has a good sense of humor. "'Hair always grows back,' she said as she examined her daughter's haircut."

Huynh, Quang Nhuong. *The Land I Lost: Adventures of a Boy in Vietnam.* Harper and Row, 1982. 115 p. Gr. 5–10.

The author recounts his childhood in a hamlet in Vietnam. Stories revolve around his prize water buffalo, Tank, and also encounters with crocodiles, snakes, and wild hogs. Some of the chapters have strong content, such as a monkey killing a human infant. This should not deter one from sharing this wonderful memoir. The author has a similar biography for slightly younger audiences titled *Water Buffalo Days* (1997).

10 Minute Selection: Read the chapter titled "So Close." A young man named Trung plans to marry his neighbor Lan. "In the evening of the wedding night Lan went to the river to take a bath." A crocodile catches her and carries her away. Trung and the relatives are heartbroken. Later that evening, Trung hears Lan's voice. He is worried "for according to an old belief a crocodile's victim must lure a new victim to his master." The next day, Lan is found safe on an island. She had escaped the crocodile. Lan and Trung have a second wedding celebration for "Lan had come back from the dead."

Second 10 Minute Selection: The chapter titled "Little Altar on the Roadside" is reminiscent of an urban tale and a good story for older audiences. A young bridegroom is found dead, and his new bride is arrested for murder. The coroner discovers that a poisonous snake was trapped in the bamboo bed, and its breath was strong enough to kill the bridegroom.

Third 10 Minute Selection: This good two-minute selection features the author's grandmother. Read a short section of the chapter titled "Opera, Karate, and Bandits," starting with the sentence, "My grandmother had married a man whom she loved with all her heart, but who was totally different from her." A bully threatens the couple in a restaurant, taunting grandfather for being weak. Grandmother dispatches the rascal with a kick to the chin. She tells everyone in the restaurant that her husband trained her. End the passage with the sentence, "And whenever anyone happened to bump into him on the street, they bowed to my grandfather in a very respectful way."

Ibbotson, Eva. *The Secret of Platform 13.* **Dutton, 1994. 231 p. Gr. 3–8.**
The title secret is a "gump," a bump that contains a hidden door to a magical world known as The Island. "The people who lived on it just called it The Island." Such doors are only open "for exactly nine days every nine years, and not one second longer, and . . . it was no good changing your mind about coming or going because nothing would open the door once the time was up." The royal heir, a baby boy, is kidnapped and held in Great Britain. Nine years later, the king and queen send a rescue squad after him: an old wizard, an agricultural fairy, a one-eyed ogre, and a young hag named Odge. Unfortunately, the team finds the prince, now called Raymond Trottle, and discovers he's grown into a terribly spoiled brat.
    10 Minute Selection: Read chapter 9. The rescue team is trying to impress Raymond with a magical presentation to show him what his life on the magical Island would be like. There are magical birds, mermaids, a fish that hiccups a ring, loud banshees, feats of strength, and magic tricks. Raymond is not impressed with any of it. For the grand finale, Cor the wizard summons a "nuckelavee," a creature with a man's head, a horse's body, and exposed internal organs. "Ugh! It's disgusting; it's creepy. I don't like it." It's not until Raymond discovers wizards can make gold—"making gold is something wizards learn to do in the nursery"—that he agrees to come to the Island.

Jacques, Brian. *Redwall.* **Philomel, 1986. 351 p. Gr. 4–8.**
Redwall Abbey is home to many good woodland creatures. Their safety is threatened by the arrival of an evil rat named Cluny, who tries to conquer the abbey with his army. A mouse named Matthias is inspired by the legend of Martin the Warrior and tries to find Martin's sword. The sword is hidden, and Matthias faces more challenges from King Bulla Sparra and Asmodeus Poisonteeth the snake. Have fun reading the unique speech patterns of the various species. This is the first of many Redwall books. The second in the series is *Mossflower* (1988).
    10 Minute Selection: Read the very short chapter 2 of "Book One," which shows us that Cluny the Scourge is on the move and heading toward Redwall Abbey. Next, read the two-page chapter 16. Cluny has taken over a church near Redwall Abbey, and he is terrorizing the Vole family. Move on to the middle of chapter 17, starting with the sentence, "Matthias expressed his wishes to the Stag." Basil the Stag Hare helps Matthias rescue the Vole family. He does so by humorously

insulting Cluny's rats, drawing them away from the Voles. "Dear, dear, don't you chaps ever take a bath? Listen here, you dreadful creature. D'you realize that you smell to high heaven?" Matthias rescues the Voles, but the chapter ends with them walking right into the sentry rats.

Jiménez, Francisco. *The Circuit: Stories from the Life of a Migrant Child.* Houghton Mifflin, 1997. 116 p. Gr. 5–8.
Author Jiménez has written several semiautobiographical short stories to give "readers an insight into the lives of migrant farm workers and their children whose backbreaking labor of picking fruits and vegetables puts food on our tables." Panchito and his family move frequently as migrant workers. He has trouble in school because of the language barrier and finds education challenging. However, Panchito values his education. "When I saw him putting on his work clothes, I remembered we were going to work, not to school. My shoulders felt heavy." There are several Spanish phrases. Be sure to share the author's afterword with your audience. Jiménez has written two more chapter books based on his life: *Breaking Through* (2001) and *Reaching Out* (2008).
   10 Minute Selection: Read the chapter titled "Inside Out." Panchito and his older brother Roberto go to school while their parents "look for work, either topping carrots or thinning lettuce." Panchito doesn't know how to speak English, so he spends most of his classroom time studying a caterpillar in a jar next to his desk. He is given a jacket from a box in the school office one cold morning. A boy named Curtis claims the jacket is his, and the two boys are punished for fighting. Near the end of the school year, Panchito wins a prize for his drawing of a butterfly. Curtis compliments the drawing. "'¿Como se dice 'es tuyo' en inglés?' I asked. 'It's yours,' answered Arthur. 'It's yours,' I repeated, handing the drawing to Curtis." This story is also the basis for the author's picture book *La Mariposa* (1998).

Johnson, Angela. *Heaven.* Simon and Schuster, 1998. 138 p. Gr. 6–10.
Fourteen-year-old Marley's idyllic life is shattered when she learns that her parents are really her aunt and uncle. She leans on the companionship of friends new to Heaven. Marley's "parents" give her the necessary time and space to come to terms with this surprise. As Pops says, "Sometimes it's easy to tell where you are. Just look around and notice the people who have always been there for you, and follow them."
   10 Minute Selection: Tell your audience that the characters live in a town called Heaven. Read most of the chapter titled "Shadow Ghosts and Cadillacs." Marley describes her friend Shoogy. "The reason we became and stayed friends was that she wasn't like anybody in her family and like everybody in mine." Marley doesn't trust Shoogy's family because of their pursuit of perfection. End with the sentence, "It makes me wonder why Shoogy stopped being beautiful and started

hating Cadillacs," and move on to the next chapter, titled "To the Amish." Marley tells how she met Bobby and came to be Feather's babysitter. She answered an ad that read "LOOKING FOR A DEPENDABLE, BABY-FRIENDLY PERSON. REFERENCES. TRANSPORTATION. MUST KNOW 'YOU ARE MY SUN-SHINE' AND LIKE *SESAME STREET.*" End with the line, "It looks to me like you're either born in Heaven or you come here from someplace else to start all over and forget what happened before."

Jordan, Sherryl. *The Raging Quiet.* Simon and Schuster, 1999. 264 p. Gr. 9–12.
Sixteen-year-old Marnie marries an older man and accompanies him to a little village by the sea. He dies in an accident a few days later. Marnie befriends a boy who the villagers believe is possessed by devils. Marnie learns that the boy she calls Raven is deaf, and she develops a series of hand signs to communicate with him. The superstitious villagers believe the "hand-words" are witch spells and that Marnie caused her husband's death. She endures ritualistic torture to prove her innocence.

    10 Minute Selection: Read the last part of chapter 23, beginning with the sentence, "The skies were blushing orange along the horizon, when they climbed over the last hill and saw their cove spread out below." Marnie and Raven are confronted by a crowd. She tells Raven to find their friend Father Brannan. The chapter ends with someone throwing a sack over Marnie's head. "There she was moving, helpless, blind, half suffocated; and there was only the rumble of the wagon wheels, and the frenzy of the crowd, savage and triumphant and screaming for a hanging." Continue reading into chapter 24. Father Brannan is accused of being bewitched by Marnie. The crowd demands a witch trial. Father Brannan reluctantly agrees to conduct the trial. End with the line, "Marnie gave a wild cry and several men rushed at her, and held her."

Juster, Norton. *The Phantom Tollbooth.* Random House, 1961. 256 p. Gr. 3–8.
Milo is unenthusiastic about everything in life. "'And worst of all,' he continued sadly, 'there's nothing for me to do, nowhere I'd care to go, and hardly anything worth seeing.' He punctuated this last thought with such a deep sigh that a house sparrow singing nearby stopped and rushed home to be with his family." He finds instructions to build a tollbooth, which takes him to a world of wordplay and strange logic where he meets many odd characters and creatures. His mission becomes to rescue Princesses Rhyme and Reason and restore, of course, rhyme and reason to the land.

    10 Minute Selection: Inform your audience that Milo is in a strange land accompanied by a watchdog—made out of a watch—named Tock. Read chapter 4,

"Confusion in the Market Place." Merchants are selling, of all things, words such as *quagmire* and *upholstery*. One particular merchant is selling letters from his wagon—on its side is a sign that reads "DO IT YOURSELF." A large bee, named the Spelling Bee, shows up and gets into an argument with a bug named the Humbug. The Spelling Bee calls the Humbug "an impostor—i-m-p-o-s-t-o-r— who can't even spell his own name." The Humbug tries to swat the bee with his cane, trips, and knocks over the merchants' stalls. The chapter ends with the bee shouting, "Help! Help! There's a little boy on me."

Kennedy, Richard. *Inside My Feet: The Story of a Giant.* Harper and Row, 1979. 71 p. Gr. 4–7.
A boy lives in the country with his mother and father. "Our nearest neighbor was out of sight and sound, and I remember always one night when both my father and mother were carried off down that road into that deep forest." Enchanted boots have carried the boy's parents to a giant, who plans to eat them. The boy cleverly destroys the boots when they come for him by having two rats eat them. The boy discovers that the enchantment now resides within the rats, so he uses them to locate his parents and confront the giant.

10 Minute Selection: Read the first section of the book. The boy and his parents awaken to a strange knocking at their door. "There on the floor were a pair of boots, common in all ways as any honest countryman's boots, except that they were as long as one of my arms, deep enough to hide a bread box in, past all size numbers, boots with leather enough in them to cover a small chair—the boots of a giant!" Later that evening, the boy's father disappears, and shortly afterward, his mother is gone, too. End the passage with the lines, "The boots were coming back for me. Somebody or something meant to carry us all off, and I was next."

Kerr, M. E. *Gentlehands.* Harper and Row, 1978. 183 p. Gr. 9–12.
Buddy Boyle is a townie. He lives year-round in Seaville, New York, where his father is the police chief. Buddy falls in love with Skye, a wealthy girl whose family spends the summer on a nearby estate called Beauregard. To impress Skye, Buddy drives her to meet his grandfather, who is estranged from the rest of the family. Grandfather Trenker charms Skye with his manner and sophistication. A writer named De Lucca accuses Trenker of being "Gentlehands," a former Nazi who worked at Auschwitz, sadistically torturing inmates, including De Lucca's cousin.

10 Minute Selection: Read most of chapter 5. Buddy has been invited to Skye's family estate. The chapter opens with, "The pool house at Beauregard is bigger than the house I live in." Buddy is introduced to Skye's mother and her dogs Janice, January, and Little Ophelia. Buddy surprisingly impresses Skye's mother with his strategy for winning at the board game Monopoly. Buddy meets some kids by the pool who are his age. One girl runs into the pool house and grabs some clothes to play Whose Is It? She holds up a sweater, and everyone makes fun of it, not realizing it belongs to Buddy. "'It's the yard boy's,' Connie said. 'It smells like the yard boy's,' Rachel said, holding the armpit to her nose and making a face." When the rich kids discover their mistake, there is an awkward silence. Some run to the beach. Rachel apologizes. "I hate myself you know." End the passage with Buddy's response to her. "'I think I'll go for a swim,' I said. I got up and dove into the pool."

King-Smith, Dick. *Babe the Gallant Pig.* **Crown, 1985. 118 p. Gr. 2–4.**
Farmer Hogget wins a pig at the fair. His collie Fly names the pig Babe and tends to him like one of her pups. Fly's task is to herd sheep, and she does it with sharp commands. Babe learns how to be a sheep-pig, but he moves the sheep around with kindness and manners. Farmer Hogget decides not to eat the pig but to enter it in the Grand Challenge Trials, a test for sheepdogs. Before this happens, Babe saves the herd from rustlers and, later, from wild dogs. Before these dogs are chased off, however, they fatally maim an old sheep named Ma. Farmer Hogget finds Babe bending over her body with blood on his snout and decides he must shoot the pig. Babe's life is spared, and he enters the trials. Side note—have fun reading Mrs. Hogget's long, run-on lines.

10 Minute Selection: Read chapter 6, "Good Pig." Farmer Hogget decides to "see if the pig would like to come, when he went around the sheep with Fly." It's the first time he sees how well the sheep mind Babe, especially after Fly yells at them. In fact, the sheep start to revolt against Fly before she bares her teeth. "'We want Babe!' they bleated. 'Babe! Babe! Ba-a-a-a-a-be!'" In contrast, Babe addresses the sheep in a civil manner. "If I might ask a great favor of you . . . could you all please be kind enough to walk down to that gate where the farmer is standing, and to go through it?" At the end of the chapter, Farmer Hogget says "Good pig."

Kjelgaard, Jim. *Outlaw Red.* **Holiday House, 1953. 180 p. Gr. 4–8.**
Sean is a champion Irish setter who has a close connection to the kennel boy Billy Dash. Billy heads into the wilderness after an altercation with his cruel uncle. Sean also finds himself surviving the wilderness after his transport crate falls off the back of a truck. The dog quickly adapts and becomes a skilled hunter. At times, he is hunted by men who mistake him for Slasher, a half-dog, half-coyote mix that kills livestock. Sean mates with another show dog who has also escaped into the wilderness, and the pair has pups. When Sean is aware that Slasher is stalking his family, the Irish setter prepares for a final battle. *Outlaw Red* is the third book in the series, following *Big Red* (1945) and *Irish Red* (1951).

10 Minute Selection: Read the second half of chapter 6, "Hound Pack." Begin with the sentence, "The big Setter first became aware of danger when a bullet from a high-powered rifle snicked into snow scarcely five feet away." A group of hill men and their dogs are on the hunt for Sean. The pack includes two dogs bred for killing and two hounds that "have never been known to leave the scent of a quarry they started." Some of the pursuing dogs follow Slasher, and the two scent dogs follow Sean. These last two dogs do indeed catch up to Sean, but their only job is to track, not to kill. The men and the other dogs are miles away. The three dogs sniff each other, and "because they were all tired from the long chase, the three curled up so they could keep each other warm, and peacefully went to sleep."

Klause, Annette Curtis. *The Silver Kiss*. Delacorte, 1990. 198 p. Gr. 7–12.
Fans of the Twilight series will enjoy this romance that also features a mortal high school girl who is attracted to a young-looking, centuries-old male vampire. Zoe's mother is dying of cancer. Zoe feels alone. Her father is distant, and her best friend is moving away. She meets a strange young man named Simon who reveals himself as a vampire. Simon is on a mission to destroy his brother Christopher, a vampire who appears as a young child but is responsible for several deaths. Zoe is enlisted to help Simon, putting her own life in danger. There are some rough words scattered throughout the text.

   10 Minute Selection: Read chapter 4. Simon is thinking about Zoe. He is fasci-nated by her. Simon leaves her house and finds himself in a vacant lot. Three boys, one with a knife, surround him. The largest boy charges Simon. "And Simon, who didn't come up to his chin, clutched the boy's belt with his free hand and lifted him into the air." Instead of running away, the boy with the knife laughs and charges Simon. Simon knocks this one down and angrily "tore the boy's wrist open with a savage scissoring of teeth." Sirens sound close by, so Simon takes the unconscious thug's leather jacket as a prize and runs to Zoe's backyard.

Kline, Suzy. *Herbie Jones*. Putnam, 1985. 95 p. Gr. K–3.
Herbie is in the lowest reading group in third grade—the Apples. He works hard to move up to the next level. His friend Raymond is worried about being the only boy left in the Apples. The two boys work on a campaign to change the group name to the Spiders based on the classic story *Charlotte's Web*. Other stories feature rumors of ghosts in the school bathrooms, the two boys leaving a class field trip to buy hamburgers, a poster contest, and Raymond's attempts to charm the teacher by dressing up and wearing what he thinks is cologne but is really perfume. This is the first in a series of books about Herbie Jones. The second book is *Herbie Jones and the Class Gift* (1987).

   10 Minute Selection: Read chapter 2, "Annabelle's Party," beginning with the sentence "The next morning at school the invitation was on Herbie's desk." Herbie and the other boys are invited to Annabelle Louisa Hodgekiss's birthday party. The invitation states "RSVP." Some sixth-graders tell them "RSVP means remove shoes very promptly." Herbie is proud of his gift—a can of pink salmon. "Herbie didn't think his mom would miss it. He remembered the can had been on the shelf a long time." Annabelle's mother opens the can so the kids can take a peek. Raymond throws up all over the table. "There's yellow barf all over the carrot dish and yellow barf floating in Margie's water glass!" Mrs. Hodgkiss calmly cleans up the mess and then serves cake with yellow icing. "And everyone was thinking the same thing. The only one who finished a piece of birthday cake was Raymond."

Konigsburg, E. L. *About the B'Nai Bagels.* **Atheneum, 1969. 172 p. Gr. 4–8.**
Mark is horrified to learn that his very own mother will be his new Little League baseball team manager. "I had no trouble with my mother, the mother; it was my mother, the manager, who gave me headaches and doubts." The team was horrible last year. Mark is worried not only about his performance on the field but also about his upcoming bar mitzvah. Surprisingly, the team does very well after the boys' initial shock of having a woman as their manager wears off. "The reason why you have a lady manager is because chlorophyll is a catalyst that enables a plant to use the energy of the sun to convert carbon dioxide and water into sugar and oxygen." In other words, it's a fact of life. The hilarious episodes and characters—Mother is a hoot—are countered with a serious look at anti-Semitism and sportsmanship.
 10 Minute Selection: Read chapter 2. Mark is alone one night with his father. "Dad and I split the soup. I put some in a bowl for him, and I spooned mine right out of the pot. Dad didn't notice until he asked for seconds." The two get into an argument, and Mark is sent to bed. Mother and Mark's older brother Spencer come home. Mother tells Spencer that he will have to help coach the team. "'Bessie!' Pause. 'Mother!' Pause. 'Mom!' Pause and louder. 'I will not. I cannot.' 'Spencer!' Pause. 'Son!' Pause. 'Boychick!' Pause and softer. 'You will. You can.'"

Konigsburg, E. L. *From the Mixed-Up Files of Mrs. Basil E. Frankweiler.*
Atheneum, 1967. 162 p. Gr. 4–6.
Claudia decides to run away from home. Actually, she doesn't think of it as running away but more like "running to somewhere." She enlists one her brothers, Jamie, to join her. They hide out in the Metropolitan Museum of Art in New York City. They become very good at remaining undetected. Claudia becomes very curious about one of the exhibits, a statue called *Angel.* Claudia is determined to solve the mystery that has stumped experts—did Michelangelo create *Angel?* The mystery leads Claudia and Jamie to the donor of the piece—Mrs. Basil E. Frankweiler.
 10 Minute Selection: Read most of chapter 3, beginning with the sentence, "As they entered the main door on Fifth Avenue, the guard clicked off two numbers on his people-counter." The children enter the museum for the first time. Because

the story is told by Mrs. Frankweiler to her lawyer, there are some asides written within parentheses. Skip these while reading. After the children check their bags, they eat in the museum's snack bar. Claudia tells Jamie how to hide in the bathroom while the museum is closing. She also selects their sleeping quarters for the night. Everything works for them. "Even the footsteps of the night watchman added only an accented quarter-note to the silence that had become a hum, a lullaby."

Korman, Gordon. *Why Did the Underwear Cross the Road?* Scholastic, **1994. 110 p. Gr. 3–6.**
Fourth-graders Justin Zeckendorf, Margaret Zachary, and Jessica Zander are known as the "Zs." The team that wins the school's Good Deeds project gets to go to Tidal Wave Water Park. Justin will do anything to win. Unfortunately, his ideas backfire, causing his team to receive negative points. He causes an accident by leaving Mrs. Milarchuk's suitcase in the middle of the road. A cement truck hits it. "KAPOW! The suitcase bounced up like a Ping-Pong ball. It hit the pavement, and broke open. There was a blizzard of underwear." His other ideas have similarly disastrous results. Fortunately, the string of hilarious events leads to the arrest of some car thieves, thanks to the Zs.

10 Minute Selection: Read chapter 6, "A Thousand Pieces of Shredded Toilet Paper," beginning with the sentence, "They started with Justin's next-door neighbors." The Zs offer their window-washing services but get turned down at the first house. Justin takes the initiative at the next house by grabbing a hose and spraying water at the window. Unfortunately, the window is open. The kids climb in the window and notice that the owners are in the basement listening to music with headphones on. The kids start mopping up the mess with paper towels and toilet paper. Justin blows the fuse when he starts the vacuum cleaner in the water. The kids hide in the closet but knock over a golf bag, open an umbrella, and step on the "release pin of Mr. McClintock's army surplus inflatable lifeboat." Jessica whispers, "'We're dead.' . . . 'Not yet!' whispered Justin." When Mr. McClintock opens the closet door, Justin says, "*Now,* we're dead."

Krull, Kathleen. *Lives of the Musicians: Good Times, Bad Times (and What the Neighbors Thought).* Harcourt, 1993. 93 p. Gr. 4–8.
Twenty musicians from Vivaldi to Woody Guthrie are chronologically featured, including little-known facts that might attract young readers, such as what they ate and their pets' names. Fun facts include Johannes Brahms "sometimes forgot to fasten his suspenders, and when he conducted, he'd have to grab his pants before they fell down," as well as the fact that William Gilbert, of Gilbert and Sullivan fame, "could swear for five minutes straight without repeating himself." Play a recording of a piece by each composer before or after you read his or her entry.

This is just one volume of Krull's fun, fact-filled Lives of series, which includes *Lives of the Writers* (1994), *Lives of the Artists* (1995), *Lives of the Athletes* (1997), *Lives of the Presidents* (1998), and *Lives of Extraordinary Women* (2000).

10 Minute Selection: Read the entry on Johann Sebastian Bach, who had twenty children and named five of them Johann, and two more Johanna. This selection opens with a brief story about Bach being attacked by six of his music students because he called one of them a "nanny-goat bassoonist." Next, read the chapter featuring Ludwig van Beethoven, who was rude to people and let his physical appearance fall apart. "Only his protruding teeth were always clean; he constantly rubbed them with his napkin." Kids will also like to learn that one of his favorite foods was macaroni and cheese. Unfortunately, Beethoven had "gradual deafness, beginning in his late twenties. . . . In his last public appearance, he began to cry when someone turned him around to make him aware of the roaring applause that he couldn't hear."

Le Guin, Ursula K. *A Wizard of Earthsea*. Parnassus, 1968. 197 p. Gr. 4–12.
Ged, or Sparrowhawk as he is known to others, is a young wizard of great power. He joins the School of Roke, a school for wizards. His pride takes over, and in an attempt to show up a fellow student, Ged tries to bring forth a dead spirit. An unknown shadow creature comes and tries to take possession of Ged. It is driven away but pursues Ged over years and distance until Ged learns that instead of being the hunted, he must become the hunter. This is the first of six books in the Earthsea series, including *The Tombs of Atuan* (1971), *The Farthest Shore* (1972), *Tehanu* (1990), *Tales from Earthsea* (2000), and *The Other Wind* (2001).

10 Minute Selection: Read a long selection from chapter 1, "Warriors in the Mist." Begin with the sentence, "In those days the Kargad Empire was strong." The people of that empire are about to attack Duny's (Ged's) village. Duny fears that he will die fighting alongside his people. He attempts a fog-weaving spell, "a binding-spell that gathers the mists together for a while in one place; with it one skilled in illusion can shape the mist into fair ghostly seemings, which last a little and fade away." The attackers are unable to tell the real villagers from the mist impressions. The villagers are able to attack the invaders, drawing some to their death over a cliff, until the Kargs run away. The villagers find Duny in a trancelike state. End the passage with the sentence, "His aunt said, 'He has overspent his power,' but she had no art to help him."

L'Engle, Madeleine. *Meet the Austins*. Farrar Straus Giroux, 1960. 216 p. Gr. 4–7.
The Austin family lives in the country, where Father is a doctor and Mother runs the household consisting of the four children—John, the oldest; twelve-year-old narrator Vicky; and the two youngest, Suzy and Rob. Their routine is jarred when

they take in newly orphaned Maggie. John best describes Maggie: "She's a spoiled brat from way back." Not only does Maggie settle in with the rest of the family but when the Austins learn that she may be taken away from them, they work hard to keep her. The chapter titled "The Anti-Muffins" was added to the revised edition and is an important part of the story linking Maggie to the rest of the family. This is the first in the Austin Family Chronicles. The other titles are *The Moon by Night* (1963), *The Young Unicorns* (1968), *A Ring of Endless Light* (1980), and *Troubling a Star* (1994).

10 Minute Selection: Read a portion of the chapter titled "The Terrible Week," beginning with the line, "So that was how the week began." John is sick with the flu and is very irritable. He and Vicky get into a fight. He goads her into doing something helpful for Mother. Vicky decides to let the air out of the upstairs radiator. "They were knocking last night and Mother said this morning she'd have to let the air out of them." Vicky makes a mess out of the task. Water is pouring out all over and no one can hear her cries for help. Mother takes care of the problem with a potato of all things. End with the sentence, "I left her holding it on the radiator and I went to the door of John's room and hissed, '*Beast*.'"

L'Engle, Madeleine. *A Wrinkle in Time.* **Farrar Straus Giroux, 1962. 211 p. Gr. 4–8.**

Meg, her young brother Charles, and their new friend Calvin go on a dangerous mission to find Meg's father. They are helped by three strange women—Mrs. Whatsit, Mrs. Who, and Mrs. Which—who aren't what they appear to be. Mrs. Who recites several quotations in various languages. One can easily read just the English translations. Mrs. Which speaks by drawing out her words, such as "Yyouu arre sstill verry yyoungg." It's not very difficult to read and actually kind of fun to say aloud. The group travels through space by means of the "tesseract," which shortens the trip via a fifth dimension. Meg learns that her father has been captured by IT, an evil force that threatens several planets, including Earth. This is the first book in a series that features Meg's family. The other titles are *A Wind in the Door* (1973), *A Swiftly Tilting Planet* (1978), and *Many Waters* (1986).

10 Minute Selection: Tell your audience that the main characters have landed on a strange planet. Read the second half of chapter 6, "The Happy Medium." Begin with the sentence, "Below them the town was laid out in harsh angular patterns." All of the residents do things in exact rhythm with each other. "Each clapped. Each child with the ball caught the ball. Each child with the skipping rope folded the rope. Each child turned and walked into the house. The doors clicked shut behind them. 'How can they do it?' Meg asked wonderingly." The three children make their way to the "CENTRAL Central Intelligence building." The chapter ends with Calvin predicting they're going into terrible danger.

Lester, Julius. *More Tales of Uncle Remus*. Dial, 1988. 141 p. Gr. 4–7.
Brer Rabbit has his way with Brer Fox, Brer Wolf, Brer Turtle, Brer Frog, and even Mr. Man in these retellings of African American folktales. Lester has a wonderful style of talking directly to the reader in some cases—"Now, let me get back to the story before it melts and ain't worth telling"—and throwing in some modern references—"He bought his wife the coffeepot and a copy of Paris *Vogue*, and he got the children the tin plates, tin cups, and some Star Wars underwear." The other books in the series are *The Tales of Uncle Remus* (1987), *Further Tales of Uncle Remus* (1990), and *The Last Tales of Uncle Remus* (1994). They have also been compiled in *Uncle Remus: The Complete Tales* (1999). All have good individual stories to read, although some may be gruesome.

10 Minute Selection: Read the story "Brer Rabbit, Brer Coon, and the Frogs." Brer Rabbit tells Brer Coon to pretend he's dead. "Don't blink your eyes; don't twitch your tail. Just lie there until you hear from me, and when I say move, you move!" Brer Rabbit tells the frogs, "Coon dead!" The frogs dig a hole around the body to bury it. When the hole is too deep for the frogs to jump out, Brer Rabbit tells Brer Coon to "RISE UP, AND GET YOUR MEAT!" Move on to the story "Brer Rabbit and Mr. Man's Chickens." Brer Rabbit humorously takes off with Mr. Man's chickens and eats them with Miz Rabbit. They wonder what to do with the chicken feathers. Brer Rabbit tricks Brer Fox into carrying the bag of chicken feathers. Mr. Man catches Brer Fox "and whipped him and whopped him." Point out that the illustration of Mr. Man resembles Jerry Pinkney, the illustrator.

Levine, Gail Carson. *The Fairy's Mistake*. HarperCollins, 1999. 87 p. Gr. 3–6.
Rosella is rewarded for her kindness by the fairy Ethelinda. Every time she speaks, jewels fall out of Rosella's mouth. Prince Harold asks her to marry him, but he's only interested in the jewels. Rosella is unhappy with her situation. "The fairy Ethelinda was getting angry. Rewards weren't supposed to work this way." When Rosella's cruel sister Myrtle is punished by the fairy for being mean, snakes and insects come out of her mouth. However, she uses this new talent to her advantage by threatening the entire village to give her gifts or else she will infest them with vile critters. "The fairy Ethelinda was getting anxious. Punishments weren't supposed to work this way." The other titles in the Princess Tales series include *The Princess Test* (1999), *Princess Sonora and the Long Sleep* (1999), *Cinderellis and the Glass Hill* (2000), *For Biddle's Sake* (2002), and *The Fairy's Return* (2002).

10 Minute Selection: Read the first three chapters. Ethelinda is disguised as an old woman when Rosella arrives at the well. Rosella kindly gives her a drink. "Your kindness merits a reward." Immediately, Rosella spits out a diamond and two opals. When Rosella's mother and sister see the jewels, Myrtle grabs the bucket and runs to the well. Ethelinda turns herself into a knight. Looking for an old woman, Myrtle is rude to the knight, and her "rudeness merits a punishment." Prince Harold sees Rosella with a sapphire coming out of her mouth and immediately asks for her hand in marriage. At the end of the passage, Myrtle opens her mouth and a garter snake slithers out, followed by two mosquitoes and a dragonfly.

Lewis, C. S. *The Lion, the Witch and the Wardrobe*. Macmillan, 1950. 208 p. Gr. 3–6.
The four Pevensie children—Peter, Susan, Edmund, and Lucy—discover a passage through a wardrobe in a country house that takes them to the magical land of Narnia. They discover the land is in perpetual winter because the evil White Witch has taken control. The White Witch tricked Edmund into delivering his siblings to her, and she is angered when he fails. She threatens to kill him, but the true king of Narnia—the lion Aslan—takes his place. This is the first book in the Chronicles of Narnia series, the second in chronological story-line order. The other titles are *Prince Caspian* (1951), *The Voyage of the Dawn Treader* (1952), *The Silver Chair* (1953), *The Horse and His Boy* (1954), *The Magician's Nephew* (1955), and *The Last Battle* (1956).

10 Minute Selection: Read the very end of chapter 3, "Edmund and the Wardrobe," beginning with the sentence, "The reindeer were about the size of Shetland ponies and their hair was so white that even the snow hardly looked white compared to them." Edmund encounters the White Witch for the first time. Continue reading chapter 4, "Turkish Delight." The witch determines that Edmund is human, "a son of Adam." He tells her about his siblings. She tricks him into believing that she is good and that he should return to her with his brother and sisters. He finds his sister Lucy, who ends the passage by making a prophetic statement: "And what wonderful adventures we shall have now that we're all in it together."

Lindgren, Astrid. *Ronia, the Robber's Daughter*. Viking, 1983. 176 p. Gr. 3–5.
A storm splits Matt's Fort in two on the night Ronia is born, leaving a large chasm between the two halves. A rival group of robbers moves into the other half, challenging Ronia's father's authority as robber chieftain. Ronia meets Birk, the son of the rival robber chief. The two become like brother and sister and save each other's lives from time to time. They run away to live in a cave after the two families continue to fight and Ronia's father disowns her. The two have several adventures in the woods, including encounters with wild horses and evil harpies.

10 Minute Selection: Read the second half of chapter 5, beginning with the sentence, "Ronia spent her time in the woods as usual." Autumn turns to winter. Ronia is skiing when she loses one ski and her foot goes "through the snow into a deep hole." She is stuck and soon surrounded by a group of strange, small creatures known as rumphobs who ask her, "Woffer did un want to do that? Broke our roof, woffor did un?" Rumphobs are usually friendly, but this group doesn't help Ronia. Instead, they hang a baby cradle on her foot inside their dwelling below. A harpy lands near the trapped Ronia, threatens her, and then flies away to get her sisters. Ronia notices dark clouds closing in. Birk finds her and helps her out of her situation. The chapter ends with Ronia saying, "I wish you were my brother," and Birk replying, "Ronia, sister mine."

Lisle, Janet. *Afternoon of the Elves.* **Orchard, 1989. 122 p. Gr. 4–6.**
Nine-year-old Hillary is invited to see an elf village by Sara-Kate, an eleven-year-old who lives in the house behind Hillary's. Sara-Kate lives alone with her mother and doesn't have any other friends. Other kids make fun of the way Sara-Kate dresses and eats. "Have you seen what Sara-Kate eats for lunch? . . . She brings white mush from home and pours sugar on top. White mush! Can you believe it?" Hillary slowly becomes convinced that Sara-Kate is an elf and sticks up for her new friend. One day, Hillary enters Sara-Kate's house uninvited and learns a terrible secret. This book is not a fantasy, as the title suggests, but a hard look at how some families cope.

  10 Minute Selection: Read chapter 4. Hillary's school friends are very critical about Sara-Kate. "It's as if Sara-Kate has put a spell on her! . . . Hillary believes everything she says. Everything!" In her backyard, Sara-Kate explains how elves live. "Sara-Kate had said 'put yourself in the position of the elf.'" At one point, Sara-Kate suddenly tells Hillary that she has to leave. Hillary notices a face in one of the upstairs windows of Sara-Kate's house. The chapter ends with, "But the face had not looked as if it belonged to a mother, any mother. It had been too white and too thin. Too frightening."

Lowry, Lois. *All about Sam.* **Houghton Mifflin, 1988. 135 p. Gr. K–4.**
In one of the funniest books on the market, we follow Anastasia Krupnik's little brother Sam coming home from the hospital shortly after his birth through his preschool years. He enters a pet worm in the library's pet contest, gives himself a punk haircut, and flushes his sister's goldfish down the toilet. At one point, his mother screams, "I CAN'T STAND THE TERRIBLE TWOS!" However, the family has more laughs together than not. There are eight Anastasia Krupnik books and three books that star Sam: *Attaboy, Sam!* (1992), *See You Around, Sam* (1996), and *Zooman Sam* (1999).

  10 Minute Selection: Practically any chapter will make a great stand-alone selection. I laughed the hardest at chapter 10. It's Show-and-Tell Day at nursery school. A girl named Leah is a big hit when she shows off her fake burp. "All of the children forgot that their lips were zipped. They shrieked with laughter." Even the teacher gives it a try. When it's Sam's turn, he takes out one of his father's pipes and starts to light it with lighter. "'HOLD IT!' said Mrs. Bennett in a loud voice. 'Stop right there, Sam Krupnik. What on earth are you doing?'" Sam starts spinning a tale about smoking a pipe with his father while his sister and mother smoke cigarettes (they don't). The teacher quickly turns the situation into a teaching moment about safety.

Second 10 Minute Selection: Read the first chapter, where we have the viewpoint of newborn Sam. He identifies his family. When they take him home, he complains about wearing a hat. "'I HATE THIS HAT,' he yelled. But it sounded like 'Waaahhh,' and they all said 'Shhhhhh' and patted his back." Continue reading the first part of chapter 2. Sam says several things to his family, but they only hear baby sounds. He tries to tell his father and sister to do a "BLURBLE BLURBLE" thing like his mother (she would put her face on his tummy and go "Blurble blurble" with her mouth). End the passage with the sentence, "Sometimes they still forgot, but he reminded them each time, and they were learning."

Lowry, Lois. *Number the Stars*. Houghton Mifflin, 1989. 132 p. Gr. 4–7.
Denmark is under occupation by the Nazis. Annamarie and her family are worried about the safety of their Jewish friends, the Rosens. Annamarie's family becomes involved in a dangerous attempt to smuggle the Rosen family out of Denmark and across the sea to Sweden. Annamarie once heard a story of how all of Denmark is the king's bodyguard. She tells her father that "now I think that all of Denmark must be bodyguard for the Jews, as well."

10 Minute Selection: Read the last half of chapter 4, "It Will Be a Long Night," starting with the sentence, "Papa's face was troubled." Annamarie learns that the Nazis have the names of her friend Ellen's family. Annamarie's parents shelter Ellen, pretending she is their daughter. Continue reading into chapter 5, "Who Is the Dark-Haired One?" beginning with the sentence, "It was hours later, but still dark, when she was awakened abruptly by the pounding on the apartment door." Nazi soldiers enter Annamarie's family's apartment at four in the morning looking for the Rosens. They question why Ellen has different colored hair than the rest of the family. Father's quick thinking saves the day. End with the chapter's closing line. "She looked down, and saw that she had imprinted the Star of David into her palm."

MacLachlan, Patricia. *Sarah, Plain and Tall*. Harper and Row, 1985. 58 p. Gr. 2–5.
Anna lives with her brother, Caleb, and their father on the prairie. Pa announces that he has advertised for a wife and has gotten a response from one Sarah Elizabeth Wheaton of Maine. When Sarah sees the prairie, she comments that "the land rolls a little like the sea." She teaches them that "ayuh" means "yes." Sarah learns how to ride a horse, drive the wagon, plow the field, and repair the roof. "'Women don't wear overalls,' said Caleb, running along behind her like one of

Sarah's chickens. 'This woman does,' said Sarah crisply." Sarah decides to stay. "I will always miss my old home, but the truth of it is I would miss you more." The book ends with Anna looking forward to the wedding. "Papa says that when the preacher asks if he will have Sarah for his wife, he will answer, 'Ayuh.'" The other titles featuring these characters are *Skylark* (1994), *Caleb's Story* (2001), *More Perfect Than the Moon* (2004), and *Grandfather's Dance* (2006).

10 Minute Selection: Read the first two chapters. Chapter 1 opens with Anna telling Caleb about the day he was born. Their mother said, "Isn't he beautiful, Anna?" Those were her last words to Anna. She died the next day. Caleb asks their father why he doesn't sing anymore. He tells them about Sarah responding to his advertisement and making plans to come out west. Anna asks Papa to "ask her if she sings." Chapter 2 features correspondence between Sarah and the children. Finally, she writes to Papa, telling him that "I will come by train. I will wear a yellow bonnet. I am plain and tall." She adds the following note: "Tell them I sing."

Magorian, Michelle. *Good Night, Mr. Tom.* Harper and Row, 1981. 318 p. Gr. 5–10.
Tom, a widower in his sixties, agrees to take in a young evacuee named Willie during the initial stages of World War II. Tom learns that Willie is an abused child who has never had any friends. Willie, later named Will, blossoms in Tom's home, makes several friends, and develops many talents, including drawing and acting. Young readers will be heartbroken when Will has to return to his mother in London, and they will also be excited when Tom makes a trip to the city to look for Will. This emotional tale will remind some readers of a Charles Dickens story.

10 Minute Selection: Warn your readers that the following passage contains strong content. Let them know that the setting is London during World War II and that Will has left the care of Mr. Tom to return home to his mother. Read a large section of the chapter titled "Home," beginning with the sentences, "'Wait. There she is,' he said, pointing to a thin, gaunt woman, standing next to a pile of sandbags." Will's mum is not happy with the changes in her boy. She demands complete obedience. Will discovers a baby in their dwelling with tape over her mouth. Mum snaps and beats Will. The chapter ends with Will discovering that he's trapped under the stairs. It's a familiar place to him, but "he felt as though he was a different person lying there in the dark. He was no longer Willie. . . . He was Will inside and out." He whispers a plea to Mr. Tom and then prays for sleep to come.

Maguire, Gregory. *Seven Spiders Spinning.* Clarion, 1994. 132 p. Gr. 3–7.
Seven venomous Siberian snow spiders each imprint themselves with a member of the girls' club known as the Tattletales. Their initial love for the girls turns into murderous hate when, one by one, each spider meets a gruesome, and sometimes

humorous, death. The surviving spiders make their way into the school and wait for the right moment to attack. This is the first in the Hamlet Chronicles series. The other titles are *Six Haunted Hairdos* (1997), *Five Alien Elves* (1998), *Four Stupid Cupids* (2000), *Three Rotten Eggs* (2002), *A Couple of April Fools* (2004), and *One Final Firecracker* (2005).

10 Minute Selection: Read chapter 1, "Falling in Love Again." Thekla Mustard, Empress of the Tattletales, calls a meeting to order. The girls defend their club name. "Does the word *tattletales* suggest a clot of simpering namby-pambies, idiotic goody-goody two-shoes, authority-bound *mushbrains*?" Unknown to the girls, the seven spiders creep close to the meeting, and each falls in love with "its own Tattletale." Move on to chapter 6, "Anna Maria Sings a High C." Miss Earth, a very popular teacher, is leading her class through spelling and geography. One of the spiders is moving about the classroom, waiting for a chance to land on Anna Maria. "The spider longed to give her a friendly little love nip, to show its undying loyalty. The poison it didn't know it had went surging through its tiny system." The spider falls on a newly sharpened pencil that Anna Maria is holding. She screams and flings the pencil "and its glob of hairy something" out the window, where the spider becomes "nothing more than a dark smoosh on the blacktop."

Mahy, Margaret. *The Great Piratical Rumbustification and The Librarian and the Robbers.* **Dent, 1978. 63 p. Gr. 2–5.**
The first story in this collection of two pirate stories features the Terrapin household. Mr. and Mrs. Terrapin are going out to dinner. They need a babysitter for their three boys—Alpha, Oliver, and Omega. A pirate named Orpheus Clinker shows up and, once the parents are gone, makes plans for a "pirate party, a Great Piratical Rumbustification—and all the pirates in town will come to drink and dine and dance." The second story features a librarian named Miss Laburnum, who is kidnapped by pirates and held for ransom. "After all, everyone knows that the library does not work properly without you." The pirates become ill, and Miss Laburnum reads to them. She returns to the library and helps the pirates turn into productive citizens. "You weren't very good at being robbers, but I think as librarians you might be excellent."

10 Minute Selection: Either story makes for a good "10 Minute Selection." Read the entire second story, or if reading the first story, begin with chapter 4, "Mr. Terrapin Rings Mother Goose." The Mother Goose Baby-Sitting Service sends "Mr. Orpheus Clinker, a naval gentleman, but retired from the sea now." Read the rest of the story to the end. Mr. and Mrs. Terrapin return to their home to find a full-blown "Rumbustification" going on. The pirates all chip in various treasures for their hosts. Everyone is satisfied, although the last chapter, "How It Ended," concludes with the sentence, "The pirates are beginning to be restless again."

Manes, Stephen. *Be a Perfect Person in Just Three Days.* **Clarion, 1982. 76 p. Gr. 3–5.**
One day at the library, Milo is struck on the head by a falling book titled *Be a Perfect Person in Just Three Days!* Milo takes the book home and follows the fairly interactive instructions by author Dr. K. Pinkerton Silverfish. One of the first instructions is to not flip to the last page. Milo does it anyway and reads the following: "BOY, ARE YOU DUMB! Didn't I tell you not to look at the last page of this book?" Over the course of the next three days, Milo is directed to wear broccoli around his neck and then avoid food for twenty-four hours. He succeeds at that, but falls short when told to do nothing for the following twenty-four hours. "Sit! Think. Relax. Be like broccoli." Milo learns that to be perfect is to be boring.

10 Minute Selection: Read the first three chapters of the book. Chapter 1 is Milo's introduction to the book. He thinks about all of the mistakes he has made and is looking forward to becoming a perfect person. In chapter 2, Milo takes some broccoli and string upstairs after receiving his instructions. Milo wears the broccoli in chapter 3 and is immediately teased by his sister. "'Sure, Dad,' said Elissa. 'Lots of people walk around with stalks of broccoli hanging from their necks. That's how you can tell the morons from the rest of us.'" At the end of the day, Milo is convinced that he is already becoming perfect.

Marsden, John. *Tomorrow, When the War Began.* **Pan Macmillan, 1993. 284 p. Gr. 7–12.**
Ellie and her six friends are camping in a remote Australian site called Hell. One night, six lots of planes thunder overhead. Ellie notices that their lights are out. The next day, everyone assumes they were part of a holiday celebration. When the teens return to their homes, they discover their families are missing. There's been an invasion, and the country has been taken over. The teens hide out back at Hell and plan guerilla attacks against the enemy. This first book in the Tomorrow series ends with Ellie and her friends still in hiding. "I just hope we can survive." The other titles in the series are *The Dead of Night* (1994), *A Killing Frost* (1995), *Darkness Be My Friend* (1996), *Burning for Revenge* (1997), *The Night Is for Hunting* (1998), and *The Other Side of Dawn* (1999).

10 Minute Selection: Introduce this passage by informing your audience that a group of teens has just returned from camping in an Australian region known as Hell. Read chapter 6, which opens with the sentence, "The dogs were dead." Ellie finds her family missing. "In the house nothing was wrong, and that is what was wrong. There was no sign of life at all." The electricity is off and the phones, television, and radio don't work. They head to another teen's place and find a similar situation. The kids remember the planes flying overhead while they were camping. The chapter ends with one of the teens stating, "If we're wrong, you can laugh as long and as loud as you want. But for now, for now, let's say it's true. Let's say we've been invaded. I think there might be a war."

Marshall, James. *Rats on the Roof and Other Stories.* **Dial, 1991. 79 p. Gr. K–4.**
Marshall has created six silly short stories featuring a cast of birds and animals. In "A Sheepish Tale," two illiterate sheep are hiking. One sheep informs the other that a sign welcomes them to the forest when, in reality, it warns about wolves. They arrive at a little house. Inside is an old starving wolf who cannot believe his luck. He disguises himself as a sheep and invites his guests to tea. The gossip that the two sheep share with each other is hilarious. The wolf falls asleep, and the sheep recognize him for what he is. After they escape, the wolf wakes up and thinks it was all a dream. In "Swan Song," a fox chases a swan. A cow directs the swan to disguise itself as a hat. The fox is fooled until the swan brags to the fox, "It's not a hat at all! It's *me*! We fooled you!" After rescuing the swan once more, the cow informs the swan, "You are nothing but a silly goose."

    10 Minute Selection: Read the title story. Two dogs complain about rats dancing on their roof and making a lot of noise. They advertise for a cat. A tomcat shows up but makes demands for a salary and nice sleeping arrangements. When the cat learns the dogs want him to chase rats, he throws a noisy fit. "Rats! I can't *stand* it!" The cat leaves, but so do the rats. They complain to the dogs about the excessive daytime noise ruining their sleep.

Mazer, Harry. *Snow Bound.* **Delacorte, 1973. 142 p. Gr. 6–12.**
Cindy is hitchhiking in a snowstorm when she's picked up by an underage driver. Tony had stolen his mother's car and was planning to live with his uncle after a family dispute. They leave the main road, become disoriented in the storm, and get stuck miles from civilization. They leave the shelter of the car and head for a cabin that Tony had found earlier. "Tony waited, while she wrote a note. 'We waited for you more than a week and you didn't come. We're trying to get back to a hunting camp Tony found. Maybe two or three miles from here going west, near a brook. Please come soon.'" On the way, Tony injures his ankle and the two are threatened by a pack of wild dogs.

    10 Minute Selection: Read the last part of chapter 4, "Cindy Takes the Wheel," beginning with the sentence, "She wiped the fog from his side of the windshield and then her side." The car is rolling down the hill. Cindy grabs the steering wheel. Read the entire chapter 5, "The Awful Snow." The car crashes into rocks and gets buried in snow. After arguing, they are able to start the engine and heater. Tony goes outside to clear the exhaust pipe. The chapter ends with Tony thinking, "It's going to be okay. It's going to be okay."

Mazer, Norma Fox. *Good Night, Maman.* **Harcourt, 1999. 181 p. Gr. 5–9.**
Twelve-year-old Karin flees France with her fourteen-year-old brother, Marc, and their mother. The children become separated from their mother and find themselves onboard the *Henry Gibbons,* part of the only group of European refugees the United States allowed during World War II. They are housed at Fort Ontario in Oswego, New York. Karin writes letters to her mother, hoping that one day they will be reunited.

10 Minute Selection: Read chapter 1, "The Visitor." Karin, Marc, and Maman are hiding in a closet in Madame Zetain's house. There is a visitor in the house so the three remain as still as possible to avoid detection. Karin worries that she will hear "heavy footsteps and voices shouting, *Come out, Jews, we know you're in there.*" Read the very short chapter 5, "Rent Money." Madame Zetain tells the family they must leave that night. Next, inform your audience that Karin, Marc, and other refugees are in quarantine behind barbed wire in Oswego, New York. Read the last half of chapter 18, "Fench Club," beginning with the sentence, "Volunteers came into the fort to teach us English and other things that would help us get along in America." Other Americans welcome the newcomers by "passing stuff like toys, clothes, and food through the fence, over the fence, under the fence." The chapter ends with a heartwarming scene of a town man taking off his shoes and throwing them to a refugee who has rags on his feet. "He walked around in the shoes. They were a little too big, but he was smiling, and he was crying."

McKay, Hilary. *The Exiles.* **Margaret K. McElderry, 1992. 217 p. Gr. 4–8.**
Four sisters—Ruth, Naomi, Rachel, and Phoebe—are "exiled" to spend the summer with Big Grandma while their parents are remodeling their house. The girls, all voracious readers, are horrified to find only a few cookbooks and a volume of Shakespeare in Big Grandma's house. There's nothing to read in the whole village. Instead of spending the summer reading, the girls find a wide assortment of things to do, ranging from badger spotting and cave exploring to fishing out of a plastic bucket. There are several hilarious moments in this, the first in a trilogy featuring the Conroy sisters. The other two titles are *The Exiles at Home* (1994) and *The Exiles in Love* (1996).

10 Minute Selection: Read the first section of chapter 7. After being cooped up in the house because of rainy weather, the girls are ready for something new. When Big Grandma informs young Phoebe that breaking into a locked house is not so easy, Phoebe chucks a rock "through the kitchen window where it smashed a neat, but rather large hole in the dead center." Big Grandma sends them off to the beach, where the girls plan to cook a meal. The villagers stare at the large amount of equipment and supplies the girls drag down to the sea. The whole chapter is a hilarious twenty-minute read. To make a shorter, ten-minute passage, end with the sentences, "This is civilization! Have you forgotten what it's like?"

McKinley, Robin. *Beauty: A Retelling of the Story of Beauty and the Beast.* Harper and Row, 1978. 247 p. Gr. 6–10.
The youngest of three daughters gains the nickname Beauty. Their father loses his business, and the family moves to the countryside. Father finds himself in a strange castle deep in the woods. He plucks a rose for Beauty but is immediately accosted by a hideous monster. In exchange for her father's life, Beauty goes to live with the Beast. Each night he asks for her hand in marriage, and each night she refuses. When Beauty is permitted to return to her family for one week, Beast is in danger of dying if Beauty doesn't return in time. Although many young listeners will be familiar with the story through the Disney movie, McKinley's version will provide a rich alternative.

10 Minute Selection: Read well into the first chapter of part 2. Begin with the sentence, "There was a table set for one, drawn snugly near the fire." Father is recounting the time when he found himself inside Beast's castle. Invisible servants took good care of him. In the morning, as Father was leaving, he spotted some roses and picked one for Beauty. "There was a roar like that of an animal." Beast accused Father of stealing but stated that he would spare Father's life "on one condition: that you will give me one of your daughters." End the passage with the line, "I was staring at the rose, silent and serene on the mantelpiece, and I heard my own voice say, 'When the month is up, Father, I will return with you.'"

Merrill, Jean. *The Pushcart War.* Scott, 1964. 223 p. Gr. 4–10.
I still remember my teacher Mrs. Robinson reading this book to our fifth-grade class in the mid-1960s. Huge trucks have taken over the city streets. They are owned by three firms led by "The Three"—Moe Mammoth, Walter Sweet, and Louie Livergreen. A war between the trucks and the owners of pushcarts begins when a trucker named Mack runs over Morris the Florist's cart. This is known as the "Daffodil Massacre." The pushcart owners retaliate with the "Pea Shooter Campaign." They shoot pins stuck in peas and cause flat tires. Things escalate in this humorous tale of war, power, revolution, politics, and conspiracy. One highlight is that author Merrill's name appears as a newspaper letter writer complaining about trucks.

10 Minute Selection: Read chapter 11, "The Secret Weapon." The pushcart peddlers design pea shooters to cause flat tires. Once the trucks have blocked the streets, the trucks will be blamed for creating traffic jams. Move on to chapter 15, "The Arrest of Frank the Flower." Frank the Flower is spotted shooting at a truck's tire. He is arrested and pleads guilty to shooting all 18,991 flat tires in the ninth day of the "Pea Shooter Campaign." He really only shot 17 or 18, but he is protecting the other pushcart owners. The police commissioner has no choice but to arrest Frank. "But treat him gently. He is a harmless crackpot." There is a hilarious exchange among the peddlers that mirrors one from chapter 11.

Morey, Walt. *Kavik the Wolf Dog.* **Dutton, 1968. 192 p. Gr. 4–8.**
Kavik, part wolf, part dog, survives a small-plane crash in Alaska. He is nursed back to health by young Andy. Kavik's wealthy owner, George Hunter, claims the animal and takes him to Washington. Hunter is only interested in showing off Kavik, since the dog won the North American Sled Dog Derby. Kavik escapes and makes the long trek back north to return to Andy. Along the way, the dog mates with a female wolf and, from her, learns the ways of the wild. After his mate dies, Kavik finishes his northward trek. Andy once again nurses the dog back to health only to find out that Hunter wants his champion dog back.

10 Minute Selection: Read chapter 2. Kavik finds himself in a cage with iron bars on a small airplane. The pilot flies into a storm. "There came a sudden abrupt crash that hurled him against the bars with savage force, a thunderous explosion and a blinding light. The cage went hurtling and spinning through space." The pilot is dead. Kavik, still trapped in his cage, goes into shock. Two coyotes try to get at the dog, "but the cage kept them suspicious and nervous." A lynx manages to reach through the bars and claw Kavik. The big cat is startled by a loud noise and runs away. The passage ends with the patient lynx planning to "return to the crate and the animal inside."

Mowat, Farley. *Owls in the Family.* **Little, Brown, 1962. 89 p. Gr. 4–8.**
A young boy in Saskatchewan rescues two owls—Wol and Weeps—and adds them to the home menagerie. In one incident, Wol returns the favor and saves the narrator from some bullies. In another, the owl joins his young owner in school by flying through an open window and landing on the teacher's lap.

10 Minute Selection: Tell your audience that a young boy has turned two wild owls into pets. Read chapter 7, which tells of Wol's relationship with Mutt, the family dog. "As far as Wol was concerned, old Mutt was something to be teased and pestered, and Wol used to tease the life half out of him." Wol would hide Mutt's bones and trick the poor dog out of his dinner. The owl would also slowly walk up to the napping dog and grab his tail. "By the time he got his bearings and was ready to take a bite out of Wol, the owl would have flown to the limb of a nearby tree from which he would peer down at Mutt as much to say: 'Good heavens! What a terrible nightmare you must have been having!'" The chapter ends with Wol bringing not one but two dead and very pungent skunks inside the house.

Murphy, Jim. *The Great Fire.* **Scholastic, 1995. 138 p. Gr. 4–8.**
This is one of the best informational books ever written for children. The Great Fire of October 1871 swept through the city of Chicago over a thirty-one-hour period. The fire took an estimated 300 lives and forced "over 100,000 people . . .

to flee the consuming flames." Author Murphy follows the lives of several individuals who survived the ordeal in a fast-flowing account. The fire began in the O'Leary barn and destroyed 17,500 buildings and 73 miles of street before rain eventually put it out.

10 Minute Selection: Read the last page of chapter 4, "A Surging Ocean of Flame," starting with the sentence, "In the middle of this smoke and fire was Claire Innes." We follow Innes as she looks for her family. "I was choking on the smoke and dust and I looked for a quiet place to rest." She finds refuge in an alley. The chapter ends with Innes realizing that both ends of the alley are blocked by fire and smoke. "Claire was now locked inside the alley, trapped, with the fire coming at her from all sides." Continue reading the next chapter, titled "Chicago Is in Flames." Claire is shielded by a pile of bricks. "There is little doubt that she had a great deal of luck on her side." Her arms and back were burned but she "scrambled over the smoldering pile of debris and made it to the street." Finish with the line, "'Now,' she said, sensing the enormity of the task facing her, 'I had to find my family in all of this.'" Skip ahead and read the last two paragraphs of the same chapter. "Nearly 100,000 people were now homeless." One of them was Claire Innes, who had some hope when she felt drops of rain on her face. Inform your audience afterward that Innes eventually found her family.

Myers, Walter Dean. *Scorpions*. Harper and Row, 1988. 216 p. Gr. 5–8.
Jamal's older brother Randy, the leader of the gang known as the Scorpions, is sent to prison. Randy wants twelve-year-old Jamal to be the new leader of the gang. Unfortunately, most of the Scorpions are older than Jamal and don't take to the idea. Jamal already has trouble at school. He rarely does his homework, skips a lot, and has trouble with some loudmouths. Randy's friend Mack gives Jamal a gun, which Jamal takes to school. Jamal's friend Tito uses the gun when Jamal is attacked by two Scorpions and one of them pulls out a knife.

10 Minute Selection: Read the last part of chapter 9, beginning with the sentence, "Jamal looked at the gun before he put it into his sneaker." Once at school, a bully named Dwayne starts giving Jamal a hard time. "You be down in the storeroom at lunchtime or I'm going to beat your butt right in the classroom." Jamal asks his friend Tito to hide the gun in the storeroom. Continue reading chapter 10. A crowd of students arrives to watch the two boys fight. Jamal locks himself and Dwayne in the storeroom. Dwayne is winning the fight when "Jamal reached up and found the bag. He took it down and pulled out the gun." Dwayne is understandably frightened of the gun. Jamal kicks him a few times and runs out of the storeroom. He leaves school and worries about what just happened. End the passage with the lines, "But if the police came and got him, they would make him take them to the place he threw it away. Things were just so messed up."

Naidoo, Beverly. *Journey to Jo'burg: A South African Story.* **Lippincott, 1986. 75 p. Gr. 4–8.**

Thirteen-year-old Naledi and her younger brother Tiro live with their baby sister, aunt, and grandmother. Their mother is working in Johannesburg, which is more than 300 kilometers away. When the baby becomes ill, Naledi and Tiro set out on foot to inform their mother. They witness the horrors of apartheid when they reach the city. Their mother hurries home with them and takes the baby to the doctor. The book ends with Naledi realizing how much she learned on her journey.

10 Minute Selection: Read chapter 7, "Mma." Naledi and Tiro find themselves in front of a wide gate with the sign "BEWARE OF THE DOG." They knock on the door and find themselves face-to-face with their mother. They explain why they traveled so far. Their mother's employer, the Madam, needs her for an important dinner party that evening but will allow her to leave with the children afterward. "I hope you realize how inconvenient this will be for me. If you are not back in a week, I shall just have to look for another maid, you understand?" Continue reading the next chapter, "The Police." The children have become separated from their new friend Grace while at the train station. The police are arresting anyone who doesn't have a pass. They try to help one young man but watch helplessly as the police van pulls away.

Namioka, Lensey. *Yang the Youngest and His Terrible Ear.* **Little, Brown, 1992. 134 p. Gr. 2–6.**

Yingtao, also known as Yang the Youngest or Fourth Brother, is the youngest of the Yang family. The musical family recently moved from China to Seattle, and they find the transition to be difficult. Father is hoping to attract violin students by showcasing the family quartet. Unfortunately, Yingtao plays second violin, and he has no ear for music. He befriends Matthew, who wants to learn how to play the violin. Matthew introduces Yingtao to baseball, and he becomes very good at it. Matthew's father doesn't want Matthew to spend time away from sports; Yingtao's father doesn't want him to do anything that takes him away from violin practice. Although the plot is fairly predictable, the story itself is heartwarming. This is the first in a series of books about the Yang family. The other titles are *Yang the Third and Her Impossible Family* (1995), *Yang the Second and Her Secret Admirers* (1998), and *Yang the Eldest and His Odd Jobs* (2000).

10 Minute Selection: Read the first chapter. Yingtao introduces his siblings. They are all practicing their musical instruments. Yingtao knows that if they could impress the audience, Father might pick up more students. Unfortunately, Yingtao has a terrible ear for music. The sound from his violin goes "SCREECH." Third Sister even calls him a mutant. "We all have our own ways of learning English and

Third Sister's is to make a list of five new words every day and memorize them. *Mutant* was on her list today." The chapter ends with Yingtao worrying. "I had to think of something to save the recital. I just had to."

Napoli, Donna Jo. *Zel.* Dutton, 1996. 227 p. Gr. 7–12.
This modern version of the folktale "Rapunzel" is told from three perspectives: Count Konrad, Rapunzel's mother, and Rapunzel, also known as Zel. Mother and Zel live in isolation. Zel notices that a goose sits on rocks in its nest. On a rare visit to town, Zel encounters Count Konrad. She helps a smith take care of Konrad's horse. The boy asks what she wants in return, and she asks for a fertile goose egg to give to the goose. From that moment on, Konrad is obsessed with the girl. Mother wants to keep Zel to herself and hides her in a tower for two years. Konrad never tires in his search for Zel.
    10 Minute Selection: Inform your audience that this story is a retelling of "Rapunzel." Read chapter 8. Mother worries that Zel is thinking about the youth she met. She worries when Zel says, "But I do love new places, new people." Mother lies and tells Zel that something evil is trying to kill her. Continue reading chapter 9. Zel and Mother rush through the woods. They reach a tower. Mother makes a nearby walnut tree grow and tells Zel to climb it. "One branch leads directly to the wide window ledge of the tower. Zel jumps down inside and turns to help Mother into the room. Her arms meet empty air. Mother isn't behind her." The chapter ends with Zel watching the tree return to its normal height.

Naylor, Phyllis Reynolds. *Shiloh.* Atheneum, 1991. 144 p. Gr. 3–6.
Marty finds a stray beagle while walking in the rural hills of West Virginia. He names the dog Shiloh. The dog ran away from its owner, Judd Travers, a man who loves to hunt and who is mean to his dogs, too mean in Marty's opinion. Shiloh runs away a second time, and Marty hides the dog in the woods. He also lies to his parents and Judd about knowing Shiloh's whereabouts. Marty's secret comes out when Shiloh is attacked by another dog and needs medical attention. This is the first book in the trilogy that includes *Shiloh Season* (1996) and *Saving Shiloh* (1997).
    10 Minute Selection: Read chapter 2. Marty and his father take Shiloh to Judd's trailer home to learn if the dog is his. Marty dislikes Judd and thinks of the time he saw Judd cheat a store owner and another time he found Judd poaching a deer. They reach the Travers place, and while Marty's father is talking to Judd, Marty holds Shiloh "low in my lap, tail between his legs, shaking like a window blind in a breeze." When they turn Shiloh over, Judd gives the dog a kick and threatens to "whup the daylights out of him." The chapter ends with "I swallow and swallow, and all the way home I can't speak a word, trying to hold the tears back."

Naylor, Phyllis Reynolds. *Witch's Sister.* **Simon and Schuster, 1975. 154 p. Gr. 5–8.**
Lynn worries that her older sister Judith is under the influence of their elderly neighbor Mrs. Tuggle, who might be a witch. Lynn finds Judith down by a creek crooning to tadpoles and coaxing them into her hands. She also observes Judith conjuring up a mysterious little boy from the same creek. Lynn's best friend, Mouse, has a book on witchcraft, and they deduce that Judith and Mrs. Tuggle are planning to murder Lynn's little brother Stevie. Her fears seem to come true when her parents ask Mrs. Tuggle to babysit the children one stormy evening. This is the first of several books in the Witch series, including *Witch Water* (1977), *The Witch Herself* (1978), *The Witch's Eye* (1990), *Witch Weed* (1991), and *The Witch Returns* (1992).

   10 Minute Selection: Read the second half of chapter 1, beginning with the lines, "Lynn bolted through the screen. 'Not here,' she said. 'We've got to go to our private place.'" Lynn tells her best friend, Mouse, "I've come to the conclusion that Judith possesses supernatural powers." She lists all of the strange things that have happened recently. Mouse tells Lynn that her father has a book titled *Spells and Potions.* When Lynn returns home, she hears Judith chanting. Judith accuses Lynn of spying. The chapter ends with Judith declaring, "Maybe I have friends you don't even know about."

Nix, Garth. *Sabriel.* **HarperCollins, 1995. 292 p. Gr. 6–12.**
Magic is strong north of the Wall, the border between Ancelstierre and the Old Kingdom. Sabriel learns that her father—Abhorsen—is lost in the realm of the dead. He is a necromancer "but not of the common kind. Where others of the art raise the dead, I lay them back to rest. And those that will not rest, I bind—or try to." Armed with her father's sword and his binding bells, Sabriel sets off on a dangerous journey through the Old Kingdom. This is the first book in a series that includes *Lirael* (2001) and *Abhorsen* (2003).

   10 Minute Selection: Read the last section of chapter 6, beginning with the sentence, "There, between gusts of snow, she saw a figure leaping from step to step; impossible leaps, that ate up the distance between them with horrible appetite." A creature known as a Mordicant is chasing Sabriel. The chapter ends with Sabriel falling through a doorway and the Mordicant's "four-taloned hand" reaching for her. Read chapter 7. A "Charter-ghost" temporarily stops the Mordicant and allows Sabriel time to go up a passage and into an island house protected by rushing water, an element a Mordicant can't cross. It turns out she's in the house of her father, safe for the moment. Outside, the Mordicant waits. "It was a sentry, guarding what might be the only exit from the island. Or perhaps, it was waiting for something to happen, or for someone to arrive . . ." The chapter ends with Sabriel meeting a cat and fainting.

Nixon, Joan Lowery. *The Kidnapping of Christina Lattimore.* **Harcourt, 1979. 158 p. Gr. 6–10.**

Christina is kidnapped for ransom shortly after she has a fight with her strict parents and her wealthy and powerful grandmother. She is locked in a basement for a few days. When she is finally led upstairs by her captors, the police arrive. Instead of freeing her, they suspect that she is the mastermind behind a plan to extort money from her grandmother. Christina works hard to prove her story and to learn the identity of the true mastermind behind the scheme.

10 Minute Selection: Read most of chapter 2, beginning with the sentence, "I run up the broad steps to the veranda and put my key in the front-door lock." Christina finds a suspicious piece of tape "over the side, to keep the lock from closing." She and Della, the housekeeper, look over the house to see if anything has been stolen. End with the sentence, "Neither can I." Tell your audience that Christina plans on going to her friend Lorna's house. Pick up the reading with the line, "I change into my old jeans and a rugby shirt and pull on an old white sweater." The two girls talk about several things, including the strange incident with the tape. The chapter ends with Christina arriving home. "Someone has stepped out of the bushes directly in front of me!" Christina feels the prick of a needle and passes out.

Norton, Mary. *The Borrowers.* **Harcourt, 1952. 148 p. Gr. 3–5.**

Borrowers are tiny people who live near "human beans" and borrow small items, such as "pencils and match boxes and sealing wax and hairpins and drawing pins and thimbles." One of the prime rules of borrowers is not to be seen by humans. Arrietty and her parents are seen by a young boy, a temporary guest in the house, and the borrowers' very existence becomes threatened. This is the first book in the series, which includes *The Borrowers Afield* (1955), *The Borrowers Afloat* (1959), *The Borrowers Aloft* (1961), *Poor Stainless* (1971), and *The Borrowers Avenged* (1982).

10 Minute Selection: Read chapter 3. Arrietty is helping her mother, Homily, prepare supper. Homily is worried about her husband, Pod. He is fetching a teacup from another part of the house, which requires him to climb up a curtain. "And your father at his age." Continue reading chapter 4. Pod has returned with the teacup. He tells Homily that he was seen by a new boy in the house. This was a surprise to them. "But there hasn't been a boy, not in this house, these twenty years." Pod was halfway down the curtain with the teacup when the boy took it. "And then, when I was down, he gave it to me." End the passage with the lines, "'Yes,' said Pod, 'but he just gave me the cup. "Here you are," he said.'"

Nye, Naomi Shihab. *Habibi.* **Simon and Schuster, 1997. 271 p. Gr. 6–10.**
Liyana is about to enter high school when her parents decide to move the family from St. Louis to her father's homeland in Jerusalem. She slowly learns to appreciate the cultural differences, especially after meeting Omer, an Israeli teen. There is some tension when she wants to bring Omer to meet her extended family. One relative hisses at Omer and says, "Remember us when you join your army." Liyana's father, Poppy, is dismayed that the tensions between the Arabs and Israelis are still present. At one point, he is arrested for trying to help a friend in trouble with the Israeli soldiers, and another time, Liyana's grandmother's house is vandalized by soldiers. Still, there is a spirit of optimism that prevails through the book.

10 Minute Selection: Read the chapter titled "Very Very Distant Relatives." Liyana comes home to find a strange woman in their house. Liyana's mother is trying to reach Poppy because the woman doesn't speak English. When he arrives, the woman tells him that they are related. "I think she's a cousin of a cousin of a cousin who died before I was born and no one ever remembered to tell me about him." The woman wants Poppy to buy her a dress as is the custom when a relative returns from America. "Liyana thought about the ten thousand relatives she'd already met." Poppy takes the woman on a drive and tricks her. "You *dumped* her?" Poppy justifies his actions. "It was a stupid custom."

O'Brien, Robert C. *Mrs. Frisby and the Rats of NIMH.* **Atheneum, 1971. 240 p. Gr. 3–5.**
Mrs. Frisby, a field mouse, consults an owl to help her save her children from the farmer's plow. She's particularly worried about her sickly son, Timothy, who is too frail to move to their summer home. The owl directs her to a group of rats who have an incredible story to tell her. The rats are escapees from a laboratory where they were given super intelligence. While the rats make plans to help Mrs. Frisby and her family, she learns that the rats themselves are in danger from humans. O'Brien's daughter, Jane Leslie Conly, wrote two NIMH sequels: *Rasco and the Rats of NIMH* (1986) and *RT, Margaret, and the Rats of NIMH* (1990).

10 Minute Selection: Read the last section of the chapter titled "A Powder for Dragon," starting with the sentence, "'Ordinarily,' said Justin, 'when we have a long project to do at night—sometimes even by day—we make sure Dragon won't bother us.'" Justin and the other rats do this by giving Dragon, a cat, a sleeping powder in his food. Mrs. Frisby volunteers for the dangerous job of putting the powder into the cat's bowl. Read to the end of the chapter, where Mrs. Frisby learns that this type of mission is how her husband died. Move to the chapter titled "Captured." Start with the sentence, "This is as far as I can go," and finish the chapter. Mrs. Frisby is caught by a human child while attempting to drug the cat. The chapter ends with the line, "The colander, upside down, was now over Mrs. Frisby."

Ortiz Cofer, Judith. *An Island like You: Stories of the Barrio.* **Orchard, 1995. 165 p. Gr. 7–12.**
Twelve stories follow Puerto Rican American teens in Paterson, New Jersey. The opening story, "Bad Influence," actually takes place in Puerto Rico. Rita is exiled to spend the summer with her grandparents because she was caught at her boyfriend's house. Rita is thrown off by the different lifestyle. "I really should have been given an instructional manual before being sent here on my own." The shoplifting Yolanda and her friend Doris star in a few of the stories. Another story features tough-guy Luis, who works in his father's junkyard after serving six months for breaking and entering. He falls for the daughter of the funeral home director. Be sure to read the opening poem, "Day in the Barrio," which ends with, "Keeping company with the pigeons, you watch the people below, / flowing in currents on the street where you live, / each one alone in a crowd, / each one an island like you."

10 Minute Selection: The most emotional story is the last one, "White Balloons." Actor Rick Sanchez used to live in the barrio. He has AIDS and, before he dies, wants to start a theater troupe in his old neighborhood. When this effort is met with hostility, Rick's partner, Joe Martini, asks Doris to help. After Rick dies, Doris manages to get several people together for a rooftop party. Many are angry when they learn the party is in honor of Rick, but they stay to release white balloons in his memory.

Park, Barbara. *Junie B. Jones Has a Monster under Her Bed.* **Random House, 1997. 69 p. Gr. K–2.**
Junie B. Jones is having a terrible time dealing with a supposed monster under her bed. "The monster's really real! 'Cause Paulie Allen Puffer told me everybody has a monster under their bed! Plus that Gracie said it can turn *invisible*." Junie B. tries everything to delay bedtime. She sneaks downstairs, she crawls into her baby brother's crib, and she still has "my worstest night ever." She learns that one of her friends vacuumed a monster up and smashed it in a trash compactor. When that doesn't work, Junie B. solves the problem by placing photos of herself making scary faces under her bed. This is one of many books featuring Junie B. Jones. The first in the series is *Junie B. Jones and the Stupid, Smelly Bus* (1992).

10 Minute Selection: Read the entire chapter 1. Junie B. explains who the cheese man is. "He takes pictures of you. And your mother has to buy them. Or else you will get your feelings hurt. School pictures is a racket, I think." Junie B. is demonstrating different faces to the school photographer. He snaps one and asks for the next person in line. Junie B. makes a fuss and has to sit with her teacher. Later on, it's time for the whole class picture. She makes another face while thinking of monsters. "And guess what? The cheese man took the class picture." I have probably read this passage to groups of kids more than any other selection.

Paterson, Katherine. *Bridge to Terabithia.* **Crowell, 1977. 128 p. Gr. 5–8.**
Jess Aarons works hard to be the fastest runner in the fifth grade. He's dismayed when he and all of the other boys are beaten by the new girl, Leslie Burke. Jess and Leslie become best friends, however, and the two create an imaginary kingdom in the woods. Inspired by the Narnia books, Leslie names the kingdom Terabithia. At one point, Jess is awed when Leslie befriends one of the school bullies and tells Jess that she now has one and one-half friends. "To be able to be Leslie's one whole friend in the world as she was his—he couldn't help being satisfied about that." Young listeners will be caught up in emotions when Jess tries to deal with Leslie's accidental death as she drowns trying to cross the creek to Terabithia.

10 Minute Selection: Read the last half of chapter 3, "The Fastest Kid in the Fifth Grade," beginning with the sentence, "The children ate lunch at their desks." The students are arguing before going outside to recess. Jess is already tired of Gary Fulcher ordering everyone around. The boys have running competitions, and this is the first day of running for the school year. Jess is very confident that his off-season training will make him the fastest boy. He waits for his heat, but when he starts running, he is dismayed that someone is pulling ahead of him. "The faded cutoffs crossed the line a full three feet ahead of him. Leslie turned to face him with a wide smile on her tanned face." Jess is worried the other boys will tease him, but he quickly defends Leslie's right to race again when Fulcher says that girls aren't allowed on the lower field. The chapter ends with Jess watching Leslie run home. "The word 'beautiful' came to his mind, but he shook it away and hurried up toward the house."

Paterson, Katherine. *Lyddie.* **Lodestar, 1991. 182 p. Gr. 5–10.**
Lyddie's father has deserted the family, and her mother is unable to cope. The children are separated, and Lyddie is hired out to a tavern as a servant girl. The overseer "watched Lyddie like a barn cat on a sparrow, but Lyddie was determined not to give her cause for complaint." She is fired from this job but eventually moves on to work in the mills in Lowell, Massachusetts. She hopes to save enough money to pay off the debt on her parents' farm. The days are long, but Lyddie is used to hard work. Lyddie shows growth and determination despite the hardship. She loses the factory job when she saves another girl from the advances of the overseer, Mr. Marsden. At the end of the book, Lyddie is off to enroll in a college, "to stare down the bear!" The companion book is *Jip, His Story* (1996).

10 Minute Selection: Start with the opening scene. A bear makes its way into the family cabin. "Lyddie looked up from the pot of oatmeal she was stirring over the fire, and there in the doorway was a massive black head, the nose up and smelling, the tiny eyes bright with hungry anticipation." The family hides in the loft as the bear looks for food. It upturns the bubbling hot oatmeal on its head and hurries out. More out of relief than the actual sight of the bear running away, the family bursts into laughter. The passage ends with Lyddie worrying about her mother. "Let her be laughing, she prayed."

Paton Walsh, Jill. *A Parcel of Patterns.* **Farrar Straus Giroux, 1983. 137 p. Gr. 8–12.**

Sixteen-year-old Mall Percival writes of the years (1665–1666) the plague struck the English mining town of Eyam. The town becomes isolated. Mall forbids her sweetheart, Thomas, from entering the village. By the time the sickness has subsided, more than three hundred villagers have died. Mall looks for a new beginning in the New World across the ocean, writing this account before she departs and leaving it behind for someone to find.

10 Minute Selection: Read the very first paragraph of the book, which begins, "A parcel of patterns brought the Plague to Eyam." There are no chapters in the book. On page 95 of the first edition hardcover book, read the section that begins with, "I had an aunt, living in the Lydgate, whom we saw seldom, and loved little." The aunt had quarreled with her brother, Mall's father. He sneaks out of Eyam to make his peace with her by her deathbed. When he returns to Eyam, he falls ill and dies. Marshall Howe, the grave digger, "had become foulmouthed and black-hearted." He treats the dead with little respect and takes what he wants from their homes. Mall and her mother don't want his services. "So my mother and I, together, carried my father's body down to the garden grave, and laid him quietly to rest, and covered him in." We also learn of a man who felt ill, dug his own grave, and laid in it for two days before dying. End the passage with the line, "I heard of this later, from Francis, who wept telling me."

Paulsen, Gary. *Hatchet.* **Simon and Schuster, 1987. 142 p. Gr. 4–8.**

Brian Robeson is stranded all alone in the Canadian wilderness when his pilot dies of a heart attack and their plane crashes into a lake. Brian slowly learns how to survive: find food, build shelter, and make fire. He faces attacks from mosquitoes and flies, a porcupine, and a moose. A tornado even hits his camp. Although it makes a mess of everything he has built, the storm flips the sunken plane and gives Brian a chance to retrieve a survival pack. The sequels are *The River* (1991), *Brian's Winter* (1996), *Brian's Return* (1999), and *Brian's Hunt* (2003). There is also a companion nonfiction work titled *Guts: The True Stories behind Hatchet and the Brian Books* (2001).

10 Minute Selection: Read chapter 8. Brian is awakened by a porcupine. He throws his hatchet and strikes with his leg. He receives eight porcupine needles, which are painful to remove. Brian is ready to give up. He falls back asleep and has a revelation in his dreams. He realizes that when he "threw the hatchet at the porcupine in the cave and missed and hit the stone wall it had showered sparks." He knows that he is able to make fire with the help of his hatchet.

Paulsen, Gary. *The Voyage of the* **Frog. Orchard, 1989. 141 p. Gr. 4–8.**
Fourteen-year-old David inherits the sailboat the *Frog* from his uncle. He takes it miles from shore to fulfill his uncle's request. "Take me to where you can't see land and scatter my ashes there on the water." David is caught in a fierce storm. He's hurt, hungry, thirsty, and miles off course. He must first find a way to save the *Frog,* which has taken on too much water, and then survive encounters with a shark and several whales, a near collision with an oil tanker, and a second storm.

10 Minute Selection: Read the second half of chapter 8, beginning with the sentence, "His eyes snapped open in the near darkness." It's nighttime on the boat, and David hears a strange scraping noise. He leans over the side and spots "gouges that went on for about three feet along the side of the boat, curving sideways and down into the water." At the last minute, he detects motion and jerks back. "The water detonated, surging up at his face, and a shark's gaping maw, teeth flashing in the moonlight, triangular-death-razor-sharp teeth, blew up and out of the darkness." The shark rams into the boat several times over the next few hours. The chapter ends with David able to rest because the "attacks stopped completely."

Pearce, Philippa. *Tom's Midnight Garden.* **Lippincott, 1958. 229 p. Gr. 3–5.**
Tom is sent to spend some time with his aunt Gwen and uncle Alan because his brother has come down with the measles. While there, he discovers a garden that appears when everyone else is asleep. He befriends a little girl named Hatty and meets her at different stages of her life. In this strange world, no one else is able to see Tom except for Hatty and the animals and birds. At one point, Hatty falls from a tree and is carried into her house by Abel the gardener. Tom learns that Abel knows of Tom's presence. "'Get you gone!' said Abel hoarsely. . . . 'I've seen you always, and thought best not to see you . . . but I've known you, and known you for what you are!'" Abel eventually accepts Tom's presence. Tom begins to plot how he can remain with his aunt and uncle in order to continue his nightly excursions to his magical world.

10 Minute Selection: Inform your audience that young Tom is spending time with his aunt and uncle in their flat, or apartment. Read the end of chapter 2, "The Clock Strikes Thirteen," beginning with the sentence, "Slow silence, and then the grandfather struck for twelve." Tom is surprised when the clock strikes thirteen. He gets out of bed to investigate. Read the entire chapter 3, "By Moonlight." Tom goes out the back door expecting "a sort of backyard, very poky, with rubbish bins" and instead finds a large lawn with a beautiful garden. He goes back in the house, but everything is different now. He sees figures that he believes are ghosts.

Peck, Richard. *The Ghost Belonged to Me.* **Viking, 1975. 183 p. Gr. 4–8.**
Alexander is told by his neighbor Blossom Culp that he is receptive to the Unseen

and that his family's barn has the ghost of a young girl in it. Alex discovers that the ghost is Inez Dumaine, and she warns him of an impending trolley disaster. Alex saves the day and becomes a local hero. The press gets wind of the story of Alex and Inez. Everyone learns where Inez is buried, and Alex, Blossom, and Uncle Miles accompany Inez's remains to be laid to rest down in New Orleans with the rest of her family. The other books in the series are *Ghosts I Have Been* (1977), *The Dreadful Future of Blossom Culp* (1983), and *Blossom Culp and the Sleep of Death* (1986).

10 Minute Selection: Read most of chapter 11, beginning with the sentence, "The barn door opened to darkness, but there was plenty of light leaking around the doorframe at the top of the stairs." Alex meets Inez in his barn. She sends him off to save the trolley. Alex flags down the motorman, and they investigate the trestle over Sand Creek. They find it vandalized and burning. Amory Timmons, the madman who set the fire, climbs aboard the trolley and drives it onto the bridge. The chapter ends with, "The trolley went end over end and hit the fallen supports in the creek. It burst open like a crate. And the bell ceased clanging."

Peck, Richard. *A Long Way from Chicago.* **Dial, 1998. 148 p. Gr. 5–8.**
Joey recalls stories about the summers of 1929–1935. He and his sister Mary Alice spent them with their outrageous grandmother. Grandma Dowdel can be quite the intimidating woman—not only to her grandchildren but also to her small-town neighbors. She battles bullies, like the Cowgill boys, who blew up her mailbox with a cherry bomb, and Sheriff Dickerson, who doesn't believe the laws apply to him. She also helps the underdogs, such as hoboes or Effie Wilcox, who is losing her home to the bank. A final story finds Joey on an army train in 1942 passing by Grandma's house. "She couldn't know what car I was in, but her hand was up, and she was waving—waving big at all the cars, hoping I'd see." The sequels include the Newbery Award winner *A Year Down Yonder* (2000) and *A Season of Gifts* (2009).

10 Minute Selection: The first story, "Shotgun Cheatham's Last Night above Ground," is one of my favorite short stories of all time. Grandma builds up the honor of the recently deceased Shotgun Cheatham because she's bothered by a big-city reporter. "He wants to get the horselaugh on us because he thinks we're nothing but a bunch of hayseeds and no-'count country people." She invites the reporter to her house, where she has volunteered to have the casket so folks could pay their respects. Late in the night, there's a movement, which causes Grandma to grab her gun. She tells Shotgun, "You've had your time," and shoots the casket. The reporter dives out the window. Joey confides that only he and Grandma saw the tomcat crawl inside the coffin. That gave Grandma the idea for showing up the reporter.

Second 10 Minute Selection: "A One Woman Crime Wave" is also a notch above the other stories as a great read-aloud. Grandma grabs the kids and tells them that they are all going fishing. They trespass onto the property of the Piatt County Rod and Gun Club and steal a rowboat. Grandma finds that her illegal fish trap is full of catfish. The members of the club, including the sheriff, are drunk and dancing in their long johns when they spot Grandma and the kids. Grandma shares the catfish with an elderly woman she knows and also with several drifters. She is also able to handle herself when the sheriff catches up with her.

Peck, Robert Newton. *Soup*. Knopf, 1974. 96 p. Gr. 4–8.
Several short stories follow the antics of narrator Rob and his best friend, Luther. "Nobody called him Luther. I called him Luther just once, which prompted Soup to break me of a very bad habit before it really got formed. As soon as the swelling went out of my lip, I called him Soup instead of Thoop." The boys make pipes out of acorns, blue daisies, and corn silk. Rob rolls down a hill in a barrel and winds up crashing into a chicken coop. They learn a lesson when they try to swindle Mr. Diskin. Fans of Gary Paulsen's *Harris and Me* will enjoy this, the first of Peck's Soup series. The second book in the series is *Soup and Me* (1975).
   10 Minute Selection: Read chapter 2, "Apples and Mrs. Stetson." Soup and Rob are on a hill flinging apples with whips made from sassafras sticks. Soup bets he can hit the Baptist church below. He breaks a stained-glass window. Mrs. Stetson runs out of the church and charges up the hill. "Her eyes burned with the wrath of the Old Testament." She grabs Rob, since Soup has quickly disappeared. Rob protests that it's impossible to fling an apple that far. Mrs. Stetson sets out to prove him wrong by flinging an apple herself. Unfortunately, she breaks a window in Old Haskin's shack. "'Run!' yelled Mrs. Stetson. 'That man's a degenerate.'" Mr. Haskin finds Soup, who has a switch in his hand, and gives the boy a licking. "In a way, it really was justice. Mrs. Stetson was right. There really is a God."

Pellowski, Anne. *Betsy's Up-and-Down Year*. Philomel, 1983. 157 p. Gr. 3–5.
Betsy, who lives on her parents' farm with her eight sisters and one brother, is interested in "sibling rivalry." She often fights with her siblings and extended family members and has occasional bouts of jealousy, but she theorizes it's all a part of growing up. Betsy has a series of mini disasters with her retainer and a strong desire to own a pair of clog shoes, which causes her to say "Heavens to me!" instead of the traditional saying "Heavens to Betsy!" This is one book in the author's Polish American Girls series. The other titles are *Stairstep Farm: Anna Rose's Story* (1981), *Willow Wind Farm: Betsy's Story* (1981), *Winding Valley Farm: Annie's Story* (1981), and *First Farm in the Valley: Anna's Story* (1982).

10 Minute Selection: Read the chapter titled "Bonfire Birthday." The extended family members have a large picnic, and they decide to celebrate Betsy's birthday at the same time. Betsy removes her retainer, places it between two bubble-gum wrappers, and puts it in her aunt Anne's purse. Unfortunately, Aunt Anne mistakes it for garbage and throws it away. Soon, everyone is digging through several trash barrels. Betsy vows never to wear this particular retainer again after noticing maggots and slugs at the bottom of one barrel.

Second 10 Minute Selection: Read the chapter titled "Friday the Thirteenth." Betsy refuses to believe in superstitions, even after witnessing a series of disasters the rest of her family experiences. Flat tires and broken casserole dishes are just a few of the accidents that make Betsy's sister Dorothy refuse to eat at the dining table. The family invited two friends over, causing Dorothy to say, "You all may want to have thirteen sitting at the table on Friday the thirteenth, but I'm moving to the kitchen."

Peterson, John. *The Littles*. Scholastic, 1967. 80 p. Gr. K–3.
The Little family lives unseen in the home of the Bigg family. The Littles are six inches tall and help keep the house in shipshape condition. They are dismayed when the Bigg family leaves the house for three months and rents it to a sloppy couple named Charles and Liz Newcomb. The Newcombs leave food lying around, and this attracts mice. The Littles do battle with the mice. The Newcombs next buy a cat, which also threatens the safety of the Little family. The text is slight but ideal for a very young audience. This is the first of several books about the Littles. The second in the series is *The Littles Take a Trip* (1968).

10 Minute Selection: Read the first chapter, which introduces the Little family. "The Littles took everything they needed from the Biggs. Usually, the Biggs didn't even know anything was missing." In return, the Littles repair electric wires and the plumbing. Tell your audience that the Biggs moved out for three months and are now renting to the Newcombs. Read the second half of chapter 5, beginning with the sentence, "The Newcombs were indeed bad housekeepers." The Littles know that the mess will attract mice, and they open up a chest of weapons. Continue reading chapter 6. Tom Little faces a mouse and is forced to shoot it with his tiny bow and arrow. "The arrows didn't stop the mouse. It crawled toward the light. A low, snarling growl came from deep in its throat."

Phelps, Ethel Johnston, ed. *Tatterhood and Other Tales*. Feminist Press, 1978. 155 p. Gr. 3–12.
Twenty-five stories from around the world feature heroines with "energy, wit, and sense." The collection includes romantic tales, tales of relationships, tales of family and community, tales of wit and humor, tales of old women, and tales

of independent women. All of the stories have interesting characters and plenty of action that will appeal to both male and female listeners. Highlights include "The Hedley Kow," the story of an elderly woman who earns the respect and becomes a companion of the hobgoblin who terrorizes the countryside; "Clever Manka," a tale of a woman who helps her father answer three riddles to earn a calf and later teaches her husband, the burgomaster, to consult her on difficult cases; and the hilarious "Kamala and the Seven Thieves," the story of a woman who continuously thwarts a gang of thieves. At one point, she tricks them into getting stung over and over by hornets.

10 Minute Selection: Read the Japanese tall tale "Three Strong Women." Forever-Mountain is the best wrestler in the country. "I'm a fine, brave man and far too modest ever to say so." He tries to tickle a little girl, but she catches his arm and drags him along the road. "'Please let me go,' he pleaded. 'I am the famous wrestler Forever-Mountain. I must go and show my strength before the Emperor'—he burst out weeping from shame and confusion—'and you're hurting my hand!'" He meets the girl's mother and grandmother and learns that these two are stronger yet. All three train him to be a better wrestler. In the end, he decides to live with them and become a farmer.

Philbrick, Rodman. *Freak the Mighty.* **Scholastic, 1993. 169 p. Gr. 6–10.**
They make an unlikely pair. Shy Maxwell is large for an eighth-grader, and he has a learning disability. Kevin, aka Freak, is the same age, but terribly small because of a birth defect. He is, however, extremely intelligent. Together they become Freak the Mighty and pursue quests. Things get rough when Max's father, Killer Kane, returns home from prison. He kidnaps Max and strangles a female acquaintance. Somehow, Kevin saves the day. Kevin's body starts to give out—"his heart just got too big for his body"—but he encourages Max to write a book about their adventures. Your audience will enjoy hearing Kevin's intelligent dialogue as well as "Freak's Dictionary," which is located at the end of the book. The sequel is *Max the Mighty* (1998).

10 Minute Selection: Read chapter 6, "Close Encounters of a Turd Kind." It's the Fourth of July, and a tough kid named Tony D is confronting Max and Freak. Freak insults Tony and calls him a cretin. Freak finds it hilarious when he learns that Max is afraid of Tony. "You mean you *couldn't* take him and I was giving him lip?" Continue reading chapter 7, "Walking High above the World." Tony and his gang chase Max and Freak into a pond. Tony follows but gets stuck in the mud. His gang starts throwing rocks at Max and Freak, but the police show up. The chapter ends with the sentence, "That's how it started, really, how we got to be Freak the Mighty, slaying dragons and fools and walking high above the world."

Pinkwater, Daniel. *The Hoboken Chicken Emergency.* **Atheneum, 1977. 102 p. Gr. 1–5.**

Arthur Bobowicz is sent out to buy a Thanksgiving turkey and returns with a 266-pound chicken he names Henrietta. He wants to keep her as a pet. His father makes him return her to Professor Mazzocchi, who creates new creatures, such as square goldfish. Henrietta escapes and soon terrorizes the city of Hoboken. "People were afraid to go shopping, to go to work, to step outside their doors. Special police chicken squads were sent to cruise the streets in cars." The mayor hires famous chicken-catcher Anthony DePalma, but he runs off with the money and the mayor's brand-new limousine. Professor Mazzocchi appears disguised as Dr. Hsu Ting Feng and successfully starts a citywide campaign to make Henrietta feel loved.

10 Minute Selection: Read the first chapter. Arthur comes home with Henrietta instead of a Thanksgiving turkey. The family has meatloaf instead. The chapter ends with Arthur's father stating, "Every boy should have a chicken." Move to the end of chapter 2, beginning with the sentence, "A door opened to a house across the street from the park, and something mostly black, and big and fast, came out, bounded across the street, over the fence, and into the park." It's a dog named Bozo. Henrietta runs away. Continue reading all of chapter 3. Arthur finds Henrietta in a tree. Arthur tries to convince the policemen and the firemen that Henrietta is not a polar bear.

Pullman, Philip. *The Ruby in the Smoke.* **Random House, 1985. 230 p. Gr. 6–10.**

Sixteen-year-old Sally Lockhart is determined to learn the truth about her father's death in this nineteenth-century-London adventure. All she has is a mysterious note that warns her to beware of "The Seven Blessings." Sally gains independence from her cruel aunt and works for a photographer. She and her newfound friends find themselves pursued by an evil, tiny woman known as Mrs. Holland, who has many contacts in the underworld. There is also a mystery man keeping to the background. At the center of everything is a missing ruby once owned by a maharajah. The opening page contains the attention-grabbing sentence, "Her name was Sally Lockhart; and within fifteen minutes, she was going to kill a man." This is the first in a trilogy about Sally Lockhart. The other two titles are *The Shadow in the North* (1988) and *The Tiger in the Well* (1990). *The Tin Princess* (1994) also features characters from the Sally Lockhart books.

10 Minute Selection: Read a portion of chapter 17, "King James's Stairs," beginning with the sentence, "Wapping in those days was very like an island." Sally's friends Frederick and Jim are on a mission to save a little girl named Adelaide from the clutches of Mrs. Holland. Jim grabs Adelaide and they run, while Frederick is confronted by Mrs. Holland's thug Mr. Berry. Jim runs into a mate named

Paddy, who helps the two hide. Unfortunately, Paddy betrays them. Finish the passage with the lines, "'Where do we go, Paddy?' said Jim, and turned—and then stopped. Mrs. Holland stood in the entrance. Paddy stood beside her."

Qualey, Marsha. *Thin Ice.* **Delacorte, 1997. 214 p. Gr. 9–12.**
High school senior Arden's parents are dead. She has been raised by her older brother Scott. He goes missing, and his snowmobile is found in the river. Everyone presumes Scott is dead except Arden. She hangs on to the hope that he's still alive. She believes that he left because he was tired of taking care of her and because his girlfriend is pregnant. Arden even spends some of her inheritance to hire a private investigator. Everyone else in their small Wisconsin community believes she's in denial. Her grades are slipping, and she's losing her friends.

10 Minute Selection: Read the first five, short chapters of part 1. The book opens with Arden's friends celebrating her seventeenth birthday. They are jumping off the roof of her house into snowbanks. We learn Arden lives with her brother because their parents have died. Scott is much older and very responsible. "While I slept, he had cleaned. What a guy." Arden has her own workshop and business—ArdenArt. "I make picture frames. This is more than a hobby; it's an art. And it's business. During the last few years I'd made a chunk of change from selling my frames through gift shops in the area." The last chapter ends with a phone call from Al Walker, a policeman. "Arden . . . bad news. Scott . . . the river . . . his sled . . . there's been an accident."

Rawls, Wilson. *Where the Red Fern Grows.* **Delacorte, 1961. 249 p. Gr. 4–8.**
Billy Colman lives with his family in the Ozarks. He works hard for two years to save enough money to buy two hunting dogs. He names them Old Dan and Little Ann. Billy and his dogs earn a great reputation for their hunting prowess. The two dogs have a fatal encounter with a mountain lion, but they save Billy's life in the fight. Red fern grows on their gravesite. I once heard Jim Trelease, author of the *Read-Aloud Handbook,* speak. He humorously told us about a time he read this book to his child and became overcome by emotion. Years later, I was reading this book to my two youngest children and had to stop. I was too choked up to read for a few moments. My own kids assured me. "It's OK, Dad." It's one of my favorite memories as a father.

10 Minute Selection: Read most of chapter 5. Billy picks up his two pups at the train station in town. He puts them in his gunny sack and prepares for a thirty-mile hike back to his place. He's quickly surrounded by some town bullies; one pulls the ear of the girl pup. Billy fights them but is overwhelmed by their numbers. The marshal chases away the gang and helps Billy set off for his trip. Stop at the sentence, "There, in a cave with a stream close by, I put up for the night." Pick up the narrative a few pages later with the sentence, "Along in the silent hours of

night, I was awakened." A mountain lion screams. The boy dog "bawled his challenge to the devil cat." The girl pup joins her brother. "What I saw in my pups
gave me courage." The three stand guard throughout the night.

Rockwell, Thomas. *How to Eat Fried Worms.* **Watts, 1973. 116 p. Gr. 3–6.**
Alan and Joe make a bet that Billy can't eat fifteen worms in fifteen days. The winner gets fifty dollars. Billy takes the bet. "How bad could a worm taste? He'd eaten
fried liver, salmon loaf, mushrooms, tongue, pigs' feet." As Billy eats worm after
worm, Joe starts to worry. He cheats by gluing two worms together and covering
them with cornmeal. He forges a doctor's signature that warns of the dangers of
eating worms. He makes a worm out of beans and hopes this will disqualify Billy.
Once Billy does indeed win the bet, he continues his strange diet. "Do you think
I could be the first person who's ever been *hooked* on worms?"
  10 Minute Selection: Read chapter 3, "Training Camp." Alan and Joe bring the
first worm. "'Luddie and gintlemin!' shouted Alan. 'I present my musterpiece
"Vurm a la Mud!"'" Continue reading the next chapter, titled "The First Worm."
The boys start arguing about whether night crawlers count as worms. Joe finds
an entry in the dictionary that proves they do. Billy manages to eat his worm. It's
covered with ketchup, mustard, salt, pepper, horseradish, and lemon. Your young
audience will delight in the grossness of eating a worm and laugh as Billy starts
acting like a bird, driving Alan and Joe away.

Rowling, J. K. *Harry Potter and the Sorcerer's Stone.* **Scholastic, 1998.
309 p. Gr. 4–12.**
What's left to say about the best-selling series of all time? All of the Harry Potter
books are wonderful read-alouds. Start at the beginning, and don't let the size of
each volume become daunting. The narrative and dialogue fly by quickly. This first
book—for those handful of people unaware of the story—features Harry's first
visit to Hogwarts School of Witchcraft and Wizardry, our own introduction to
a wonderful cast of characters, and Harry's first encounter with "this wizard who
went . . . bad. As bad as you could go. Worse. Worse than worse . . . Voldemort."
The second book in the series is *Harry Potter and the Chamber of Secrets* (1999).
  10 Minute Selection: Read the second half of chapter 10, "Halloween," beginning with the sentence, "On Halloween morning they woke to the delicious smell
of baking pumpkin wafting through the corridors." Ron hurts Hermione's feelings, and she runs off to the girls' bathroom. Professor Quirrell announces that a
troll has been seen in the dungeons. Harry and Ron run to the girls' bathroom to
warn Hermione, and they find the troll advancing toward her. Harry manages to
knock it out with "the first spell that came into his head." The chapter ends with,
"But from that moment on, Hermione Granger became their friend. There are

some things you can't share without ending up liking each other, and knocking out a twelve-foot mountain troll is one of them."

Rylant, Cynthia. *Every Living Thing.* **Bradbury, 1985. 81 p. Gr. K–5.**
Twelve very short, gentle stories feature the bonds between animals and humans. Many of the stories are simple yet heartwarming. Turtles, dogs, wild boars, parrots, goldfish, cats, squirrels, robins, cows, and hermit crabs make appearances. One highlight is "Papa's Parrot." Harry's father owns a candy store, complete with a parrot. As Harry grows older, he spends less and less time with his father. Harry takes over the store when his father is rushed to the hospital. He is surprised to hear the parrot say, "Where's Harry?" Harry soon understands that the parrot is repeating what his father must have said over and over. "He checked the furnace so the bird wouldn't get cold. Then he left to go visit his papa."

10 Minute Selection: Read the two stories "Retired" and "Shells," both of which feature elderly people. In the first story, Miss Cutcheon, a retired schoolteacher, gets an old collie. "And she, too, was retired. A retired collie. She had belonged to a family who lived around the corner from Miss Cutcheon. The dog had helped raise three children, and she had been loved." The two fall into a quiet routine when one day they pass the school playground. The children run over to pet the dog. Both the retired teacher and collie are rejuvenated from their reconnection with children. The other story features Michael, who lives with his elderly aunt after his parents have died. The two don't get along until one day Michael purchases a hermit crab. His aunt takes an interest and purchases a thirty-gallon tank and an additional twenty hermit crabs.

Sachar, Louis. *Holes.* **Farrar Straus Giroux, 1998. 233 p. Gr. 4–8.**
Stanley Yelnats is sent to Camp Green Lake as punishment for stealing Clyde "Sweet Feet" Livingston's sneakers. The inmates at Camp Green Lake must each dig a hole every day. The reasons for doing so become clear as Stanley's story, the story of his "no-good-dirty-rotten-pig-stealing-great-great-grandfather" and Madame Zeroni, and the story of Stanley's great-grandfather and Kissin' Kate Barlow dance around each other and provide clues for the audience. This is one of the best-selling award-winning children's books of all time, very popular with young readers, and my personal favorite children's book. The companion book *Small Steps* (2006) features Armpit and X-Ray from *Holes*.

10 Minute Selection: Read chapter 19. The boys are all different races, but "on the lake they were the same reddish brown color—the color of dirt." Stanley is accused of stealing Mr. Sir's sack of sunflower seeds. Move on to chapter 20. The Warden is upset that Mr. Sir brought Stanley to her. She strikes Mr. Sir with her rattlesnake venom nail polish on her fingernails. "He had three long red marks slanting across the side of his face. . . . It took a moment for the venom to sink in. Suddenly, Mr. Sir screamed and clutched his face with both hands."

Second 10 Minute Selection: Read chapter 30. Zero saves Stanley from Zigzag. The Warden and Mr. Pendanski start ridiculing Zero for being illiterate. "He's so stupid, he doesn't even know he's stupid." Zero takes a shovel, hits Pendanski with it, and runs away. "'He's going to have to come back for water,' said the Warden." Finish the passage by reading chapter 32. Stanley steals Mr. Sir's truck and drives it into a hole. Stanley then runs into the desert.

Sachar, Louis. *Sideways Stories from Wayside School.* **Morrow, 1978. 124 p. Gr. 3–5.**

The builder was sorry that he built Wayside School "thirty stories high, with one classroom on each story." This collection of absurd short stories features the students from the thirtieth story of the school. Mrs. Jewls becomes the new teacher after the previous teacher, Mrs. Gorf, was turned into an apple. The other books in the series include *Wayside School Is Falling Down* (1989) and *Wayside School Gets a Little Stranger* (1995). There are also two companion activity books: *Sideways Arithmetic from Wayside School* (1989) and *More Sideways Arithmetic from Wayside School* (1994).

10 Minute Selection: Read chapter 10, "Paul." Paul sits in the best seat in the class—the back row. Paul loves to pull Leslie's pigtails. "'Pigtails are meant to be pulled,' Paul concluded." He's worked out a system that allows him to pull her pigtails twice each day, one tug short of Mrs. Jewls's "three strikes" rule. Leslie outsmarts him when she gives a sudden yell. Mrs. Jewls orders Paul to go home early on the kindergarten bus. Move from this short story back to chapter 3, "Joe." Joe has trouble counting. Mrs. Jewls keeps him inside from recess to give him extra practice. Joe fails to count correctly the conventional way, but he manages to get the right answer—to Mrs. Jewls's chagrin—when he goes about it in his own style. "Joe counted the potatoes. 'Seven, five, three, one, two, four, six, eight. There are eight potatoes, Mrs. Jewls.' 'No, there are eight,' said Mrs. Jewls. . . . 'You got the right answer, but you counted the wrong way again.'"

Selections from Other Books in the Series: Each of the two direct sequels has an outstanding selection to share. In *Wayside School Is Falling Down,* read chapter 1, "A Package for Mrs. Jewls." Louis, the yard teacher (modeled after author Sachar), delivers a heavy package marked "Fragile" all the way up to the thirtieth floor of Wayside School. Mrs. Jewls holds a spelling bee to see which student will let Louis in. In the meantime, Louis is struggling to hold the heavy package. The class opens the package, which turns out to be a computer. Mrs. Jewls pushes it out the window to teach the class about gravity. The other selection is from *Wayside School Gets a Little Stranger.* Read chapter 3, "Poetry." Mrs. Jewls works hard to teach the concept of poetry to the children. Their final written results are hilarious.

San Souci, Robert D. *Cut from the Same Cloth: American Women of Myth, Legend, and Tall Tale.* **Philomel, 1993. 128 p. Gr. 4–8.**
Strong and clever female protagonists are featured from Anglo-American, African American, American Indian, and Mexican American sources. San Souci groups these fifteen stories by region, including Alaska and Hawaii. Highlights include "Pale-Faced Lightning," where the title character protects her adopted tribe from Zuni warriors; and "Hekeke," the story of a tiny woman who finds a way to defeat the cannibal giant ogre Yayali.
   10 Minute Selection: Read the chapter titled "Bess Call." Strongmen from all over the world try their luck against Joe Call. Lewis Giant of England makes several attempts to best Joe. Lewis runs away when he sees Joe lift an ox with one hand. After he leaves, Bess lifts the other ox over her head. When he returns, Lewis wrestles Bess. She tosses him "body, boots, and britches over the fence, where he landed in a muddy ditch." She then tosses his horse after him. Bess confides, "I didn't have the heart t'tell him that I've been feelin' a mite under the weather."
   Second 10 Minute Selection: Read the chapter titled "Susanna and Simon." Susanna's father is a powerful witch who states his daughter can only marry a man "who cleared six acres of land and rolled up the logs and piled the brush in one day." Susanna uses her own magic to help Simon succeed at this task. The angry father chases them "with his knife in his hand." Susanna successfully slows him down by changing Simon's boat into a forest, throwing down an egg that creates fog, turning a meal sack into a pond of water, altering a skillet into a dark cloud, and then ordering Simon to drop red pebbles, which grow into mountains. She finally creates a rock wall so tall that her father gives up.

Scieszka, Jon. *Knights of the Kitchen Table.* **Viking, 1991. 55 p. Gr. 2–6.**
Joe, Fred, and Sam are the Time Warp Trio, three boys who travel back and forth in time with the help of a magic book. In this, the first book in the popular humorous series, the boys go back in time to the days of King Arthur. After defeating the Black Knight, the boys meet King Arthur and the knights and ladies of Camelot. Everyone believes the boys are enchanters. Merlin the magician is skeptical and wants the boys to show their magical powers. Joe shows them a simple card trick, but then the boys are put to a bigger test when Bloeb, an unbelievably smelly giant, and Smaug, a dragon, both attack the castle. The second in the series is *The Not-So-Jolly Roger* (1991).
   10 Minute Selection: Read the first three chapters. Chapter 1 immediately starts with the Black Knight charging the three boys. Joe states, "We were about to be killed more than a thousand years before we were even born." Chapter 2 gives background information on how the boys found themselves in the time of King Arthur, and chapter 3 finishes the story line of the Black Knight. The boys humorously taunt the Black Knight. "Your mother was a sardine can!" They repeatedly

jump out of the way each time the Black Knight charges, successfully wearing down the fighter. Fred smacks the Black Knight in the head with a stick, knocking him out. The chapter ends with the cliff-hanging line, "Three more knights on horses, with swords drawn, were galloping down the path toward us." Over the years, I read this selection to hundreds and hundreds of children touring the library.

Silvey, Anita, ed. *Help Wanted: Short Stories about Young People Working.* **Little, Brown, 1997. 169 p. Gr. 6–12.**

Twelve short stories feature teens and their work—sometimes at jobs, sometimes personal projects. Several boys decide to haul dirt up to the roof of their housing complex to grow grass and watermelons in Bordon Deal's "Antaeus." Gaston Major has to serve community hours at a run-down retirement home in Peter Sieruta's "Hands in the Darkness." Lucy gets a job as a secretary and finds herself battling the ghost of a previous secretary in the whimsical story "QWERTYUI-OP," by Vivien Alcock. Other authors featured include Ray Bradbury, Michael Dorris, Francisco Jiménez, Cherylene Lee, Norma Fox Mazer, Tim Wynne-Jones, Judith Ortiz Cofer, Gary Soto, and Budge Wilson.

10 Minute Selection: Read the first story, "The Original Recipe," by Michael Dorris. Rayona, who has appeared in other Dorris books, gets a job at Kentucky Fried Chicken. One day, her father comes in with Rayona's grandmother and aunt Edna. Father and Rayona's boss rush Derek the cook to the hospital. Rayona and another worker, Tiffany, are left alone with the two older women moments before the dinner crowd arrives. "We are approaching the hour of the wolf, that point in every twenty-four-hour cycle when a little pilot light goes on in the stomachs of Montanans and they believe themselves not only ready but entitled as American citizens to eat." Aunt Edna confides that she once knew Colonel Sanders's wife and leaps into action. At one point, she convinces "a man bursting out of a black Sturgis Biker Rally T-shirt, with a skull-and-crossbones tattoo on each forearm" that, instead of KFC's Cajun-style chicken, he really wants the new special of the day.

Singer, Isaac Bashevis. *Zlateh the Goat and Other Stories.* **Harper and Row, 1966. 90 p. Gr. 3–6.**

Isaac Bashevis Singer shares seven Jewish stories—some with supernatural themes, such as "The Devil's Trick," and some revolving around the foolish citizens of Chelm, such as "The Snow in Chelm." One highlight is "Fool's Paradise," a tale of a young man who hears that paradise is perfect, so he imagines that he has died and entered the heavenly kingdom. A doctor cleverly "cures" him of this notion. Another fun story is titled "The First Shlemiel." A lazy man's wife gives him orders to follow, and so that he won't eat up all of the jam, she tells him that the jam jar contains poison. The poor man ruins everything and decides to kill himself by eating the jam.

10 Minute Selection: The gem of this collection is the title story. Winter has been overly mild, and Aaron's father, a furrier, has little business. He decides to sell their goat Zlateh to the butcher. This will help pay for Hanukkah candles, gifts, and food. On the way to deliver the goat to town, Aaron and Zlateh find themselves in a fierce blizzard. Aaron finds a haystack and the two make shelter inside. The storm keeps them trapped for three days. Aaron survives on not only Zlateh's milk but also her companionship. When the storm subsides, Aaron brings the goat back home, to the delight of his family. "Nobody ever again thought of selling Zlateh."

Smith, Dodie. *The Hundred and One Dalmatians*. Viking, 1956. 184 p. Gr. 2–5.
Mr. and Mrs. Dearly of London own a pair of Dalmatians named Pongo and Missus, who give birth to fifteen pups. Cruella de Vil is a former classmate of Mrs. Dearly. "'What a strange name "de Vil" is,' said Mr. Dearly. 'If you put the two words together, they make "devil."'" Indeed, Cruella wants to buy the puppies, kill them, and turn them into fur coats. She arranges for the Baddun brothers to kidnap the pups and hide them in the country until they are bigger. When Pongo and Missus, with the aid of several animals, find their pups, they discover many more Dalmatian pups that have been kidnapped—a total of 100 dogs (the author asks the reader to discover who the 101st dog is). All of the dogs set out on the perilous journey home.

10 Minute Selection: Read the last part of the chapter titled "Cruella de Vil Pays Two Calls," beginning with the sentence, "By now it was December, but the days were fine and surprisingly warm, so the puppies were able to play in the area several times a day." Nanny Cook discovers that the puppies are missing. Continue reading the entire next, long chapter, "Hark, Hark, the Dogs Do Bark!" Pongo and Missus send out a message to other dogs through "Twilight Barking." The puppies have been spotted miles away in an old house. "The place is *seething* with Dalmatian puppies."

Smith, Janice Lee. *The Monster in the Third Dresser Drawer and Other Stories about Adam Joshua*. Harper and Row, 1981. 86 p. Gr. K–3.
Adam Joshua deals with many changes in his life, including moving to a new house and losing a tooth. When his newborn baby sister, Amanda Jane, comes home from the hospital and shares his bedroom, Adam Joshua writes "WILL BE LEAVING SOON!" across the bottom of her diaper. When their parents work hard at getting Amanda Jane her own room, Adam Joshua tells them to work harder. Of course, once she's gone from his room, he carries her back to his own

bed and tucks her in. "'I'm right here,' he said." There are many more Adam Joshua books. The second book in the series is *The Kid Next Door and Other Headaches: Stories about Adam Joshua* (1984).

10 Minute Selection: Read the chapter titled "The Loose Tooth." Adam Joshua tries to wiggle his loose tooth and is impatient when it doesn't come out. His father tells him to be patient. Adam Joshua's friend Nelson ties a string from the tooth to a doorknob. The tooth doesn't come out. "Adam Joshua went to supper, rubbing the sore loose tooth that was still in his mouth. 'Usually works fine!' Nelson yelled after him." The tooth finally pops loose while Adam Joshua is eating cereal. Unfortunately, he swallows the tooth. He writes a note to the Tooth Fairy and finds forty-three cents under his pillow. Now, he has to be patient for the new tooth. When it finally arrives, Adam Joshua says, "I've been waiting for you."

Sneve, Virginia Driving Hawk. *High Elk's Treasure.* **Holiday House, 1972. 96 p. Gr. 2–5.**
Joe High Elk and his sister are dismissed from school because of threatening weather. They try to hurry home, but their horse Star becomes lame. The two children seek shelter in a cave, but their horse runs away. Joe finds a leather object in the cave. He later looks for Star and runs into two horse catchers, "hunting the wild herd illegally on the preserve." One of them threatens Joe, but with the support of a family friend, Mr. Blue Shield, Joe is able to prove Star belongs to him. Joe and his family eventually learn the historical significance of the object Joe found in the cave. A pictograph narrative on leather gives a firsthand account of the Battle of the Little Big Horn.

10 Minute Selection: Read the chapter titled "The Lost Filly." Joe and his sister Marie are riding home from school when their horse Star is frightened by thunder and falls down. "Joe whistled to her and was horrified to see her limping as she came to him." They find shelter in a cave that once belonged to their great-grandfather High Elk. The chapter ends with Star falling into the swollen creek and being swept downstream until "she broke free of the swiftly flowing waters and scrambled out onto the bank." Joe watches helplessly as Star disappears "into the trees on the other side."

Snicket, Lemony. *The Bad Beginning.* **Scholastic, 1999. 162 p. Gr. 4–8.**
The first book in the popular A Series of Unfortunate Events features the Baudelaire orphans—Violet, Klaus, and Sunny—matching wits with the evil Count Olaf. The mock-gothic tone of the book matches the narrator's wordplay—"Occasionally his eyes would close. He found himself reading the same sentence over and over. He found himself reading the same sentence over and over. He found himself reading the same sentence over and over"—as well as the translations of baby Sunny—"For instance, this morning she was saying 'Gack!' over

and over, which probably meant, 'Look at that mysterious figure emerging from the fog!'" *The Bad Beginning* features an elaborate plan by Count Olaf to marry Violet and take control of the family fortune. The second book in the series is *The Reptile Room* (1999).

10 Minute Selection: Read the first page of chapter 1, which sets the tone. The book has no happy beginning, middle, or end. "I'm sorry to tell you this, but that is how the story goes." Move on to chapter 4 and begin with the lines, "'Orphans?' Count Olaf called out in his scratchy voice. 'Where are you, orphans?'" and read to the end of the chapter. Count Olaf is angry that the children did not cook roast beef for him and his motley, yet menacing, theatrical troupe. He later strikes Klaus in the face. At one point, a member of the troupe warns Violet, "If I were you I would try not to anger Count Olaf, or he might wreck that pretty little face of yours." The chapter ends with the children crying in their bedroom.

Soto, Gary. *Baseball in April and Other Stories.* Harcourt, 1990. 107 p. Gr. 5–8.
Several Latino kids are portrayed along with their families and friends throughout eleven short stories. Lupe Medrano is a smart girl who is no good at sports. Then she discovers marbles and becomes a champion by practicing and exercising her thumb to the point that others ask her why her thumb is swollen. Alfonso, on the other hand, pushes against his teeth for hours, trying to straighten them out to impress girls. Yollie is embarrassed because she and her mother are too poor to buy a new dress. Her mother dyes an old dress for Yollie, but when the dye starts dripping, Yollie flees the dance. Soto includes a glossary for the numerous Spanish words, phrases, and expressions used in this quiet, charming book.

10 Minute Selection: Read the short story "Seventh Grade," with its universal implications for all middle-school-age kids. Victor is trying to get the attention of Teresa, a girl in his French class. He practices scowling because all the male models in *GQ* magazine "would sit at a pool, their rippled stomachs dark with shadow, and *scowl.*" On the first day of class, the French teacher asks if anyone speaks French. Victor raises his hand, "wanting to impress Teresa." Unfortunately, he doesn't really know French. He bluffs his way by saying, "La me vava me con le grandma." When the teacher looks at him funny, Victor goes on to say, "Frenchie oh wewe gee in September." Victor is totally embarrassed until, after class, Teresa says, "I didn't know you knew French. . . . That was good," and asks him to help her with homework.

Soto, Gary. *Crazy Weekend.* Scholastic, 1994. 139 p. Gr. 6–8.
Seventh-grader Hector and his friend Mando leave East Los Angeles for the weekend to spend time in Fresno with Hector's uncle Julio. Julio is a photographer, and he takes the boys with him on an aerial shoot. High in the sky, they witness the

robbery of an armored vehicle. Julio snaps a shot of the getaway car. The newspaper publishes the pictures, and the teens are interviewed. Unfortunately, the two robbers—Freddie and Huey—decide to take revenge on Hector, Mando, and Julio. This lighthearted book is full of slapstick, as the thugs are inept not only at robbing but at retrieving the incriminating negatives. Spanish words and phrases are interspersed throughout the story.

10 Minute Selection: Read the very short chapter 4. Freddie and Huey read the paper and decide to "take care of those two punks!" Move on to chapter 8. Freddie and Huey steal a different car and track down Julio and the boys. They slam into Julio's car with their stolen vehicle. "They were so close that Freddie reached out his hand and tried to grab Uncle's hair. But Uncle dodged his hand and slammed Freddie's face with the heel of his palm." Meanwhile, one of the boys picks up the camera and takes several pictures of the criminals. The chapter ends with Julio's car crashing into a tree.

Speare, Elizabeth George. *The Witch of Blackbird Pond.* Houghton Mifflin, 1958. 249 p. Gr. 5–8.

In 1687, sixteen-year-old Kit leaves her home in Barbados and travels to the Connecticut Colony to live with her only remaining family. She has a hard time fitting in with the Puritan ways of Aunt Rachel's family and village. Even before she arrives at her relative's house, Kit upsets one of the townsfolk, Goodwife Cruff. Kit had committed the offensive act of swimming in order to rescue a girl's doll. "We do not welcome strangers in this town, and you be the kind we like the least." Kit befriends a Quaker widow named Hannah, who many believe is a witch. The townspeople later turn their attention on Kit, believing that she, too, is practicing witchcraft.

10 Minute Selection: Read the first part of chapter 17. Many children and young people are stricken with a mysterious illness, including Kit's cousins Judith and Mercy. Several townspeople believe Hannah has put a curse on their children. Kit rushes to warn Hannah. They escape moments before the crowd sets fire to Hannah's house. End the passage with the line, "Kit flung both arms around the trembling woman, and together they huddled against the log and watched till the red glow lessened and died away."

Spinelli, Jerry. *Maniac Magee.* Little, Brown, 1990. 184 p. Gr. 4–8.

Orphan Jeffrey Lionel Magee runs away from his aunt and uncle and becomes legendary for his amazing feats. He's fast, he can run on train rails, he can untie a knot that has stumped even magicians, and he goes back and forth between West End, where the white folks live, and East End, made up of black folks. He tries hard to let each side know that there are few differences between the races. He lives with the Beale family in the East End. He lives in a band shell with an old man named Grayson. He lives in the buffalo pen at the zoo. It's not until the very end of the book that "finally, truly, at long last, someone was calling him home."

10 Minute Selection: Read chapter 7. John McNab is large kid who is in the middle of striking out thirty-five batters in a row when Jeffrey Magee shows up at the ballpark. The new kid not only hits the fastball but also knocks McNab's hat off his head with the ball. Jeffrey hits everything thrown to him. McNab even throws a frog, which Jeffrey promptly bunts and runs around the bases, making McNab look foolish. Read the first part of chapter 8. Jeffrey gets his nickname: Maniac. End the passage with the sentence, "The legend had a name."

Spinelli, Jerry. *Who Put That Hair in My Toothbrush?* **Little, Brown, 1984. 220 p. Gr. 6–9.**

Megan and her older brother Greg have a bad case of sibling rivalry, or, as their father states, sibling homicide. Megan is brash, sloppy, and athletic. Besides being irritated by her brother, she becomes annoyed with the new girl, who has moved from California. Greg is all business in his quest to impress Jennifer Wade. He lifts weights and constantly primps. Many scenes are hilarious. The mood of the book shifts at the very end; it becomes overly melodramatic. This shouldn't deter one from sharing this funny book with young teens.

10 Minute Selection: Each chapter is titled "Megan" or "Greg" as the two characters alternate stories. Read the first Greg story. It is summer, and Greg has become obsessed with Jennifer Wade. "I got subscriptions to *Muscles* and *Body Beautiful*. I exercised and lifted weights. I covered myself with Coppertone and tanned in the sun. I used Sassoon shampoo and Sassoon conditioner and Sassoon rinse, and I brushed my teeth with Close-up at least four times every day." He imagines scenarios between Jennifer and himself. At the end of the chapter, he learns that Jennifer has moved.

Second 10 Minute Selection: Read the sixth "Megan" chapter, the one that begins with "Romeo and Juliet Get Down and Boogie." Megan helps backstage for the school's modern version of *Romeo and Juliet*. She sees a roach and backpedals from it, crashing into scenery and knocking arches around the lead actress. She later finds that the roach came home with her. She catches it and carries it to her brother's bedroom. "The door was shut. I crouched. I pressed my little surprise to the threshold. I tilted the postcard, lifted the cup. The roach ran under the door."

Steig, William. *Abel's Island.* **Farrar Straus Giroux, 1976. 117 p. Gr. 2–4.**

A mouse named Abelard Hassam di Chirico Flint—Abel for short—is swept away in a hurricane and marooned on an island "12,000 tails long, 5,000 wide." The island is near a waterfall, and the river current is too swift for a mouse to swim. Abel comes up with many ways to get off of the island, but they all fail. He eventually spends an entire year trapped. His only visitors are a hungry owl and an elderly frog. Abel finally finds a way to the main shore only to run into a cat. The only thing on his mind is to return to his wife, Amanda.

10 Minute Selection: Read the first three chapters. Chapter 1 finds Abel and Amanda picnicking. The rain begins to fall. It gets heavier and heavier, so the couple dashes to a cave, where a variety of animals have taken shelter. The fierce wind grabs Amanda's scarf in chapter 2, and Abel runs out of the cave to retrieve it. "But when he tried to climb back with his trophy, the wind walloped and sent him spinning like weightless tumbleweed, his sweetheart's scarf in his paw." He's tossed onto a board with a nail sticking out of it. This becomes his boat when the rain and wind carry him to a river and over a waterfall. Abel awakes in chapter 3 to find his "boat" in a tree on an island. He looks forward to greeting the rescue team and sharing stories of his adventures. He goes back to sleep, confident "that he had the strength, the courage, and the intelligence to survive."

Streatfield, Noel. *Skating Shoes.* **Random House, 1951. 245 p. Gr. 3–5.**
Ten-year-old Harriet is encouraged by her doctor to strengthen her legs by ice-skating. At the local rink, she meets skating sensation Lalla, who has been skating since the age of three. The two become good friends. Lalla is hungry for companionship because her aunt Claudia forces her to spend all day practicing to become a world champion. When Harriet shows signs of being a great skater herself, Lalla displays some spiteful behavior. It's interesting how the modern-day issues of adults obsessed with children attaining perfection are captured in this novel from the 1950s. Streatfield has several "Shoes" books featuring different characters, including *Ballet Shoes* (1936), *Tennis Shoes* (1937), *Circus Shoes* (1938), *Theater Shoes* (1944), *Party Shoes* (1946), *Movie Shoes* (1949), *Family Shoes* (1954), *Dancing Shoes* (1957), and *Traveling Shoes* (1962).

10 Minute Selection: Read chapter 6. Harriet is worried about Lalla's first visit to her house because "it looked shabby compared to Lalla's home." However, Lalla is thrilled to meet Harriet's parents and brothers. She is thrown off when they ask her what she does besides skating. "Lalla was puzzled. 'I do lessons.'" She admits she is lonely for companionship but proudly declares, "I'm going to be a world champion. Everybody knows it." The kids make plans to grow a secret garden and make a pledge "on our uncle's stomach because it's probably the best filled." At the end of the day, Lalla declares, "Oh giggerty-geggerty, it was the nicest Sunday I've ever, ever had."

Taylor, Theodore. *The Trouble with Tuck.* **Doubleday, 1981. 110 p. Gr. 3–6.**
Helen is upset because her golden lab, Tuck, is becoming blind. As Tuck loses his sight, he becomes a problem dog. At one point, he is hit by a car. Helen is very loyal to Tuck. He saved her life on one occasion and from an attacker on another. She is worried that her parents will put Tuck to sleep and runs away with him. She

doesn't get far before she realizes her decision is foolish. She is inspired to contact the California Companion Dogs for the Blind School. Helen's family gets the use of Daisy, a retired guide dog. However, Tuck refuses to have anything to do with the training and threatens to bite both Daisy and Helen. The sequel is *Tuck Triumphant* (1991).

10 Minute Selection: Read the first chapter. Tuck crashes through a screen door in pursuit of some cats. Helen and her mother try to notice "anything different about Tuck." They conclude that something is wrong with his eyes and make an appointment with the veterinarian. Move on and read the second half of chapter 9, beginning with the sentence, "Monday morning, I did something that I seldom did in summer—I got up early." Helen takes Tuck for a walk and notices that he walks into traffic. "Without warning, he dropped off the curb and began to angle across to the other side of Wickenham. Suddenly I saw a car coming our way, fast." At dinner that night, Helen tells the rest of her family, "He needs one of those dogs that help the blind." They all look at her as if she was "bedbug crazy."

Temple, Frances. *Grab Hands and Run*. Orchard, 1993. 165 p. Gr. 4–8.
Felipe lives in El Salvador during dangerous times with his parents and sister Romy. His father warns Felipe's mother, "Listen: if they come for me, you and the children grab hands and run. Go north, all the way to Canada." Felipe's mother springs into action when Father's motorcycle is found outside of the city, "not wrecked but abandoned." The three manage to get across the border into Guatemala and again into Mexico. They follow rules they made: "Avoid the authorities. Be polite. Let Mama do the talking. Like a chameleon, blend in wherever you are." They are eventually caught in the United States and sent to a detention center. There, they consider a few options, including returning to El Salvador. Help finally arrives to get them into Canada. There are several Spanish words and phrases scattered throughout the text.

10 Minute Selection: Read chapter 6, "The Madman of Guija." The family negotiates with a man to help them cross Lago de Guija, "the lake shared by El Salvador and Guatemala." He charges three hundred *colones* for the boat ride. Once across, he charges them another three hundred *colones* and threatens to blow a whistle that will attract soldiers if they don't comply. The chapter ends with the man getting his money and leaving the family alone in the dark.

Thomas, Jane Resh. *The Comeback Dog*. Clarion, 1981. 62 p. Gr. 3–5.
While still grieving over the death of his dog, Captain, Daniel finds another dog. The dog, which Daniel names Lady, is injured. Daniel nurses her back to health, but Lady is wary of humans. Daniel loses patience with her. "'She's worse than

nothing!' Daniel cried. 'I wish she had died that first day. I wish I'd never found her!'" In the spring, he takes off her choke chain while they are walking in the fields and lets her run away. She returns later with her face and body full of porcupine quills. She lets only Daniel get close enough to take them out. The book ends with Lady licking his hand and Daniel saying, "'Maybe this time,' he said, 'you'll stay.'"

10 Minute Selection: Read the first chapter. Daniel is angry that Captain has died. "I don't want another dog! I hate dogs!" He wanders the farm field and begins to throw rocks into a culvert. "He threw the first stone sidearm as hard as he could, but it made no sound." After throwing more rocks, Daniel peers into the culvert and finds a dog barely breathing. Continue reading chapter 2. Daniel runs to the farm to get his rusty wagon and burlap sacks. He returns to the farm with the dog. His father and the vet are there. "'She's sick to death,' said Doc. 'We can speed her along. I've got some stuff in my bag. One shot will put her out nice and easy.'" Daniel decides that he'll take care of her.

Uchida, Yoshiko. *Journey to Topaz.* **Scribner, 1971. 149 p. Gr. 4–6.**
Eleven-year-old Yuki and her Japanese American family live in Berkeley, California, in 1942. Yuki's father is sent away to an internment camp in Montana shortly after Pearl Harbor is bombed. Yuki, her mother, and her older brother are later forced to leave their home. At first, they don't believe it will happen. "You children are American citizens. . . . How can they do anything like that to citizens?" When President Roosevelt signs the executive order, Yuki is confused. "The United States should be at war with Italy and Germany too, but . . . it was only the Japanese who were considered so dangerous to the country." First, they live in modified horse stalls in a converted race track and then are eventually sent to the desert of Utah. Yuki's brother soon leaves with other young men when the U.S. Army decides to make "an all-Nisei unit" of the military comprised of children of Japanese heritage who were born in this country.

10 Minute Selection: Read the first chapter, "Strangers at the Door." Yuki is excited about the approach of Christmas. Her family turns on the radio and hears, "'This is a repeat of the news bulletin,' a newscaster said harshly, his voice trembling with urgency. 'Japanese planes have attacked Pearl Harbor.'" Shortly afterward, policemen and FBI agents appear at their door. Father is taken away because "he is employed by one of Japan's largest business firms." One FBI agent and two policemen stay at the home. The chapter ends with Yuki feeling like a stranger in her own home. "She had no way of knowing that this was only the beginning of a terrible war and that her small comfortable world would be turned upside down."

Van Draanen, Wendelin. *Sammy Keyes and the Hotel Thief.* **Knopf, 1998. 163 p. Gr. 3–6.**

Sammy lives secretly with her grandmother in a seniors-only building. Her irresponsible mother dumped her there while pursuing a career as an actress in Hollywood. Sammy has to avoid attracting attention so her grandmother won't be in trouble for harboring her. It's hard for Sammy to keep a low profile. She's suspended on the first day of junior high for punching another girl in the nose. She manages to find her way into most buildings in the neighborhood, including the roof of the mall. The local police officers quickly become very familiar with her. Sammy spends most of her time trying to solve the mystery behind a rash of neighborhood burglaries. The second book in this series is *Sammy Keyes and the Skeleton Man* (1998).

10 Minute Selection: Read the one-page prologue, which starts, "Grams told me my binoculars were going to get me into trouble." Sammy thinks Grams is worrying about nothing. "That is, until I saw a man stealing money from a hotel room across the street—and he saw me." Continue reading chapter 1. Sammy tells us why she spends so much time looking out of Gram's window with the binoculars. She sees a man on the fourth floor of the Heavenly Hotel digging through a purse. He looks up and spots Sammy. "He kind of leaned into the window and stared, and I stared right back through the binoculars. Then I did something really, really stupid. I waved." Later on, the doorbell rings and Sammy jumps and yelps. The chapter ends with, "And all of a sudden I know who it is. It's the guy I saw at the Heavenly Hotel, come to shut me up for good."

Voigt, Cynthia. *Bad Girls.* **Scholastic, 1996. 277 p. Gr. 4–7.**

Fifth-graders Margalo and Mikey are two new girls at Washington Street Elementary. They check each other out. "'Is something bothering you?' Margalo asked. 'You have a problem with my face?' Mikey answered." They become friends, but they have their disagreements, too. Margalo is a sneaky plotter, while Mikey actively confronts other students, sometimes with physical violence. At one point, Mikey says to Margalo, "You're really bad," to which Margalo responds, "Why thank you." Mikey's nemesis, Louis, gets so enraged at Mikey that he cuts off her braids and is transferred to another class. Margalo manipulated these actions. Another time, Margalo admits to putting a dead squirrel in Rhonda's lunch bag. Mikey sticks up for her, and the two become outcasts. They sing to each other, "Nobody likes me. Everybody hates me. Going to the garden to eat worms." Other books featuring Margalo and Mikey are *Bad, Badder, Baddest* (1997), *It's Not Easy Being Bad* (2000), *Bad Girls in Love* (2002), and *Bad Girls, Bad Girls, Whatcha Gonna Do?* (2006).

10 Minute Selection: Read the last portion of chapter 2, "Are We Friends Yet?" beginning with the sentence, "Margalo arrived on Pet Day carrying a small cage made out of wire mesh; its handle was a twisted rope." The school is having a Pet Day. Margalo brings a rat that one of her stepbrothers trapped at the dump. Mrs. Chemsky, the teacher, maintains her cool. Mikey brings a shoe box that Louis knocks to the floor. Leaves fall out. Margalo announces that Mikey had told her she was bringing a black widow spider, implying it was now loose in the classroom. Then the rat escapes. Students climb on their desks. "'Stand still,' Mrs. Chemsky said, her voice very calm now. 'Or sit quietly.' She followed her own advice, sitting on her desk chair, and gathering her knees up to her chest."

Voigt, Cynthia. *Homecoming*. Atheneum, 1981. 312 p. Gr. 4–8.
The four Tillerman children are abandoned by their mother in a shopping-mall parking lot. Dicey, the oldest, is only thirteen. They decide to walk to their great-aunt Cilla's house, miles away, even though they have never met her. They arrive after many hardships only to learn that Cilla has passed away. Her daughter Eunice takes them in. The children take to the road once more when they learn that they may be separated. They make their way to their grandmother's farm, unsure if they'll be welcomed or not. This is the first book that features the Tillerman family. The second in the series is Newbery Award winner *Dicey's Song* (1982).

10 Minute Selection: Read most of chapter 5 in part 2 of the book, beginning with the sentence, "At midday, they saw another sign that said: PICKERS WANTED." It's August and the children have been walking for several miles. They decide to make money and approach a farmhouse. Mr. Rudyard takes them in his pickup truck to a field. He tells them to start picking tomatoes. "I'll be by at dark." Dicey knows that something is wrong, "something she couldn't put her finger on." Rudyard returns with his dog. "Mr. Rudyard tied the dog to a tree, using the end of the long rope. . . . 'I keep him hungry,' he remarked. He backed the truck around and drove off." The children eventually escape by crashing his truck and paddling across a nearby river.

Vuong, Lynette Dyer. *The Brocaded Slipper and Other Vietnamese Tales*. Addison-Wesley, 1982. 100 p. Gr. 3–6.
The title story of this collection of five Vietnamese folktales is a "Cinderella" variant. The author compares the other stories to Western folklore. "Little Finger of the Watermelon Patch," the tale of a girl "no bigger than your finger," is reminiscent of "Thumbelina." "The Fairy Grotto," in which a human marries a fairy and learns that a day in her world equals a year in his, may remind some listeners of Rip Van Winkle. "Master Frog" has similarities to "The Frog Prince." The last story, "The Lampstand Princess," has characteristics of several princess stories as well as "The Goose Girl." A pronunciation guide is provided.

10 Minute Selection: Your audience may enjoy comparing the story "The Brocaded Slipper" with the well known Disney version of "Cinderella." Tam is the victim of her cruel stepmother and her stepsister Cam. The crown prince marries Tam, but shortly after their marriage, the stepmother kills Tam. Cam takes her place as the prince's wife. Tam's spirit comes back in the form of a bird, two peach trees, and a persimmon before she resumes human form. Of course, in the end, she "lived happily with the prince for many years, loved by all of the people of the kingdom, first as their princess and later as their queen."

Walter, Mildred Pitts. *Justin and the Best Biscuits in the World.* **Lothrop, Lee and Shepard, 1986. 122 p. Gr. 2–4.**
Ten-year-old Justin is frustrated with his mother and two sisters. They constantly criticize him, especially when it comes to cleaning around the house, something he considers "woman's work." He visits his grandfather's horse ranch without the rest of his family. His grandfather teaches Justin how to make his bed, clean fish, and cook. Justin also learns a lot of his family's history. It wasn't easy for his ancestors—former slaves—to move to Missouri in 1879. Justin takes pride in his new skills when he makes a batch of biscuits for his mother and sisters upon his return.

    10 Minute Selection: Read chapter 6, "Riding Fence." Grandpa makes breakfast, but when he asks Justin, "Would you rather wash or dry?" Justin replies, "Neither." Justin feels guilty and learns how to make his bed and put away his clothes so they will look sharp for the upcoming festival. Justin and Grandpa find a fawn caught in fence wire while riding around on the property. Continue reading chapter 7, "About Black Cowboys." Justin learns stories of black cowboys, such as Bill Pickett and Nate Love. Grandpa also tells Justin, "All the cooks on the cattle trail were men," and that housework is for everyone. "All work is that way. It doesn't matter who does the work, man or woman, when it needs to be done." The chapter ends with Justin wishing he knew how to tell Grandpa that he loves him.

Werlin, Nancy. *The Killer's Cousin.* **Delacorte, 1998. 229 p. Gr. 7–12.**
Seventeen-year-old David Yaffe is acquitted of the murder of his girlfriend. His parents ship him off to Boston to live with his aunt and uncle, who are dealing with the suicide of their daughter Kathy. David learns that their marriage is rocky and that their eleven-year-old daughter, Lily, his cousin, is manipulating her parents. Lily and David soon wage a psychological war in this tense thriller. There is one use of the "*f*-word," which Lily uses to shock David. Your audience will be surprised when they deduce the book's title has more than one meaning. There's also a slight supernatural twist to the book when David believes his dead cousin, Kathy, is telling him to "help Lily."

    10 Minute Selection: Inform your audience that high school senior David is living with his aunt, uncle, and eleven-year-old cousin, Lily. Read chapter 26, which opens with the lines, "The next two weeks were quiet. Too quiet." David finds that someone has wiped out his computer's hard drive. The only person at home is Lily. When David accuses her of the vandalism, Lily smiles. "'You're *craaazy*,' said Lily. 'My parents think you're *craaazy*.'" She also says, "What are you going to do . . . dust for fingerprints?" He tells her to keep away from his stuff, and she runs to her bedroom giggling and saying, "Make me!" David realizes that Lily is convincing his aunt and uncle that he is indeed crazy. The chapter ends with the sentence, "I wondered if maybe I was."

White, E. B. *Charlotte's Web*. Harper and Row, 1952. 184 p. Gr. 1–5.
A farm girl named Fern saves a runt pig from her father's ax. She names the little pig Wilbur. When Wilbur reaches a certain size, he is moved down the road to the Zuckerman farm. He's lonely until he hears a voice overhead. It is Charlotte, a spider. The two become the best of friends, despite their differences. When they learn that Wilbur will most likely be killed for Christmas dinner, Charlotte makes it her mission to save her friend. The importance of this heartwarming novel in the history of children's literature cannot be overstated.

10 Minute Selection: Read chapter 9, "Wilbur's Boast." Wilbur believes he can spin a web like his friend Charlotte. "'I could spin a web if I tried,' said Wilbur, boasting. 'I've just never tried.'" Templeton, the cranky rat, ties a piece of string to Wilbur's tail. Wilbur jumps and lands on his head. "I guess I was just trying to show off. Serves me right." Later that evening, Wilbur confesses that he doesn't want to die. Charlotte decides she must do something to help the pig. "The plan is still in its early stages and hasn't completely shaped up yet, but I'm working on it."

White, Ruth. *Belle Prater's Boy*. Farrar Straus Giroux, 1996. 196 p. Gr. 4–6.
Gypsy lives with a terrible secret about her father's death. Her cousin, Woodrow, moves in next door after his mother mysteriously disappears. The two become close as they deal with their own situations. Woodrow sidetracks inquiries about his mother with his storytelling skills. Gypsy is concerned that people don't see her for who she is. The story is set in a 1950s small-town Appalachian community where everybody knows each other's business. When Woodrow helps Gypsy recover from a bully's taunts, he offers clues about his mother's disappearance. The sequel is *The Search for Belle Prater* (2005).

10 Minute Selection: Read a very short section of chapter 11 to help young audience members know what chiggers are. Read the paragraph that begins, "It was true that there was a bumper crop of chiggers that year," and end with the line, "Chigger city." Move on and read the entire chapter 12. A bully named Buzz insists on sitting on a tree stump during an evening bonfire. After Buzz tells a story, Woodrow tells what seems to be a ghost story about his aunt Millie, who died and was buried. After the funeral, Aunt Millie showed up with a bleeding hand. It turned out she wasn't really dead. The Sloan sisters dug her up to steal her diamond ring. When they cut Millie's finger, she woke up. Buzz denounces the story and insults Woodrow. Later, when Gypsy apologizes for letting Buzz come, Woodrow tells her not to worry and that the stump that Buzz was sitting on was "chiggers national headquarters."

Williams, Vera. *Scooter.* Greenwillow, 1993. 147 p. Gr. 1–4.
Elana Rose Rosen moves to a new apartment in the city—apartment 8E to be exact. "The highest up I ever lived . . ." Elana relates her first two months and one week (or 5,961,600 seconds) living there. After she gets injured in an accident with her scooter, she meets the rest of the kids in the building, including young Petey. Petey, whose mother is very sickly, never talks. Elana spends a lot of time with him and Mrs. Greiner, his babysitter, whom Elana refers to as "Mrs. Greiner the whiner." Acrostic poems are scattered throughout the text, including chapter headings. These and various signs, lists, charts, and instructions should also be read aloud. The story builds up to a big Field Day, which turns into a "zigzag day," a day with ups and downs.

10 Minute Selection: Read chapter 2, the chapter heading that features an acrostic poem made out of the word *emergency.* Elana is outside in front of her building practicing her jumps. "Then I started practicing my double heel click. That's a very special trick I invented." She hits a loose piece of sidewalk and lands on her face. She is rushed to the emergency room in a taxi. The taxi driver doesn't even charge Elana's mother for the ride. When Elana gets home, she finds her scooter "right in the place I had made for it by the window." She learns that the boy named Petey returned the scooter and went away without saying a word. The passage ends with Elana polishing her scooter.

Wrede, Patricia C. *Dealing with Dragons.* Harcourt, 1990. 212 p. Gr. 4–8.
Princess Cimorene is fed up trying to live the life of a princess. She hates lessons in dancing, embroidery, drawing, and etiquette—"from the proper way to curtsey before a visiting prince to how loudly it was permissible to scream when being carried off by a giant." Her father forbids her from learning fencing and magic. When she learns she is to be married to Prince Therandil, Cimorene runs away to live with the dragons. She volunteers to become the princess to the wise dragon Kazul. Her duties include cooking and cataloging the dragon's library. Cimorene gets involved helping the dragons escape from the crooked dealings of several wizards. This is the first book in the Enchanted Forest Chronicles. The other titles are *Searching for Dragons* (1991), *Calling on Dragons* (1993), and *Talking to Dragons* (1993).

10 Minute Selection: Read the second half of chapter 2, "In Which Cimorene Discovers the Value of a Classical Education and Has Some Unwelcome Visitors." Begin with the sentence, "The first of the knights arrived at the end of the second week." Cimorene is frustrated to learn that the knights of the kingdom are lining up to rescue her from the dragons. The first knight is confused when Cimorene tells him, "I'd rather not be rescued, thank you just the same." Later on, her intended, Prince Therandil, shows up. "'Aren't you a little slow?' she asked irritably. 'There've been eight knights here before you.'" The passage ends with Cimorene sending the prince packing because it's time to make dinner.

Wright, Betty Ren. *Christina's Ghost.* **Holiday House, 1985. 105 p. Gr. 4–5.**
Christina's parents are on a long trip, and her grandmother is in the hospital, so Christina is forced to stay with her crabby uncle Ralph. The two are staying at a large, foreboding lakeside house. Christina begins to see a little boy and eventually determines that he is a ghost. She also hears thumping in the attic and, when she tries to go up the stairs, is met with a cold force. She learns that a child and his tutor were murdered in the house several years ago, killed over valuable stamps that were never recovered. After Uncle Ralph begins to believe in the ghosts, the two work together to locate the stamps and hopefully send the malevolent attic ghost away.

10 Minute Selection: Read chapter 5, "The Boy Comes Back." Christina is wondering if she really saw a little boy. She decides to teach herself to be a better swimmer. While in the water, she sees a boy on the dock. "As she stared, he raised a hand in greeting." She swims over to him, but he is no longer in sight. She is convinced that she has seen a ghost. Continue reading chapter 6, "Footsteps in the Hall." It is midnight and the attic door is open. Christina hears a thud overhead and quickly shuts the door. She places a large chest against the door. In the morning, "there was nothing unusual to see, except for the chest. It stood out from the attic door at an angle, as if it had been roughly thrust aside."

Yee, Paul. *Tales from Gold Mountain: Stories of the Chinese in the New World.* **Macmillan, 1989. 62 p. Gr. 4–8.**
These eight original stories give a sense of the experience of Chinese immigrants on America's West Coast in the nineteenth century. They portray a wide cast of characters, from the greedy aspirations of Merchant Moy, who disowns his own daughters and replaces them with two boys, to the clever trickiness of the hard-working Lee Jim, who teaches his selfish employer a lesson. Many of the stories have a supernatural element to them. "Spirits of the Railway" tells of Chu, who crosses the ocean to find his father. Instead, he locates his father's spirit and helps it find its final resting place.

10 Minute Selection: Share the story "Rider Chan and the Night River." Rider Chan is hardworking and dependable. His brother is the opposite. Their mother sends them to the New World to seek their fortunes. Rider Chan finds a job as a courier, while his brother "disappeared into the gold territory." Rider Chan is on an important mission to deliver medicine when he is grabbed by a frightful water spirit. He is able to get free, but the ghost wants a favor. "Bury my body on the shore. Wait, and when only my bones are left, dig them up and send them back to China." It turns out Rider Chan's brother killed the spirit when it was human but died himself because of his greed. The ghost tells Rider Chan where their gold can be found. Rider Chan sends the gold to his mother in China. "Not long after, she died, too, but with a peaceful smile on her face."

Yep, Laurence. *The Ghost Fox.* **Scholastic, 1994. 69 p. Gr. 3–5.**
Near the docks, Little Lee is working with his father, Big Lee, a trader. Little Lee bumps into a stranger, and the man, wearing a red robe, goes to strike the boy. Big Lee intervenes, and Red Robe, as Little Lee calls him, vows revenge. Little Lee and his mother are bothered by strange scratching noises at their door, windows, and roof. Little Lee's mother starts acting strange. The boy learns that Red Robe is a ghost fox trying to catch their souls.

10 Minute Selection: Read the first chapter, "Wind to the Sea." This chapter sets up the conflict between Little Lee's family and the man Little Lee calls Red Robe. The chapter ends with Big Lee leaving on a big trip. Continue reading the next chapter, "Prowlers." Little Lee notices Red Robe following him at a distance. "When they stopped at their front door, Little Lee tugged at his mother's robe. 'I think someone followed us home.'" That night, Little Lee sees a fox outside his window. "Father says they can steal people's souls." Move on to chapter 7, "The Guardian." The fox gets inside the house. Little Lee strikes it with a knife as it escapes. Mother throws Little Lee out of the house. The neighbors hear the commotion. "A ghost fox has cast a spell on my mother. I tried to catch it, but it got away." The neighbors don't believe Little Lee. The chapter ends with Little Lee realizing "only he could save his mother."

Yolen, Jane. *Briar Rose.* **Tor, 1992. 239 p. Gr. 8–12.**
Gemma repeatedly tells the story of Sleeping Beauty, also known as Briar Rose, to her three granddaughters. Years later, Gemma tells Becca, the youngest granddaughter, that she—Gemma—is Briar Rose and that Becca should find "the castle in the sleeping woods." Little does Becca realize that this mysterious search of her grandmother's past will lead her to Poland and the World War II extermination camp known as Chelmno. Becca discovers how much of the fairy tale was true in Gemma's life. The book contains many German and Polish names and words.

10 Minute Selection: Read chapter 1, which demonstrates the beauty of Gemma's storytelling abilities. Baby Rebecca asks for the story "Seepin Boot." Continue reading chapter 2. Becca and her sisters, Sylvia and Shana, know that their grandmother is dying, and they pay her a visit in the nursing home. Becca remains after her sisters go home. Gemma tells her, "I was the princess in the castle in the sleeping woods." Read the short chapter 3, which goes back in time to another of Gemma's retellings of the story. Gemma mentions the bad fairy, "the one in black with big black boots and silver eagles on her hat." Read two more pages into chapter 4. Becca says good-bye to Gemma at the funeral. She leaves with her father. End the passage with the line, "They walked back to the limo arm in arm, and she hadn't the heart to pry his fingers away, though she was sure he was leaving bruises."

Yolen, Jane. *The Devil's Arithmetic.* **Viking, 1988. 170 p. Gr. 5–12.**
Twelve-year-old Hannah is transported from modern times to 1942 Nazi-occupied Poland. She is called Chaya, which is her actual Hebrew name. Her entire new family and community are captured by Nazi soldiers. With the knowledge she possesses, Hannah tries to warn the others that "resettlement" really means gas chambers. Chaya/Hannah's memories start to fade as she goes through her ordeal in a concentration camp.

10 Minute Selection: Read the second half of chapter 6, starting with the sentence, "Near the barn, Shmuel and the other men stood smoking and laughing at one joke after another." Hannah, as Chaya, meets other girls her age. She tries to tell them about her life in America, but she "realizes it would be useless telling them she lived in New Rochelle." She begins to tell them stories. Continue reading the next chapter. Hannah has mesmerized the others with the stories of *Star Wars, Yentl, Conan the Barbarian, Fiddler on the Roof, Little Women,* and *The Wizard of Oz.* End a few pages into this chapter when Yente asks, "What happened next to this Dorothy Gale?" Move on and read the entire chapter 8. Hannah is going with the others to her uncle Shmuel's wedding. She meets his bride-to-be, Fayge, and the two become fast friends. They all find Nazi soldiers waiting for them. Hannah recognizes the real danger. The chapter ends with the chilling lines, "As they moved closer, more men in dark uniforms got out of cars and truck cabs. They made a perfect half circle in front of the synagogue doors, like a steel trap with gaping jaws ready to be sprung."

Titles by Decade and Year

1950s

1950—Lewis, C. S. *The Lion, the Witch and the Wardrobe.*

1951—Gannett, Ruth Stiles. *The Dragons of Blueland.*

1951—Streatfield, Noel. *Skating Shoes.*

1952—Norton, Mary. *The Borrowers.*

1952—White, E. B. *Charlotte's Web.*

1953—Henry, Marguerite. *Brighty of the Grand Canyon.*

1953—Kjelgaard, Jim. *Outlaw Red.*

1954—Cameron, Eleanor. *The Wonderful Flight to the Mushroom Planet.*

1954—DeJong, Meindert. *The Wheel on the School.*

1955—Boston, L. M. *The Children of Green Knowe.*

1956—Butterworth, Oliver. *The Enormous Egg.*

1956—Smith, Dodie. *The Hundred and One Dalmatians.*

1957—Enright, Elizabeth. *Gone-Away Lake.*

1958—Bond, Michael. *A Bear Called Paddington.*

1958—Pearce, Philippa. *Tom's Midnight Garden.*

1958—Speare, Elizabeth George. *The Witch of Blackbird Pond.*

1959—George, Jean Craighead. *My Side of the Mountain.*

1960s

1960—Burnford, Sheila. *The Incredible Journey.*

1960—Estes, Eleanor. *The Witch Family.*

1960—L'Engle, Madeleine. *Meet the Austins.*

1961—Juster, Norton. *The Phantom Tollbooth.*

1961—Rawls, Wilson. *Where the Red Fern Grows.*

1962—Ball, Zachary. *Bristle Face.*

1962—L'Engle, Madeleine. *A Wrinkle in Time.*

1962—Mowat, Farley. *Owls in the Family.*

1963—Alexander, Lloyd. *Time Cat: The Remarkable Journeys of Jason and Gareth.*

1963—Fleischman, Sid. *By the Great Horn Spoon.*

1964—Fitzhugh, Louise. *Harriet the Spy.*

1964—Fleming, Ian. *Chitty-Chitty-Bang-Bang.*

1964—Hunt, Irene. *Across Five Aprils.*

1964—Merrill, Jean. *The Pushcart War.*

1965—Cleary, Beverly. *The Mouse and the Motorcycle.*

1966—Burch, Robert. *Queenie Peavy.*

1966—Singer, Isaac Bashevis. *Zlateh the Goat and Other Stories.*

1967—Christopher, John. *The White Mountains.*

1967—Hinton, S. E. *The Outsiders.*

1967—Hoban, Russell. *The Mouse and His Child.*

1967—Konigsburg, E. L. *From the Mixed-Up Files of Mrs. Basil E. Frankweiler.*

1967—Peterson, John. *The Littles.*

1968—Cleary, Beverly. *Ramona the Pest.*

1968—Hamilton, Virginia. *The House of Dies Drear.*

1968—Hautzig, Esther. *The Endless Steppe: Growing Up in Siberia.*

1968—Le Guin, Ursula K. *A Wizard of Earthsea.*

1968—Morey, Walt. *Kavik the Wolf Dog.*

1969—Chew, Ruth. *The Wednesday Witch.*

1969—Cleaver, Vera, and Bill Cleaver. *Where the Lilies Bloom.*

1969—Konigsburg, E. L. *About the B'Nai Bagels.*

1970s

1970—Babbitt, Natalie. *Kneeknock Rise.*

1970—Dahl, Roald. *Fantastic Mr. Fox.*

1971—O'Brien, Robert C. *Mrs. Frisby and the Rats of NIMH.*

1971—Uchida, Yoshiko. *Journey to Topaz.*

1972—Sneve, Virginia Driving Hawk. *High Elk's Treasure.*

1973—Bellairs, John. *The House with a Clock in Its Walls.*

1973—Cooper, Susan. *The Dark Is Rising.*

1973—Mazer, Harry. *Snow Bound.*

1973—Rockwell, Thomas. *How to Eat Fried Worms.*

1974—Holman, Felice. *Slake's Limbo.*

1974—Peck, Robert Newton. *Soup.*

1975—Babbitt, Natalie. *Tuck Everlasting.*

1975—Naylor, Phyllis Reynolds. *Witch's Sister.*

1975—Peck, Richard. *The Ghost Belonged to Me.*

1976—Steig, William. *Abel's Island.*

1977—Byars, Betsy. *The Pinballs.*

1977—Paterson, Katherine. *Bridge to Terabithia.*

1977—Pinkwater, Daniel. *The Hoboken Chicken Emergency.*

1978—Kerr, M. E. *Gentlehands.*

1978—Mahy, Margaret. *The Great Piratical Rumbustification and The Librarian and the Robbers.*

1978—McKinley, Robin. *Beauty: A Retelling of the Story of Beauty and the Beast.*

1978—Phelps, Ethel Johnston, ed. *Tatterhood and Other Tales.*

1978—Sachar, Louis. *Sideways Stories from Wayside School.*

1979—Catling, Patricia Skene. *The Chocolate Touch.*

1979—Clifford, Eth. *Help! I'm a Prisoner in the Library.*

1979—Howe, Deborah, and James Howe. *Bunnicula: A Rabbit-Tale of Mystery.*

1979—Kennedy, Richard. *Inside My Feet: The Story of a Giant.*

1979—Nixon, Joan Lowery. *The Kidnapping of Christina Lattimore.*

1980s

1980—Burch, Robert. *Ida Early Comes over the Mountain.*

1980—Fleischman, Paul. *The Half-a-Moon Inn.*

1981—Cameron, Ann. *The Stories Julian Tells.*

1981—Magorian, Michelle. *Good Night, Mr. Tom.*

1981—Smith, Janice Lee. *The Monster in the Third Dresser Drawer and Other Stories about Adam Joshua.*

1981—Taylor, Theodore. *The Trouble with Tuck.*

1981—Thomas, Jane Resh. *The Comeback Dog.*

1981—Voigt, Cynthia. *Homecoming.*

1982—Dahl, Roald. *The BFG.*

1982—Huynh, Quang Nhuong. *The Land I Lost: Adventures of a Boy in Vietnam.*

1982—Manes, Stephen. *Be a Perfect Person in Just Three Days.*

1982—Vuong, Lynette Dyer. *The Brocaded Slipper and Other Vietnamese Tales.*

1983—Cassedy, Sylvia. *Behind the Attic Wall.*

1983—Lindgren, Astrid. *Ronia, the Robber's Daughter.*

1983—Paton Walsh, Jill. *A Parcel of Patterns.*

1983—Pellowski, Anne. *Betsy's Up-and-Down Year.*

1984—Bunting, Eve. *Someone Is Hiding on Alcatraz Island.*

1984—Fox, Paula. *One-Eyed Cat.*
1984—Spinelli, Jerry. *Who Put That Hair in My Toothbrush?*
1985—Hamilton, Virginia. *The People Could Fly: American Black Folktales.*
1985—King-Smith, Dick. *Babe the Gallant Pig.*
1985—Kline, Suzy. *Herbie Jones.*
1985—MacLachlan, Patricia. *Sarah, Plain and Tall.*
1985—Pullman, Philip. *The Ruby in the Smoke.*
1985—Rylant, Cynthia. *Every Living Thing.*
1985—Wright, Betty Ren. *Christina's Ghost.*
1986—Bauer, Marion Dane. *On My Honor.*
1986—Fleischman, Sid. *The Whipping Boy.*
1986—Hahn, Mary Downing. *Wait Till Helen Comes.*
1986—Jacques, Brian. *Redwall.*
1986—Naidoo, Beverly. *Journey to Jo'burg: A South African Story.*
1986—Walter, Mildred Pitts. *Justin and the Best Biscuits in the World.*
1987—Avi. *Romeo and Juliet—Together (and Alive!) at Last.*
1987—Brittain, Bill. *Dr. Dredd's Wagon of Wonders.*
1987—Paulsen, Gary. *Hatchet.*
1988—Deuker, Carl. *On the Devil's Court.*
1988—Henkes, Kevin. *The Zebra Wall.*
1988—Lester, Julius. *More Tales of Uncle Remus.*
1988—Lowry, Lois. *All about Sam.*
1988—Myers, Walter Dean. *Scorpions.*
1988—Yolen, Jane. *The Devil's Arithmetic.*
1989—Cooney, Caroline B. *The Fog.*
1989—Duncan, Lois. *Don't Look Behind You.*
1989—Hurwitz, Johanna. *Russell and Elisa.*
1989—Lisle, Janet. *Afternoon of the Elves.*
1989—Lowry, Lois. *Number the Stars.*
1989—Paulsen, Gary. *The Voyage of the* Frog.
1989—Yee, Paul. *Tales from Gold Mountain: Stories of the Chinese in the New World.*

1990s

1990—Blume, Judy. *Fudge-a-Mania.*
1990—DeFelice, Cynthia. *Weasel.*
1990—Klause, Annette Curtis. *The Silver Kiss.*
1990—Soto, Gary. *Baseball in April and Other Stories.*

1990—Spinelli, Jerry. *Maniac Magee.*

1990—Wrede, Patricia C. *Dealing with Dragons.*

1991—Berry, James. *Ajeemah and His Son.*

1991—Ho, Minfong. *The Clay Marble.*

1991—Marshall, James. *Rats on the Roof and Other Stories.*

1991—Naylor, Phyllis Reynolds. *Shiloh.*

1991—Paterson, Katherine. *Lyddie.*

1991—Scieszka, Jon. *Knights of the Kitchen Table.*

1992—Dorris, Michael. *Morning Girl.*

1992—Greenfield, Eloise. *Koya Delaney and the Good Girl Blues.*

1992—McKay, Hilary. *The Exiles.*

1992—Namioka, Lensey. *Yang the Youngest and His Terrible Ear.*

1992—Yolen, Jane. *Briar Rose.*

1993—Cooper, Susan. *The Boggart.*

1993—Krull, Kathleen. *Lives of the Musicians: Good Times, Bad Times (and What the Neighbors Thought).*

1993—Marsden, John. *Tomorrow, When the War Began.*

1993—Philbrick, Rodman. *Freak the Mighty.*

1993—San Souci, Robert D. *Cut from the Same Cloth: American Women of Myth, Legend, and Tall Tale.*

1993—Temple, Frances. *Grab Hands and Run.*

1993—Williams, Vera. *Scooter.*

1994—Cushman, Karen. *Catherine, Called Birdy.*

1994—Danziger, Paula. *Amber Brown Is Not a Crayon.*

1994—Farmer, Nancy. *The Ear, the Eye and the Arm.*

1994—Hesse, Karen. *Sable.*

1994—Ibbotson, Eva. *The Secret of Platform 13.*

1994—Korman, Gordon. *Why Did the Underwear Cross the Road?*

1994—Maguire, Gregory. *Seven Spiders Spinning.*

1994—Soto, Gary. *Crazy Weekend.*

1994—Yep, Laurence. *The Ghost Fox.*

1995—Avi. *Poppy.*

1995—Ayer, Eleanor. *Parallel Journeys.*

1995—Curtis, Christopher Paul. *The Watsons Go to Birmingham—1963.*

1995—Gallo, Don, ed. *Ultimate Sports: Short Stories by Outstanding Writers for Young Adults.*

1995—Murphy, Jim. *The Great Fire.*

1995—Nix, Garth. *Sabriel.*

1995—Ortiz Cofer, Judith. *An Island like You: Stories of the Barrio.*

1996—Clements, Andrew. *Frindle.*
1996—Dickinson, Peter. *Chuck and Danielle.*
1996—Dorris, Michael. *Sees Behind Trees.*
1996—Hobbs, Will. *Far North.*
1996—Napoli, Donna Jo. *Zel.*
1996—Voigt, Cynthia. *Bad Girls.*
1996—White, Ruth. *Belle Prater's Boy.*
1997—Bloor, Edward. *Tangerine.*
1997—Bruchac, Joseph. *Eagle Song.*
1997—Creech, Sharon. *Chasing Redbird.*
1997—Giff, Patricia Reilly. *Lily's Crossing.*
1997—Hesse, Karen. *Out of the Dust.*
1997—Jiménez, Francisco. *The Circuit: Stories from the Life of a Migrant Child.*
1997—Nye, Naomi Shihab. *Habibi.*
1997—Park, Barbara. *Junie B. Jones Has a Monster under Her Bed.*
1997—Qualey, Marsha. *Thin Ice.*
1997—Silvey, Anita, ed. *Help Wanted: Short Stories about Young People Working.*
1998—Armstrong, Jennifer. *Shipwreck at the Bottom of the World: The Extraordinary True Story of Shackleton and the* Endurance.
1998—Bauer, Joan. *Rules of the Road.*
1998—Bruchac, Joseph, and James Bruchac. *When the Chenoo Howls: Native American Tales of Terror.*
1998—Grimes, Nikki. *Jazmin's Notebook.*
1998—Johnson, Angela. *Heaven.*
1998—Peck, Richard. *A Long Way from Chicago.*
1998—Rowling, J. K. *Harry Potter and the Sorcerer's Stone.*
1998—Sachar, Louis. *Holes.*
1998—Van Draanen, Wendelin. *Sammy Keyes and the Hotel Thief.*
1998—Werlin, Nancy. *The Killer's Cousin.*
1999—Almond, David. *Skellig.*
1999—English, Karen. *Francie.*
1999—Erdrich, Louise. *The Birchbark House.*
1999—Haddix, Margaret Peterson. *Just Ella.*
1999—Herrera, Juan Felipe. *Crashboomlove: A Novel in Verse.*
1999—Horvath, Polly. *The Trolls.*
1999—Jordan, Sherryl. *The Raging Quiet.*
1999—Levine, Gail Carson. *The Fairy's Mistake.*
1999—Mazer, Norma Fox. *Good Night, Maman.*
1999—Snicket, Lemony. *The Bad Beginning.*

Books by Subject

African/African American

Berry, James. *Ajeemah and His Son.*
Cameron, Ann. *The Stories Julian Tells.*
Curtis, Christopher Paul. *The Watsons Go to Birmingham—1963.*
English, Karen. *Francie.*
Farmer, Nancy. *The Ear, the Eye and the Arm.*
Greenfield, Eloise. *Koya Delaney and the Good Girl Blues.*
Grimes, Nikki. *Jazmin's Notebook.*
Hamilton, Virginia. *The House of Dies Drear.*
———. *The People Could Fly: American Black Folktales.*
Johnson, Angela. *Heaven.*
Lester, Julius. *More Tales of Uncle Remus.*
Myers, Walter Dean. *Scorpions.*
Naidoo, Beverly. *Journey to Jo'burg: A South African Story.*
Walter, Mildred Pitts. *Justin and the Best Biscuits in the World.*

American Indian/Indians of West Indies

Bruchac, Joseph. *Eagle Song.*
Bruchac, Joseph, and James Bruchac. *When the Chenoo Howls: Native American Tales of Terror.*
Dorris, Michael. *Morning Girl.*
———. *Sees Behind Trees.*
Erdrich, Louise. *The Birchbark House.*
Sneve, Virginia Driving Hawk. *High Elk's Treasure.*

ANIMALS

Alexander, Lloyd. *Time Cat: The Remarkable Journeys of Jason and Gareth.*
Avi. *Poppy.*
Ball, Zachary. *Bristle Face.*
Bond, Michael. *A Bear Called Paddington.*
Burnford, Sheila. *The Incredible Journey.*
Butterworth, Oliver. *The Enormous Egg.*
Cleary, Beverly. *The Mouse and the Motorcycle.*
Dahl, Roald. *Fantastic Mr. Fox.*
Dickinson, Peter. *Chuck and Danielle.*
Fox, Paula. *One-Eyed Cat.*
George, Jean Craighead. *My Side of the Mountain.*
Henry, Marguerite. *Brighty of the Grand Canyon.*
Hesse, Karen. *Sable.*
Hoban, Russell. *The Mouse and His Child.*
Howe, Deborah, and James Howe. *Bunnicula: A Rabbit-Tale of Mystery.*
Huynh, Quang Nhuong. *The Land I Lost: Adventures of a Boy in Vietnam.*
Jacques, Brian. *Redwall.*
King-Smith, Dick. *Babe the Gallant Pig.*
Kjelgaard, Jim. *Outlaw Red.*
Lester, Julius. *More Tales of Uncle Remus.*
Maguire, Gregory. *Seven Spiders Spinning.*
Marshall, James. *Rats on the Roof and Other Stories.*
Morey, Walt. *Kavik the Wolf Dog.*
Mowat, Farley. *Owls in the Family.*
Naylor, Phyllis Reynolds. *Shiloh.*
O'Brien, Robert C. *Mrs. Frisby and the Rats of NIMH.*
Pinkwater, Daniel. *The Hoboken Chicken Emergency.*
Rawls, Wilson. *Where the Red Fern Grows.*
Rylant, Cynthia. *Every Living Thing.*
Smith, Dodie. *The Hundred and One Dalmatians.*
Sneve, Virginia Driving Hawk. *High Elk's Treasure.*
Steig, William. *Abel's Island.*
Taylor, Theodore. *The Trouble with Tuck.*
Thomas, Jane Resh. *The Comeback Dog.*
White, E. B. *Charlotte's Web.*

Asian/Asian American

Ho, Minfong. *The Clay Marble.*
Huynh, Quang Nhuong. *The Land I Lost: Adventures of a Boy in Vietnam.*
Namioka, Lensey. *Yang the Youngest and His Terrible Ear.*
Uchida, Yoshiko. *Journey to Topaz.*
Vuong, Lynette Dyer. *The Brocaded Slipper and Other Vietnamese Tales.*
Yee, Paul. *Tales from Gold Mountain: Stories of the Chinese in the New World.*
Yep, Laurence. *The Ghost Fox.*

Biographies/Fictionalized Memoirs/Informational

Armstrong, Jennifer. *Shipwreck at the Bottom of the World: The Extraordinary True Story of Shackleton and the* Endurance.
Ayer, Eleanor. *Parallel Journeys.*
Hautzig, Esther. *The Endless Steppe: Growing Up in Siberia.*
Huynh, Quang Nhuong. *The Land I Lost: Adventures of a Boy in Vietnam.*
Jiménez, Francisco. *The Circuit: Stories from the Life of a Migrant Child.*
Krull, Kathleen. *Lives of the Musicians: Good Times, Bad Times (and What the Neighbors Thought).*
Murphy, Jim. *The Great Fire.*

Elderly Characters

Bauer, Joan. *Rules of the Road.*
Clements, Andrew. *Frindle.*
Fox, Paula. *One-Eyed Cat.*
Giff, Patricia Reilly. *Lily's Crossing.*
Kerr, M. E. *Gentlehands.*
Konigsburg, E. L. *From the Mixed-Up Files of Mrs. Basil E. Frankweiler.*
Magorian, Michelle. *Good Night, Mr. Tom.*
McKay, Hilary. *The Exiles.*
Naylor, Phyllis Reynolds. *Witch's Sister.*
Peck, Richard. *A Long Way from Chicago.*
Rylant, Cynthia. *Every Living Thing.*
Van Draanen, Wendelin. *Sammy Keyes and the Hotel Thief.*
Voigt, Cynthia. *Homecoming.*
Walter, Mildred Pitts. *Justin and the Best Biscuits in the World.*
Yolen, Jane. *Briar Rose.*

FAMILY

Almond, David. *Skellig.*

Babbitt, Natalie. *Tuck Everlasting.*

Bauer, Joan. *Rules of the Road.*

Berry, James. *Ajeemah and His Son.*

Bloor, Edward. *Tangerine.*

Blume, Judy. *Fudge-a-Mania.*

Burch, Robert. *Ida Early Comes over the Mountain.*

————. *Queenie Peavy.*

Byars, Betsy. *The Pinballs.*

Cameron, Ann. *The Stories Julian Tells.*

Cleaver, Vera, and Bill Cleaver. *Where the Lilies Bloom.*

Creech, Sharon. *Chasing Redbird.*

Curtis, Christopher Paul. *The Watsons Go to Birmingham—1963.*

Cushman, Karen. *Catherine, Called Birdy.*

Dorris, Michael. *Morning Girl.*

Duncan, Lois. *Don't Look Behind You.*

English, Karen. *Francie.*

Enright, Elizabeth. *Gone-Away Lake.*

Erdrich, Louise. *The Birchbark House.*

Farmer, Nancy. *The Ear, the Eye and the Arm.*

Fox, Paula. *One-Eyed Cat.*

Giff, Patricia Reilly. *Lily's Crossing.*

Greenfield, Eloise. *Koya Delaney and the Good Girl Blues.*

Grimes, Nikki. *Jazmin's Notebook.*

Hahn, Mary Downing. *Wait Till Helen Comes.*

Hautzig, Esther. *The Endless Steppe: Growing Up in Siberia.*

Henkes, Kevin. *The Zebra Wall.*

Hesse, Karen. *Out of the Dust.*

Hinton, S. E. *The Outsiders.*

Ho, Minfong. *The Clay Marble.*

Hoban, Russell. *The Mouse and His Child.*

Horvath, Polly. *The Trolls.*

Hunt, Irene. *Across Five Aprils.*

Hurwitz, Johanna. *Russell and Elisa.*

Huynh, Quang Nhuong. *The Land I Lost: Adventures of a Boy in Vietnam.*

Jiménez, Francisco. *The Circuit: Stories from the Life of a Migrant Child.*

Johnson, Angela. *Heaven.*

Kerr, M. E. *Gentlehands.*

Klause, Annette Curtis. *The Silver Kiss.*

Konigsburg, E. L. *About the B'Nai Bagels.*

————. *From the Mixed-Up Files of Mrs. Basil E. Frankweiler.*

L'Engle, Madeleine. *Meet the Austins.*

————. *A Wrinkle in Time.*

Lisle, Janet. *Afternoon of the Elves.*

Lowry, Lois. *All about Sam.*

MacLachlan, Patricia. *Sarah, Plain and Tall.*

Magorian, Michelle. *Good Night, Mr. Tom.*

Mazer, Norma Fox. *Good Night, Maman.*

McKay, Hilary. *The Exiles.*

McKinley, Robin. *Beauty: A Retelling of the Story of Beauty and the Beast.*

Myers, Walter Dean. *Scorpions.*

Naidoo, Beverly. *Journey to Jo'burg: A South African Story.*

Namioka, Lensey. *Yang the Youngest and His Terrible Ear.*

Napoli, Donna Jo. *Zel.*

Naylor, Phyllis Reynolds. *Witch's Sister.*

Norton, Mary. *The Borrowers.*

Nye, Naomi Shihab. *Habibi.*

Park, Barbara. *Junie B. Jones Has a Monster under Her Bed.*

Peck, Richard. *A Long Way from Chicago.*

Pellowski, Anne. *Betsy's Up-and-Down Year.*

Qualey, Marsha. *Thin Ice.*

Smith, Janice Lee. *The Monster in the Third Dresser Drawer and Other Stories about Adam Joshua.*

Sneve, Virginia Driving Hawk. *High Elk's Treasure.*

Snicket, Lemony. *The Bad Beginning.*

Spinelli, Jerry. *Who Put That Hair in My Toothbrush?*

Temple, Frances. *Grab Hands and Run.*

Uchida, Yoshiko. *Journey to Topaz.*

Voigt, Cynthia. *Homecoming.*

Walter, Mildred Pitts. *Justin and the Best Biscuits in the World.*

Werlin, Nancy. *The Killer's Cousin.*

White, Ruth. *Belle Prater's Boy.*

Williams, Vera. *Scooter.*

Yep, Laurence. *The Ghost Fox.*

Yolen, Jane. *Briar Rose.*

FANTASY AND SCIENCE FICTION

Alexander, Lloyd. *Time Cat: The Remarkable Journeys of Jason and Gareth.*
Almond, David. *Skellig.*
Avi. *Poppy.*
Babbitt, Natalie. *Tuck Everlasting.*
Bellairs, John. *The House with a Clock in Its Walls.*
Bond, Michael. *A Bear Called Paddington.*
Boston, L. M. *The Children of Green Knowe.*
Brittain, Bill. *Dr. Dredd's Wagon of Wonders.*
Butterworth, Oliver. *The Enormous Egg.*
Cameron, Eleanor. *The Wonderful Flight to the Mushroom Planet.*
Cassedy, Sylvia. *Behind the Attic Wall.*
Catling, Patricia Skene. *The Chocolate Touch.*
Chew, Ruth. *The Wednesday Witch.*
Christopher, John. *The White Mountains.*
Cleary, Beverly. *The Mouse and the Motorcycle.*
Cooper, Susan. *The Boggart.*
———. *The Dark Is Rising.*
Dahl, Roald. *The BFG.*
———. *Fantastic Mr. Fox.*
Estes, Eleanor. *The Witch Family.*
Farmer, Nancy. *The Ear, the Eye and the Arm.*
Fleming, Ian. *Chitty-Chitty-Bang-Bang.*
Gannett, Ruth Stiles. *The Dragons of Blueland.*
Hahn, Mary Downing. *Wait Till Helen Comes.*
Hoban, Russell. *The Mouse and His Child.*
Howe, Deborah, and James Howe. *Bunnicula: A Rabbit-Tale of Mystery.*
Ibbotson, Eva. *The Secret of Platform 13.*
Jacques, Brian. *Redwall.*
Juster, Norton. *The Phantom Tollbooth.*
Kennedy, Richard. *Inside My Feet: The Story of a Giant.*
King-Smith, Dick. *Babe the Gallant Pig.*
Klause, Annette Curtis. *The Silver Kiss.*
Le Guin, Ursula K. *A Wizard of Earthsea.*
L'Engle, Madeleine. *A Wrinkle in Time.*
Levine, Gail Carson. *The Fairy's Mistake.*
Lewis, C. S. *The Lion, the Witch and the Wardrobe.*
Lindgren, Astrid. *Ronia, the Robber's Daughter.*

Maguire, Gregory. *Seven Spiders Spinning.*
Marshall, James. *Rats on the Roof and Other Stories.*
McKinley, Robin. *Beauty: A Retelling of the Story of Beauty and the Beast.*
Napoli, Donna Jo. *Zel.*
Naylor, Phyllis Reynolds. *Witch's Sister.*
Nix, Garth. *Sabriel.*
Norton, Mary. *The Borrowers.*
O'Brien, Robert C. *Mrs. Frisby and the Rats of NIMH.*
Pearce, Philippa. *Tom's Midnight Garden.*
Peck, Richard. *The Ghost Belonged to Me.*
Peterson, John. *The Littles.*
Pinkwater, Daniel. *The Hoboken Chicken Emergency.*
Rowling, J. K. *Harry Potter and the Sorcerer's Stone.*
Sachar, Louis. *Holes.*
Scieszka, Jon. *Knights of the Kitchen Table.*
Smith, Dodie. *The Hundred and One Dalmatians.*
Steig, William. *Abel's Island.*
White, E. B. *Charlotte's Web.*
Wrede, Patricia C. *Dealing with Dragons.*
Wright, Betty Ren. *Christina's Ghost.*
Yep, Laurence. *The Ghost Fox.*
Yolen, Jane. *The Devil's Arithmetic.*

FOLKLORE/DERIVATIVE LITERATURE

Bruchac, Joseph, and James Bruchac. *When the Chenoo Howls: Native American Tales of Terror.*
Haddix, Margaret Peterson. *Just Ella.*
Hamilton, Virginia. *The People Could Fly: American Black Folktales.*
Lester, Julius. *More Tales of Uncle Remus.*
McKinley, Robin. *Beauty: A Retelling of the Story of Beauty and the Beast.*
Napoli, Donna Jo. *Zel.*
Phelps, Ethel Johnston, ed. *Tatterhood and Other Tales.*
San Souci, Robert D. *Cut from the Same Cloth: American Women of Myth, Legend, and Tall Tale.*
Vuong, Lynette Dyer. *The Brocaded Slipper and Other Vietnamese Tales.*
Yep, Laurence. *The Ghost Fox.*

Friendship

Avi. *Romeo and Juliet—Together (and Alive!) at Last.*
Bauer, Marion Dane. *On My Honor.*
Bloor, Edward. *Tangerine.*
Burch, Robert. *Ida Early Comes over the Mountain.*
Byars, Betsy. *The Pinballs.*
Cameron, Ann. *The Stories Julian Tells.*
Cleary, Beverly. *The Mouse and the Motorcycle.*
Danziger, Paula. *Amber Brown Is Not a Crayon.*
English, Karen. *Francie.*
Enright, Elizabeth. *Gone-Away Lake.*
Giff, Patricia Reilly. *Lily's Crossing.*
Greenfield, Eloise. *Koya Delaney and the Good Girl Blues.*
Hinton, S. E. *The Outsiders.*
Kline, Suzy. *Herbie Jones.*
Lindgren, Astrid. *Ronia, the Robber's Daughter.*
Lisle, Janet. *Afternoon of the Elves.*
Lowry, Lois. *Number the Stars.*
Namioka, Lensey. *Yang the Youngest and His Terrible Ear.*
Paterson, Katherine. *Bridge to Terabithia.*
Pearce, Philippa. *Tom's Midnight Garden.*
Peck, Robert Newton. *Soup.*
Philbrick, Rodman. *Freak the Mighty.*
Sachar, Louis. *Holes.*
Spinelli, Jerry. *Maniac Magee.*
Streatfield, Noel. *Skating Shoes.*
Voigt, Cynthia. *Bad Girls.*
White, E. B. *Charlotte's Web.*
Williams, Vera. *Scooter.*

Historical Fiction

Ball, Zachary. *Bristle Face.*
Berry, James. *Ajeemah and His Son.*
Burch, Robert. *Ida Early Comes over the Mountain.*
Curtis, Christopher Paul. *The Watsons Go to Birmingham—1963.*
Cushman, Karen. *Catherine, Called Birdy.*

DeFelice, Cynthia. *Weasel.*
Dorris, Michael. *Morning Girl.*
————. *Sees Behind Trees.*
English, Karen. *Francie.*
Erdrich, Louise. *The Birchbark House.*
Fleischman, Sid. *By the Great Horn Spoon.*
Fox, Paula. *One-Eyed Cat.*
Giff, Patricia Reilly. *Lily's Crossing.*
Grimes, Nikki. *Jazmin's Notebook.*
Henry, Marguerite. *Brighty of the Grand Canyon.*
Hesse, Karen. *Out of the Dust.*
Ho, Minfong. *The Clay Marble.*
Hunt, Irene. *Across Five Aprils.*
Jiménez, Francisco. *The Circuit: Stories from the Life of a Migrant Child.*
Jordan, Sherryl. *The Raging Quiet.*
Lowry, Lois. *Number the Stars.*
MacLachlan, Patricia. *Sarah, Plain and Tall.*
Magorian, Michelle. *Good Night, Mr. Tom.*
Mazer, Norma Fox. *Good Night, Maman.*
Paterson, Katherine. *Lyddie.*
Paton Walsh, Jill. *A Parcel of Patterns.*
Peck, Richard. *A Long Way from Chicago.*
Peck, Robert Newton. *Soup.*
Pullman, Philip. *The Ruby in the Smoke.*
Rawls, Wilson. *Where the Red Fern Grows.*
Speare, Elizabeth George. *The Witch of Blackbird Pond.*
Taylor, Theodore. *The Trouble with Tuck.*
Uchida, Yoshiko. *Journey to Topaz.*
White, Ruth. *Belle Prater's Boy.*
Yee, Paul. *Tales from Gold Mountain: Stories of the Chinese in the New World.*
Yolen, Jane. *The Devil's Arithmetic.*

Horror/Ghost Stories

Bellairs, John. *The House with a Clock in Its Walls.*
Boston, L. M. *The Children of Green Knowe.*
Brittain, Bill. *Dr. Dredd's Wagon of Wonders.*

Bruchac, Joseph, and James Bruchac. *When the Chenoo Howls: Native American Tales of Terror.*
Cooney, Caroline B. *The Fog.*
Cooper, Susan. *The Dark Is Rising.*
Hahn, Mary Downing. *Wait Till Helen Comes.*
Kennedy, Richard. *Inside My Feet: The Story of a Giant.*
Klause, Annette Curtis. *The Silver Kiss.*
Maguire, Gregory. *Seven Spiders Spinning.*
Naylor, Phyllis Reynolds. *Witch's Sister.*
Nix, Garth. *Sabriel.*
Peck, Richard. *The Ghost Belonged to Me.*
Rowling, J. K. *Harry Potter and the Sorcerer's Stone.*
Wright, Betty Ren. *Christina's Ghost.*
Yee, Paul. *Tales from Gold Mountain: Stories of the Chinese in the New World.*
Yep, Laurence. *The Ghost Fox.*

Humor

Avi. *Romeo and Juliet—Together (and Alive!) at Last.*
Blume, Judy. *Fudge-a-Mania.*
Bond, Michael. *A Bear Called Paddington.*
Butterworth, Oliver. *The Enormous Egg.*
Catling, Patricia Skene. *The Chocolate Touch.*
Cleary, Beverly. *The Mouse and the Motorcycle.*
————. *Ramona the Pest.*
Clements, Andrew. *Frindle.*
Dahl, Roald. *The BFG.*
————. *Fantastic Mr. Fox.*
Fleischman, Sid. *The Whipping Boy.*
Horvath, Polly. *The Trolls.*
Juster, Norton. *The Phantom Tollbooth.*
Konigsburg, E. L. *About the B'Nai Bagels.*
Korman, Gordon. *Why Did the Underwear Cross the Road?*
Lester, Julius. *More Tales of Uncle Remus.*
Lowry, Lois. *All about Sam.*
Maguire, Gregory. *Seven Spiders Spinning.*
Mahy, Margaret. *The Great Piratical Rumbustification and The Librarian and the Robbers.*

Manes, Stephen. *Be a Perfect Person in Just Three Days.*
Marshall, James. *Rats on the Roof and Other Stories.*
McKay, Hilary. *The Exiles.*
Merrill, Jean. *The Pushcart War.*
Namioka, Lensey. *Yang the Youngest and His Terrible Ear.*
Park, Barbara. *Junie B. Jones Has a Monster under Her Bed.*
Peck, Richard. *A Long Way from Chicago.*
Peck, Robert Newton. *Soup.*
Pinkwater, Daniel. *The Hoboken Chicken Emergency.*
Rockwell, Thomas. *How to Eat Fried Worms.*
Sachar, Louis. *Sideways Stories from Wayside School.*
Scieszka, Jon. *Knights of the Kitchen Table.*
Soto, Gary. *Crazy Weekend.*
Spinelli, Jerry. *Who Put That Hair in My Toothbrush?*
Wrede, Patricia C. *Dealing with Dragons.*

LATINA/LATINO

Herrera, Juan Felipe. *Crashboomlove: A Novel in Verse.*
Jiménez, Francisco. *The Circuit: Stories from the Life of a Migrant Child.*
Ortiz Cofer, Judith. *An Island like You: Stories of the Barrio.*
Soto, Gary. *Baseball in April and Other Stories.*
————. *Crazy Weekend.*
Temple, Frances. *Grab Hands and Run.*

MYSTERY AND SUSPENSE

Babbitt, Natalie. *Kneeknock Rise.*
Bellairs, John. *The House with a Clock in Its Walls.*
Bunting, Eve. *Someone Is Hiding on Alcatraz Island.*
Clifford, Eth. *Help! I'm a Prisoner in the Library.*
Cooney, Caroline B. *The Fog.*
Duncan, Lois. *Don't Look Behind You.*
Fleischman, Paul. *The Half-a-Moon Inn.*
Hahn, Mary Downing. *Wait Till Helen Comes.*
Hamilton, Virginia. *The House of Dies Drear.*
Howe, Deborah, and James Howe. *Bunnicula: A Rabbit-Tale of Mystery.*
Konigsburg, E. L. *From the Mixed-Up Files of Mrs. Basil E. Frankweiler.*

Naylor, Phyllis Reynolds. *Witch's Sister.*
Nixon, Joan Lowery. *The Kidnapping of Christina Lattimore.*
Pearce, Philippa. *Tom's Midnight Garden.*
Peck, Richard. *The Ghost Belonged to Me.*
Pullman, Philip. *The Ruby in the Smoke.*
Qualey, Marsha. *Thin Ice.*
Sachar, Louis. *Holes.*
Van Draanen, Wendelin. *Sammy Keyes and the Hotel Thief.*
Werlin, Nancy. *The Killer's Cousin.*
Wright, Betty Ren. *Christina's Ghost.*
Yolen, Jane. *Briar Rose.*

Outdoor Survival

Armstrong, Jennifer. *Shipwreck at the Bottom of the World: The Extraordinary True Story of Shackleton and the* Endurance.
Burnford, Sheila. *The Incredible Journey.*
George, Jean Craighead. *My Side of the Mountain.*
Hobbs, Will. *Far North.*
Holman, Felice. *Slake's Limbo.*
Kjelgaard, Jim. *Outlaw Red.*
Lindgren, Astrid. *Ronia, the Robber's Daughter.*
Mazer, Harry. *Snow Bound.*
Morey, Walt. *Kavik the Wolf Dog.*
Paulsen, Gary. *Hatchet.*
————. *The Voyage of the* Frog.
Steig, William. *Abel's Island.*
Voigt, Cynthia. *Homecoming.*

People with Disabilities

Bloor, Edward. *Tangerine.*
DeJong, Meindert. *The Wheel on the School.*
Dorris, Michael. *Sees Behind Trees.*
Fleischman, Paul. *The Half-a-Moon Inn.*
Hesse, Karen. *Out of the Dust.*
Jordan, Sherryl. *The Raging Quiet.*
Lisle, Janet. *Afternoon of the Elves.*

Magorian, Michelle. *Good Night, Mr. Tom.*
Philbrick, Rodman. *Freak the Mighty.*
Taylor, Theodore. *The Trouble with Tuck.*
Voigt, Cynthia. *Homecoming.*

SCHOOL

Avi. *Romeo and Juliet—Together (and Alive!) at Last.*
Bloor, Edward. *Tangerine.*
Bruchac, Joseph. *Eagle Song.*
Burch, Robert. *Queenie Peavy.*
Cleary, Beverly. *Ramona the Pest.*
Clements, Andrew. *Frindle.*
Danziger, Paula. *Amber Brown Is Not a Crayon.*
DeJong, Meindert. *The Wheel on the School.*
Fitzhugh, Louise. *Harriet the Spy.*
Herrera, Juan Felipe. *Crashboomlove: A Novel in Verse.*
Kline, Suzy. *Herbie Jones.*
Korman, Gordon. *Why Did the Underwear Cross the Road?*
Maguire, Gregory. *Seven Spiders Spinning.*
Park, Barbara. *Junie B. Jones Has a Monster under Her Bed.*
Rowling, J. K. *Harry Potter and the Sorcerer's Stone.*
Sachar, Louis. *Sideways Stories from Wayside School.*
Voigt, Cynthia. *Bad Girls.*

SHORT STORY COLLECTIONS (SEE ALSO FOLKLORE/DERIVATIVE LITERATURE)

Dickinson, Peter. *Chuck and Danielle.*
Gallo, Don, ed. *Ultimate Sports: Short Stories by Outstanding Writers for Young Adults.*
Hurwitz, Johanna. *Russell and Elisa.*
Jiménez, Francisco. *The Circuit: Stories from the Life of a Migrant Child.*
Marshall, James. *Rats on the Roof and Other Stories.*
Ortiz Cofer, Judith. *An Island like You: Stories of the Barrio.*
Peck, Richard. *A Long Way from Chicago.*
Peck, Robert Newton. *Soup.*
Rylant, Cynthia. *Every Living Thing.*
Sachar, Louis. *Sideways Stories from Wayside School.*

Silvey, Anita, ed. *Help Wanted: Short Stories about Young People Working.*

Singer, Isaac Bashevis. *Zlateh the Goat and Other Stories.*

Smith, Janice Lee. *The Monster in the Third Dresser Drawer and Other Stories about Adam Joshua.*

Soto, Gary. *Baseball in April and Other Stories.*

Yee, Paul. *Tales from Gold Mountain: Stories of the Chinese in the New World.*

SPORTS

Bloor, Edward. *Tangerine.*

Deuker, Carl. *On the Devil's Court.*

Gallo, Don, ed. *Ultimate Sports: Short Stories by Outstanding Writers for Young Adults.*

Greenfield, Eloise. *Koya Delaney and the Good Girl Blues.*

Konigsburg, E. L. *About the B'Nai Bagels.*

Streatfield, Noel. *Skating Shoes.*

STORIES/ACCOUNTS SET OUTSIDE THE UNITED STATES

Alexander, Lloyd. *Time Cat: The Remarkable Journeys of Jason and Gareth.*

Almond, David. *Skellig.*

Armstrong, Jennifer. *Shipwreck at the Bottom of the World: The Extraordinary True Story of Shackleton and the* Endurance.

Ayer, Eleanor. *Parallel Journeys.*

Berry, James. *Ajeemah and His Son.*

Bond, Michael. *A Bear Called Paddington.*

Boston, L. M. *The Children of Green Knowe.*

Burnford, Sheila. *The Incredible Journey.*

Cooper, Susan. *The Boggart.*

———. *The Dark Is Rising.*

Cushman, Karen. *Catherine, Called Birdy.*

Dahl, Roald. *The BFG.*

DeJong, Meindert. *The Wheel on the School.*

Dickinson, Peter. *Chuck and Danielle.*

Dorris, Michael. *Morning Girl.*

Farmer, Nancy. *The Ear, the Eye and the Arm.*

Fleischman, Paul. *The Half-a-Moon Inn.*

Fleming, Ian. *Chitty-Chitty-Bang-Bang.*

Hautzig, Esther. *The Endless Steppe: Growing Up in Siberia.*

Ho, Minfong. *The Clay Marble.*

Hobbs, Will. *Far North.*

Huynh, Quang Nhuong. *The Land I Lost: Adventures of a Boy in Vietnam.*

Ibbotson, Eva. *The Secret of Platform 13.*

Lowry, Lois. *Number the Stars.*

Magorian, Michelle. *Good Night, Mr. Tom.*

Mahy, Margaret. *The Great Piratical Rumbustification and The Librarian and the Robbers.*

Marsden, John. *Tomorrow, When the War Began.*

Mazer, Norma Fox. *Good Night, Maman.*

McKay, Hilary. *The Exiles.*

Morey, Walt. *Kavik the Wolf Dog.*

Mowat, Farley. *Owls in the Family.*

Naidoo, Beverly. *Journey to Jo'burg: A South African Story.*

Napoli, Donna Jo. *Zel.*

Nye, Naomi Shihab. *Habibi.*

Paton Walsh, Jill. *A Parcel of Patterns.*

Paulsen, Gary. *Hatchet.*

Pearce, Philippa. *Tom's Midnight Garden.*

Phelps, Ethel Johnston, ed. *Tatterhood and Other Tales.*

Pullman, Philip. *The Ruby in the Smoke.*

Rowling, J. K. *Harry Potter and the Sorcerer's Stone.*

Singer, Isaac Bashevis. *Zlateh the Goat and Other Stories.*

Smith, Dodie. *The Hundred and One Dalmatians.*

Streatfield, Noel. *Skating Shoes.*

Temple, Frances. *Grab Hands and Run.*

Vuong, Lynette Dyer. *The Brocaded Slipper and Other Vietnamese Tales.*

Yep, Laurence. *The Ghost Fox.*

Yolen, Jane. *Briar Rose.*

———. *The Devil's Arithmetic.*

TRAVEL

Armstrong, Jennifer. *Shipwreck at the Bottom of the World: The Extraordinary True Story of Shackleton and the* Endurance.

Avi. *Poppy.*

Bauer, Joan. *Rules of the Road.*

Christopher, John. *The White Mountains.*
Fleischman, Sid. *By the Great Horn Spoon.*
Le Guin, Ursula K. *A Wizard of Earthsea.*
L'Engle, Madeleine. *A Wrinkle in Time.*
Mazer, Norma Fox. *Good Night, Maman.*
Morey, Walt. *Kavik the Wolf Dog.*
Naidoo, Beverly. *Journey to Jo'burg: A South African Story.*
Nix, Garth. *Sabriel.*
Paulsen, Gary. *The Voyage of the* Frog.
Temple, Frances. *Grab Hands and Run.*
Voigt, Cynthia. *Homecoming.*

Grade-Level Recommendations

EARLY ELEMENTARY (GRADES K-2)

Blume, Judy. *Fudge-a-Mania.*

Bond, Michael. *A Bear Called Paddington.*

Bruchac, Joseph. *Eagle Song.*

Cameron, Ann. *The Stories Julian Tells.*

Catling, Patricia Skene. *The Chocolate Touch.*

Chew, Ruth. *The Wednesday Witch.*

Cleary, Beverly. *The Mouse and the Motorcycle.*

————. *Ramona the Pest.*

Clifford, Eth. *Help! I'm a Prisoner in the Library.*

Dahl, Roald. *The BFG.*

————. *Fantastic Mr. Fox.*

Danziger, Paula. *Amber Brown Is Not a Crayon.*

Estes, Eleanor. *The Witch Family.*

Gannett, Ruth Stiles. *The Dragons of Blueland.*

Hamilton, Virginia. *The People Could Fly: American Black Folktales.*

Hesse, Karen. *Sable.*

Hoban, Russell. *The Mouse and His Child.*

Howe, Deborah, and James Howe. *Bunnicula: A Rabbit-Tale of Mystery.*

Hurwitz, Johanna. *Russell and Elisa.*

King-Smith, Dick. *Babe the Gallant Pig.*

Kline, Suzy. *Herbie Jones.*

Lowry, Lois. *All about Sam.*

MacLachlan, Patricia. *Sarah, Plain and Tall.*

Mahy, Margaret. *The Great Piratical Rumbustification and The Librarian and the Robbers.*

Marshall, James. *Rats on the Roof and Other Stories.*

Namioka, Lensey. *Yang the Youngest and His Terrible Ear.*
Park, Barbara. *Junie B. Jones Has a Monster under Her Bed.*
Peterson, John. *The Littles.*
Pinkwater, Daniel. *The Hoboken Chicken Emergency.*
Rylant, Cynthia. *Every Living Thing.*
Scieszka, Jon. *Knights of the Kitchen Table.*
Smith, Dodie. *The Hundred and One Dalmatians.*
Smith, Janice Lee. *The Monster in the Third Dresser Drawer and Other Stories about Adam Joshua.*
Sneve, Virginia Driving Hawk. *High Elk's Treasure.*
Walter, Mildred Pitts. *Justin and the Best Biscuits in the World.*
White, E. B. *Charlotte's Web.*
Williams, Vera. *Scooter.*

Upper Elementary (Grades 3–5)

Alexander, Lloyd. *Time Cat: The Remarkable Journeys of Jason and Gareth.*
Almond, David. *Skellig.*
Armstrong, Jennifer. *Shipwreck at the Bottom of the World: The Extraordinary True Story of Shackleton and the* Endurance.
Avi. *Poppy.*
———. *Romeo and Juliet—Together (and Alive!) at Last.*
Babbitt, Natalie. *Kneeknock Rise.*
———. *Tuck Everlasting.*
Ball, Zachary. *Bristle Face.*
Bauer, Marion Dane. *On My Honor.*
Bellairs, John. *The House with a Clock in Its Walls.*
Blume, Judy. *Fudge-a-Mania.*
Bond, Michael. *A Bear Called Paddington.*
Boston, L. M. *The Children of Green Knowe.*
Brittain, Bill. *Dr. Dredd's Wagon of Wonders.*
Bruchac, Joseph. *Eagle Song.*
Bruchac, Joseph, and James Bruchac. *When the Chenoo Howls: Native American Tales of Terror.*
Bunting, Eve. *Someone Is Hiding on Alcatraz Island.*
Burch, Robert. *Ida Early Comes over the Mountain.*
———. *Queenie Peavy.*
Burnford, Sheila. *The Incredible Journey.*
Butterworth, Oliver. *The Enormous Egg.*

Byars, Betsy. *The Pinballs.*

Cameron, Eleanor. *The Wonderful Flight to the Mushroom Planet.*

Cassedy, Sylvia. *Behind the Attic Wall.*

Catling, Patricia Skene. *The Chocolate Touch.*

Chew, Ruth. *The Wednesday Witch.*

Christopher, John. *The White Mountains.*

Cleary, Beverly. *The Mouse and the Motorcycle.*

————. *Ramona the Pest.*

Cleaver, Vera, and Bill Cleaver. *Where the Lilies Bloom.*

Clements, Andrew. *Frindle.*

Clifford, Eth. *Help! I'm a Prisoner in the Library.*

Cooper, Susan. *The Boggart.*

————. *The Dark Is Rising.*

Creech, Sharon. *Chasing Redbird.*

Curtis, Christopher Paul. *The Watsons Go to Birmingham—1963.*

Dahl, Roald. *The BFG.*

————. *Fantastic Mr. Fox.*

Danziger, Paula. *Amber Brown Is Not a Crayon.*

DeFelice, Cynthia. *Weasel.*

DeJong, Meindert. *The Wheel on the School.*

Dickinson, Peter. *Chuck and Danielle.*

Dorris, Michael. *Morning Girl.*

————. *Sees Behind Trees.*

English, Karen. *Francie.*

Enright, Elizabeth. *Gone-Away Lake.*

Erdrich, Louise. *The Birchbark House.*

Estes, Eleanor. *The Witch Family.*

Farmer, Nancy. *The Ear, the Eye and the Arm.*

Fitzhugh, Louise. *Harriet the Spy.*

Fleischman, Paul. *The Half-a-Moon Inn.*

Fleischman, Sid. *By the Great Horn Spoon.*

————. *The Whipping Boy.*

Fleming, Ian. *Chitty-Chitty-Bang-Bang.*

Fox, Paula. *One-Eyed Cat.*

Gannett, Ruth Stiles. *The Dragons of Blueland.*

George, Jean Craighead. *My Side of the Mountain.*

Giff, Patricia Reilly. *Lily's Crossing.*

Greenfield, Eloise. *Koya Delaney and the Good Girl Blues.*

Haddix, Margaret Peterson. *Just Ella.*

Hahn, Mary Downing. *Wait Till Helen Comes.*

Hamilton, Virginia. *The House of Dies Drear.*

————. *The People Could Fly: American Black Folktales.*

Hautzig, Esther. *The Endless Steppe: Growing Up in Siberia.*

Henkes, Kevin. *The Zebra Wall.*

Henry, Marguerite. *Brighty of the Grand Canyon.*

Hesse, Karen. *Out of the Dust.*

————. *Sable.*

Ho, Minfong. *The Clay Marble.*

Hoban, Russell. *The Mouse and His Child.*

Horvath, Polly. *The Trolls.*

Howe, Deborah, and James Howe. *Bunnicula: A Rabbit-Tale of Mystery.*

Hunt, Irene. *Across Five Aprils.*

Huynh, Quang Nhuong. *The Land I Lost: Adventures of a Boy in Vietnam.*

Ibbotson, Eva. *The Secret of Platform 13.*

Jacques, Brian. *Redwall.*

Jiménez, Francisco. *The Circuit: Stories from the Life of a Migrant Child.*

Juster, Norton. *The Phantom Tollbooth.*

Kennedy, Richard. *Inside My Feet: The Story of a Giant.*

King-Smith, Dick. *Babe the Gallant Pig.*

Kjelgaard, Jim. *Outlaw Red.*

Kline, Suzy. *Herbie Jones.*

Konigsburg, E. L. *About the B'Nai Bagels.*

————. *From the Mixed-Up Files of Mrs. Basil E. Frankweiler.*

Korman, Gordon. *Why Did the Underwear Cross the Road?*

Krull, Kathleen. *Lives of the Musicians: Good Times, Bad Times (and What the Neighbors Thought).*

Le Guin, Ursula K. *A Wizard of Earthsea.*

L'Engle, Madeleine. *Meet the Austins.*

————. *A Wrinkle in Time.*

Lester, Julius. *More Tales of Uncle Remus.*

Levine, Gail Carson. *The Fairy's Mistake.*

Lewis, C. S. *The Lion, the Witch and the Wardrobe.*

Lindgren, Astrid. *Ronia, the Robber's Daughter.*

Lisle, Janet. *Afternoon of the Elves.*

Lowry, Lois. *All about Sam.*

————. *Number the Stars.*

MacLachlan, Patricia. *Sarah, Plain and Tall.*

Magorian, Michelle. *Good Night, Mr. Tom.*

Maguire, Gregory. *Seven Spiders Spinning.*

Mahy, Margaret. *The Great Piratical Rumbustification and The Librarian and the Robbers.*

Manes, Stephen. *Be a Perfect Person in Just Three Days.*

Marshall, James. *Rats on the Roof and Other Stories.*

Mazer, Norma Fox. *Good Night, Maman.*

McKay, Hilary. *The Exiles.*

Merrill, Jean. *The Pushcart War.*

Morey, Walt. *Kavik the Wolf Dog.*

Mowat, Farley. *Owls in the Family.*

Murphy, Jim. *The Great Fire.*

Myers, Walter Dean. *Scorpions.*

Naidoo, Beverly. *Journey to Jo'burg: A South African Story.*

Namioka, Lensey. *Yang the Youngest and His Terrible Ear.*

Naylor, Phyllis Reynolds. *Shiloh.*

———. *Witch's Sister.*

Norton, Mary. *The Borrowers.*

O'Brien, Robert C. *Mrs. Frisby and the Rats of NIMH.*

Paterson, Katherine. *Bridge to Terabithia.*

———. *Lyddie.*

Paulsen, Gary. *Hatchet.*

———. *The Voyage of the* Frog.

Pearce, Philippa. *Tom's Midnight Garden.*

Peck, Richard. *The Ghost Belonged to Me.*

———. *A Long Way from Chicago.*

Peck, Robert Newton. *Soup.*

Pellowski, Anne. *Betsy's Up-and-Down Year.*

Peterson, John. *The Littles.*

Phelps, Ethel Johnston, ed. *Tatterhood and Other Tales.*

Pinkwater, Daniel. *The Hoboken Chicken Emergency.*

Rawls, Wilson. *Where the Red Fern Grows.*

Rockwell, Thomas. *How to Eat Fried Worms.*

Rowling, J. K. *Harry Potter and the Sorcerer's Stone.*

Rylant, Cynthia. *Every Living Thing.*

Sachar, Louis. *Holes.*

———. *Sideways Stories from Wayside School.*

San Souci, Robert D. *Cut from the Same Cloth: American Women of Myth, Legend, and Tall Tale.*

Scieszka, Jon. *Knights of the Kitchen Table.*

Singer, Isaac Bashevis. *Zlateh the Goat and Other Stories.*

Smith, Dodie. *The Hundred and One Dalmatians.*

Smith, Janice Lee. *The Monster in the Third Dresser Drawer and Other Stories about Adam Joshua.*

Sneve, Virginia Driving Hawk. *High Elk's Treasure.*

Snicket, Lemony. *The Bad Beginning.*

Soto, Gary. *Baseball in April and Other Stories.*

Speare, Elizabeth George. *The Witch of Blackbird Pond.*

Spinelli, Jerry. *Maniac Magee.*

Steig, William. *Abel's Island.*

Streatfield, Noel. *Skating Shoes.*

Taylor, Theodore. *The Trouble with Tuck.*

Temple, Frances. *Grab Hands and Run.*

Thomas, Jane Resh. *The Comeback Dog.*

Uchida, Yoshiko. *Journey to Topaz.*

Van Draanen, Wendelin. *Sammy Keyes and the Hotel Thief.*

Voigt, Cynthia. *Bad Girls.*

————. *Homecoming.*

Vuong, Lynette Dyer. *The Brocaded Slipper and Other Vietnamese Tales.*

Walter, Mildred Pitts. *Justin and the Best Biscuits in the World.*

White, E. B. *Charlotte's Web.*

White, Ruth. *Belle Prater's Boy.*

Williams, Vera. *Scooter.*

Wrede, Patricia C. *Dealing with Dragons.*

Wright, Betty Ren. *Christina's Ghost.*

Yee, Paul. *Tales from Gold Mountain: Stories of the Chinese in the New World.*

Yep, Laurence. *The Ghost Fox.*

Yolen, Jane. *The Devil's Arithmetic.*

MIDDLE SCHOOL (GRADES 6–8)

Almond, David. *Skellig.*

Armstrong, Jennifer. *Shipwreck at the Bottom of the World: The Extraordinary True Story of Shackleton and the* Endurance.

Avi. *Romeo and Juliet—Together (and Alive!) at Last.*

Ayer, Eleanor. *Parallel Journeys.*

Babbitt, Natalie. *Kneeknock Rise.*

———. *Tuck Everlasting.*

Ball, Zachary. *Bristle Face.*

Bauer, Joan. *Rules of the Road.*

Bellairs, John. *The House with a Clock in Its Walls.*

Berry, James. *Ajeemah and His Son.*

Bloor, Edward. *Tangerine.*

Brittain, Bill. *Dr. Dredd's Wagon of Wonders.*

Bruchac, Joseph, and James Bruchac. *When the Chenoo Howls: Native American Tales of Terror.*

Bunting, Eve. *Someone Is Hiding on Alcatraz Island.*

Burch, Robert. *Queenie Peavy.*

Cassedy, Sylvia. *Behind the Attic Wall.*

Christopher, John. *The White Mountains.*

Cleaver, Vera, and Bill Cleaver. *Where the Lilies Bloom.*

Clements, Andrew. *Frindle.*

Cooney, Caroline B. *The Fog.*

Cooper, Susan. *The Boggart.*

———. *The Dark Is Rising.*

Creech, Sharon. *Chasing Redbird.*

Curtis, Christopher Paul. *The Watsons Go to Birmingham—1963.*

Cushman, Karen. *Catherine, Called Birdy.*

DeFelice, Cynthia. *Weasel.*

Deuker, Carl. *On the Devil's Court.*

Dickinson, Peter. *Chuck and Danielle.*

Dorris, Michael. *Morning Girl.*

———. *Sees Behind Trees.*

Duncan, Lois. *Don't Look Behind You.*

English, Karen. *Francie.*

Erdrich, Louise. *The Birchbark House.*

Farmer, Nancy. *The Ear, the Eye and the Arm.*

Fleischman, Paul. *The Half-a-Moon Inn.*

Fleischman, Sid. *The Whipping Boy.*

Fox, Paula. *One-Eyed Cat.*

Gallo, Don, ed. *Ultimate Sports: Short Stories by Outstanding Writers for Young Adults.*

George, Jean Craighead. *My Side of the Mountain.*

Giff, Patricia Reilly. *Lily's Crossing.*

Greenfield, Eloise. *Koya Delaney and the Good Girl Blues.*

Grimes, Nikki. *Jazmin's Notebook.*

Haddix, Margaret Peterson. *Just Ella.*

Hahn, Mary Downing. *Wait Till Helen Comes.*

Hamilton, Virginia. *The House of Dies Drear.*

———. *The People Could Fly: American Black Folktales.*

Hautzig, Esther. *The Endless Steppe: Growing Up in Siberia.*

Hesse, Karen. *Out of the Dust.*

Hinton, S. E. *The Outsiders.*

Ho, Minfong. *The Clay Marble.*

Hobbs, Will. *Far North.*

Holman, Felice. *Slake's Limbo.*

Hunt, Irene. *Across Five Aprils.*

Huynh, Quang Nhuong. *The Land I Lost: Adventures of a Boy in Vietnam.*

Ibbotson, Eva. *The Secret of Platform 13.*

Jacques, Brian. *Redwall.*

Jiménez, Francisco. *The Circuit: Stories from the Life of a Migrant Child.*

Johnson, Angela. *Heaven.*

Juster, Norton. *The Phantom Tollbooth.*

Kennedy, Richard. *Inside My Feet: The Story of a Giant.*

Kjelgaard, Jim. *Outlaw Red.*

Klause, Annette Curtis. *The Silver Kiss.*

Konigsburg, E. L. *About the B'Nai Bagels.*

———. *From the Mixed-Up Files of Mrs. Basil E. Frankweiler.*

Korman, Gordon. *Why Did the Underwear Cross the Road?*

Krull, Kathleen. *Lives of the Musicians: Good Times, Bad Times (and What the Neighbors Thought).*

Le Guin, Ursula K. *A Wizard of Earthsea.*

L'Engle, Madeleine. *Meet the Austins.*

———. *A Wrinkle in Time.*

Lester, Julius. *More Tales of Uncle Remus.*

Levine, Gail Carson. *The Fairy's Mistake.*

Lewis, C. S. *The Lion, the Witch and the Wardrobe.*

Lisle, Janet. *Afternoon of the Elves.*

Lowry, Lois. *Number the Stars.*

Magorian, Michelle. *Good Night, Mr. Tom.*

Maguire, Gregory. *Seven Spiders Spinning.*

Marsden, John. *Tomorrow, When the War Began.*

Mazer, Harry. *Snow Bound.*

Mazer, Norma Fox. *Good Night, Maman.*

McKay, Hilary. *The Exiles.*

McKinley, Robin. *Beauty: A Retelling of the Story of Beauty and the Beast.*

Merrill, Jean. *The Pushcart War.*

Morey, Walt. *Kavik the Wolf Dog.*

Mowat, Farley. *Owls in the Family.*

Murphy, Jim. *The Great Fire.*

Myers, Walter Dean. *Scorpions.*

Naidoo, Beverly. *Journey to Jo'burg: A South African Story.*

Namioka, Lensey. *Yang the Youngest and His Terrible Ear.*

Napoli, Donna Jo. *Zel.*

Naylor, Phyllis Reynolds. *Shiloh.*

————. *Witch's Sister.*

Nix, Garth. *Sabriel.*

Nixon, Joan Lowery. *The Kidnapping of Christina Lattimore.*

Nye, Naomi Shihab. *Habibi.*

Ortiz Cofer, Judith. *An Island like You: Stories of the Barrio.*

Paterson, Katherine. *Bridge to Terabithia.*

————. *Lyddie.*

Paton Walsh, Jill. *A Parcel of Patterns.*

Paulsen, Gary. *Hatchet.*

————. *The Voyage of the* Frog.

Peck, Richard. *The Ghost Belonged to Me.*

————. *A Long Way from Chicago.*

Peck, Robert Newton. *Soup.*

Phelps, Ethel Johnston, ed. *Tatterhood and Other Tales.*

Philbrick, Rodman. *Freak the Mighty.*

Pullman, Philip. *The Ruby in the Smoke.*

Rawls, Wilson. *Where the Red Fern Grows.*

Rockwell, Thomas. *How to Eat Fried Worms.*

Rowling, J. K. *Harry Potter and the Sorcerer's Stone.*

Sachar, Louis. *Holes.*

San Souci, Robert D. *Cut from the Same Cloth: American Women of Myth,*

Legend, and Tall Tale.
Scieszka, Jon. *Knights of the Kitchen Table.*
Silvey, Anita, ed. *Help Wanted: Short Stories about Young People Working.*
Singer, Isaac Bashevis. *Zlateh the Goat and Other Stories.*
Snicket, Lemony. *The Bad Beginning.*
Soto, Gary. *Baseball in April and Other Stories.*
————. *Crazy Weekend.*
Speare, Elizabeth George. *The Witch of Blackbird Pond.*
Spinelli, Jerry. *Maniac Magee.*
————. *Who Put That Hair in My Toothbrush?*
Taylor, Theodore. *The Trouble with Tuck.*
Temple, Frances. *Grab Hands and Run.*
Uchida, Yoshiko. *Journey to Topaz.*
Van Draanen, Wendelin. *Sammy Keyes and the Hotel Thief.*
Voigt, Cynthia. *Bad Girls.*
————. *Homecoming.*
Vuong, Lynette Dyer. *The Brocaded Slipper and Other Vietnamese Tales.*
Werlin, Nancy. *The Killer's Cousin.*
White, Ruth. *Belle Prater's Boy.*
Wrede, Patricia C. *Dealing with Dragons.*
Yee, Paul. *Tales from Gold Mountain: Stories of the Chinese in the New World.*
Yolen, Jane. *Briar Rose.*
————. *The Devil's Arithmetic.*

HIGH SCHOOL (GRADES 9–12)

Armstrong, Jennifer. *Shipwreck at the Bottom of the World: The Extraordinary True Story of Shackleton and the* Endurance.
Ayer, Eleanor. *Parallel Journeys.*
Bauer, Joan. *Rules of the Road.*
Berry, James. *Ajeemah and His Son.*
Bloor, Edward. *Tangerine.*
Cooper, Susan. *The Dark Is Rising.*
Cushman, Karen. *Catherine, Called Birdy.*
Deuker, Carl. *On the Devil's Court.*
Duncan, Lois. *Don't Look Behind You.*
English, Karen. *Francie.*
Gallo, Don, ed. *Ultimate Sports: Short Stories by Outstanding Writers for Young Adults.*

Grimes, Nikki. *Jazmin's Notebook.*

Haddix, Margaret Peterson. *Just Ella.*

Hamilton, Virginia. *The People Could Fly: American Black Folktales.*

Hautzig, Esther. *The Endless Steppe: Growing Up in Siberia.*

Herrera, Juan Felipe. *Crashboomlove: A Novel in Verse.*

Hinton, S. E. *The Outsiders.*

Hobbs, Will. *Far North.*

Holman, Felice. *Slake's Limbo.*

Huynh, Quang Nhuong. *The Land I Lost: Adventures of a Boy in Vietnam.*

Johnson, Angela. *Heaven.*

Jordan, Sherryl. *The Raging Quiet.*

Kerr, M. E. *Gentlehands.*

Klause, Annette Curtis. *The Silver Kiss.*

Le Guin, Ursula K. *A Wizard of Earthsea.*

Magorian, Michelle. *Good Night, Mr. Tom.*

Marsden, John. *Tomorrow, When the War Began.*

Mazer, Harry. *Snow Bound.*

Mazer, Norma Fox. *Good Night, Maman.*

McKinley, Robin. *Beauty: A Retelling of the Story of Beauty and the Beast.*

Merrill, Jean. *The Pushcart War.*

Napoli, Donna Jo. *Zel.*

Nix, Garth. *Sabriel.*

Nixon, Joan Lowery. *The Kidnapping of Christina Lattimore.*

Nye, Naomi Shihab. *Habibi.*

Ortiz Cofer, Judith. *An Island like You: Stories of the Barrio.*

Paterson, Katherine. *Lyddie.*

Paton Walsh, Jill. *A Parcel of Patterns.*

Phelps, Ethel Johnston, ed. *Tatterhood and Other Tales.*

Philbrick, Rodman. *Freak the Mighty.*

Pullman, Philip. *The Ruby in the Smoke.*

Qualey, Marsha. *Thin Ice.*

Rowling, J. K. *Harry Potter and the Sorcerer's Stone.*

Silvey, Anita, ed. *Help Wanted: Short Stories about Young People Working.*

Spinelli, Jerry. *Who Put That Hair in My Toothbrush?*

Werlin, Nancy. *The Killer's Cousin.*

Yolen, Jane. *Briar Rose.*

———. *The Devil's Arithmetic.*

You may also be interested in

More Family Storytimes: This book features stories, fingerplays, songs, and movement activities to enhance the time families spend at the library. Brimming with all new material, it offers practical, creative, and active storytime programs that will captivate audiences of all ages.

Something Musical Happened at the Library: Drawing on thousands of hours listening and programming, Reid selects the best of the best, presenting eight ready-to-use, comprehensive lesson plans to help you make music an everyday part of your programs.

Cool Story Programs for the School-Age Crowd: What kid wouldn't love literary explorations of the stinky, creepy, and dirty? Throw in rats, witches, aliens, and underwear and it's irresistible. This proven, adaptable resource is for anyone who wants to help literature come alive for kids in grades K–4.

Check out these and other great titles at www.alastore.ala.org!

....

Book Links: The magazine that has been helping librarians, teachers, and parents connect children with high-quality books for more than fifteen years is where Reid began the "Reid-Aloud Alert" column that inspired *Reid's Read-Alouds*. Subscribe to *Book Links* at www.ala.org/booklinks.